PANSIES, VIOLAS & VIOLETTAS

Pansies, Violas & Violettas

The Complete Guide

Rodney Fuller

The Crowood Press

First published in 1990 by
The Crowood Press Ltd
Ramsbury, Marlborough
Wiltshire SN8 2HR

Paperback edition 1993

This impression 1993

British Library Cataloguing-in-Publication Data

A catalogue record for this book is available from the British Library.

ISBN 1 85223 748 1

Acknowledgements
Line illustrations by Claire Upsdale-Jones.
All colour photographs are by the author other than the nineteenth-
century reproductions which were photographed by Eileen Tweedy.

Printed in Great Britain by
Redwood Books, Trowbridge, Wiltshire

Contents

Acknowledgements

There are many people to whom I wish to record my gratitude for their assistance and encouragement throughout the creation of this book.

I am grateful to Dennis Cove of the Crowood Press whose initial invitation that I should write such a book was instrumental in setting the whole project in motion, and to Delphine Verroest and her colleagues for their subsequent organisation of its production.

Much of the historical material has inevitably been acquired from literature and illustrations handed down from earlier generations, access to which would have been far from easy but for the friendly and most efficient help and co-operation of Dr Brent Elliott, Ruth Howell and Jenny Vine of the Lindley Library of the Royal Horticultural Society.

I am grateful to the many seed merchants who have provided details of their products. In this connection I particularly wish to thank the following: Mark Heath of Samuel Yates Ltd, Dr Jim Reid and Cliff Utting of Royal Sluis Ltd, Vernon Francis of W W Johnson & Son Ltd, Marcus White of Breeders Seeds Ltd, Philip Bailey of Nutting & Sons Ltd and Christine Birne of Unwins Seeds Ltd.

I have particular reason to wish to thank Tom Pitt, President of the National Viola and Pansy Society who has so freely shared with me his enthusiasm for and knowledge of pansies and violas and generously supplied much fascinating detail concerning a subject to which he is devoted.

I am grateful to Wilf Winstanley for generously providing material relating to the North of England Pansy and Viola Society.

No one could possibly have been more generous with her encouragement, support and practical assistance than my very good friend Aafje van Dijk of the Netherlands. Aafje has not only shared with me her enthusiasm and unrivalled knowledge of the entire genus *Viola* but she has also made available to me a wealth of valuable material from her extensive library on the subject. I hereby extend to Aafje my extreme respect and gratitude.

Acknowledgements

Last but by no means least my especial thanks go to Liz Bly without whose constant encouragement and moral support the book would quite simply never have materialised. With great generosity of spirit she has undertaken the formidable task of converting my scribble into a typescript acceptable to the publisher and her enormous contribution to the whole project has been such that her name should appear on the title page alongside my own.

Preface

It is now some thirty years or more since literature has afforded to the pansy, the viola and the violetta the degree of attention that they truly deserve.

Since its introduction in the early years of the nineteenth century, the garden pansy has without doubt enjoyed continuous and widespread popularity. The garden viola, a more recent introduction to our gardens, and the violetta have, for reasons that the true enthusiast will find difficult to comprehend, enjoyed rather more fluctuating popularity with the effect that it is only in recent years that positive steps have been taken to rescue from obscurity and possible extinction and to re-introduce to the gardening public varieties that could so easily have become no more than fading memories. Along with this renewal of interest in the violas and violettas of the past a considerable number of new varieties have been introduced within the last few years.

Few of our flowering garden plants are as accommodating and bloom so profusely for such a long period whilst requiring so little attention and it is a source of surprise to those of us who love them that they are not now more universally appreciated and cultivated in our gardens.

The object of this little book is to encourage and inspire the reader to become acquainted with and further involved in the cultivation of the pansy, the viola and the violetta in the belief that they will fall victim to their charms and subsequently perhaps make some small contribution towards ensuring the maintenance, improvement and preservation for posterity of these splendid little flowering plants.

Should this object not be achieved, all will not be lost, the author having so thoroughly enjoyed immersing himself in a subject dear to his heart that he asks for no more.

Rodney Fuller
Bratton Seymour 1990

Preface to the Second Edition

The second edition of this book has allowed me the opportunity to incorporate a few minor amendments and, in particular, to update the information relating to nurserymen, seed merchants and their currently available varieties.

Rodney Fuller
Bratton Seymour 1993

Introduction

There is understandable confusion in the minds of many as to the precise difference between the Pansy, the Viola and the Violetta and it must be acknowledged at the outset that in attempting to define the differences it is, in fact, far from easy to be absolutely precise in the matter.

Initial confusion arises as a result of the fact that gardeners have adopted the name 'viola' for what is no more than a relatively small group of plants within the very much larger order, or family, Violaceae. To the botanist, the name 'viola' signifies a genus of more than 400 species, subspecies and varieties of plants which include not only garden pansies, garden violas and violettas but also countless violets such as out native dog violet, *Viola canina* and sweet violet, *Viola odorata*. It is therefore inherent that confusion may arise when gardeners refer to what to them is simply a viola, as opposed to a pansy or violetta. The name 'tufted pansy' was originally suggested for what has subsequently become known as the garden 'viola' but for reasons not readily apparent the name was never universally adopted.

THE PANSY

There can be few amongst us who do not form some sort of acquaintanceship with the pansy from an early age and at the mention of the name will immediately visualise a large round, five-petalled bloom with the characteristic dark almost black blotch which virtually covers the lower petals. To many of us this is the true garden pansy although the blotch is by no means an essential characteristic, there being many strains of pansy with plain flowers without blotches.

The modern pansy is an annual, or at best biennial plant with significantly large flowers borne throughout much of the summer on a plant which as it matures will – if left to grow naturally – become somewhat lax and straggling in habit. It is a plant developed directly from our wild pansies, chiefly *Viola tricolor* or heartsease and it exhibits many of the characteristics of its more diminutive ancestor. Undoubtedly, both *Viola lutea* and *Viola tricolor* played most important roles in the ancestry of the garden pansies of today.

The pansy has been further divided into two categories by those who show and enter into competitive exhibition. They are the Show pansy and the Fancy pansy which will be discussed in greater detail in a later chapter.

THE VIOLA

The garden viola is the result of cross-breeding between the garden pansy and other species of viola, chiefly *Viola lutea* and *Viola cornuta* as a result of which it has inherited a more compact and tufted habit than the single-stemmed pansy, making for a rather more robust, floriferous and perennial plant with a particularly long flowering season. The blotch is not a characteristic of the viola although it is by no means unknown. There is great variety amongst violas both in terms of flower size and colour. Many bear flowers of just one colour, others are bi-coloured with the two top petals being of a contrasting shade of colour to that of the lower three petals and others have an outer margin or belting of a contrasting colour. More bizarre markings are by no means unusual producing striped and mottled flowers and convoluted petals. As with the pansy, the central eye of the flower is white, cream, yellow or orange.

The viola has likewise been sub-divided into two basic sections – Bedding violas and Exhibition violas, both names being almost self-explanatory and discussed in greater detail in a later chapter.

There is a third category of viola which embraces all the many small-flowered violas that do not qualify for inclusion under the heading of violettas. To this section has been given the appropriate name Miniature viola.

THE VIOLETTA

The violetta is in many respects a miniature viola but with particular emphasis placed upon it having not only a flower totally devoid of the rays or whiskers that radiate from the centre of most violas but also a distinct fragrance – characteristics shared by some but by no means all violas.

The violetta is derived from the combined breeding between garden pansies and *Viola cornuta*, from which it inherits its particularly vigorous root system and its neat, compact habit of growth.

It is inevitable that the dividing lines between various categories of pansies, violas and violettas are on occasion somewhat blurred, rendering precise allocation difficult if not almost impossible. It is to the credit of the specialist societies, in particular the National Viola and Pansy Society, The North of England Pansy and Viola Society, the Scottish Pansy and Viola Association and other bodies that have gone before that specific efforts have been taken over the years to define the requirements for each category and in so doing to establish a basis upon which standards towards perfection should not only be maintained but improved.

1

Viola – a Botanical Introduction

'Viola' is an ancient Latin name which appears as early as 40BC in the writings of the Roman poet Virgil. It was the equivalent of the contemporary Greek name *ion* and both names were originally applied to what are now three separate groups of plants. The true violets were, to the Romans, *Viola purpurea* and to the Greeks, *ion melan*. *Viola alba* and *leukoion* were the names used for what we now call Matthiola or Stock and *Viola lutea* and *ion melinon* were the early names for what are now called Cheiranthus or Wall-flower. The *Viola lutea* in this connection must not be confused with our native *Viola lutea* or mountain pansy which was subsequently to play a part in the development of modern day violas and violettas.

Pansies, violas and violettas, as classified today, are all members of the botanical family *Violaceae*, containing more than 400 main species, the majority of which are more akin to those plants commonly referred to as violets, which include amongst many others our native dog violet, *Viola canina* and the ever popular sweet violet, *Viola odorata*. For botanical clarity, the genus viola has been divided into a number of sections and sub-sections but when considering pansies, violas and violettas we are concerned only with that section of the genus which is called Melanium, with its four sub-sections which are called *Scaposae, Elongatae, Integrifoliae* and *Crenatifoliae*. Beneath these headings fall all the species and sub-species, the interbreeding of which have given rise to all the pansies, violas and violettas that we now grow in our gardens. It is somewhat beyond the scope of a book of this nature to define in precise botanical detail all the characteristics which combine to qualify a species viola as a member of the section Melanium. Basically a plant of the Melanium section is, in its most common form, a perennial but sometimes an annual or biennial herbaceous plant which is either stemless, stemmed or even long-stemmed. A characteristic of all the plants in this section is the free-standing, deeply-cut stipules or small leaf-like appendages which are found at the base of the petiole or leaf stalk at the point at which it joins the stem from which it grows. The most common flower colours found in these species are shades of yellow and blue. Occasionally white or shades of pinkish-purple are also found and it is a significant characteristic that two or more colours are often found combined in a variety of ways within a single flower. The three lower petals are bearded at their bases where they unite at the centre of the flower. All these characteristics are immediately apparent upon close inspection of our native wild pansy or heartsease.

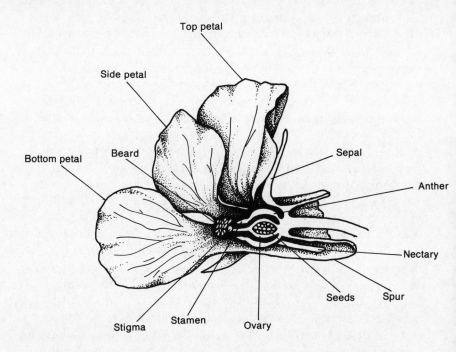

A botanical cross-section of a pansy or viola flower with the principal parts identified

The sub-section *Scaposae* is represented by only one species, *Viola alpina*, a stemless plant with small membrane-like stipules that are united with the petioles or leaf stalks.

The sub-section *Elongatae* is represented by plants with significantly long, well-developed stems although, if only to confuse, there are some members of this sub-section with very short stems, notably some of the high alpine species. This sub-section contains plants with noticeably large, green, leafy stipules.

Finally we have the subsection *Crenatifoliae* which, as the name would imply, is composed of plants of which the leaves have crenated or wavy edges. We need not attach undue importance to the nature of the stipules or to other relatively minor physical characteristics of our pansies, violas and violettas other than to appreciate that the closer we study a plant the greater is our understanding of its construction and consequently our ability to recognise the relationship that one species may have with another.

All garden hybrid pansies are grouped botanically under the heading *Viola × Wittrockiana* and all viola and violetta hybrids are grouped botanically under the heading *Viola × Williamsii* or *Viola × Visseriana*. *Viola × Williamsii* are those hybrid varieties derived from the interaction of *Viola × Wittrockiana*, the garden pansy, and the species *Viola cornuta*. *Viola × Visseriana* is the collective name for all hybrids derived from both *Viola cornuta* and *Viola gracilis*. Both groups shelter amongst many other species under the main heading of *Violaceae* Melanium section.

If it is correct to assume that the reader is a gardener rather than a botanist we need concern ourselves with no greater detail in this particular respect other than to append a list of the most significant members of the Melanium section.

VIOLACEAE (MELANIUM SECTION)

V. aetolica: A variety of *V. saxatilis*.
V. allchariensis: A member of the sub-section *Crenatifoliae*. A perennial plant that forms a network of branches from ground level and reaches a height of about 4in (10cm). The leaves and stems are coated with short grey hairs. The flowers are violet-blue and approximately $1\frac{1}{4}$in (3cm) long. It is a native of Yugoslavia.
V. alpestris: A synonym of *V. saxatilis*.
V. alpina: The sole member of sub-section *Scaposae*. A stemless perennial no more than about 4in (10cm) high with rich purple or violet, white-eyed flowers up to 1in (2.5cm) long. An alpine pansy found native in Austria, Romania and eastwards. It flowers in May and June.
V. altaica: A member of the sub-section *Crenatifoliae*. A creeping perennial, leafy-stemmed plant growing to a height of about 5in (12.5cm). The flowers which are commonly yellow, occasionally violet, can be as long as $1\frac{1}{2}$in (4cm). It is native to the Crimea, Turkistan and the Altai Mountains where it flowers between

March and June. It is a pansy with characteristics to suggest that it may well be an ancestor of some garden pansies. Cultivated in English gardens as early as 1816.

V. amoena: A variety of *V. lutea* with blue-purple flowers. A native of Scotland.

V. arsenica: A member of sub-section *Crenatifoliae*. A native of Yugoslavia with rich yellow-rayed flowers about $1\frac{1}{4}$in (3cm) long, and rounded leaves with slightly crenated edges.

V. arvensis: The native field pansy and another member of the sub-section *Crenatifoliae*. It is a rather tall, straggly plant not unlike the wild pansy or heartsease, *V. tricolor*, but with very much smaller flowers of cream with a yellow eye. A common plant throughout Europe including the British Isles. It is classified by some as a variety of *V. tricolor* and described rather unkindly by some as a weed on cultivated ground.

V. Bertolonii: Again a member of the sub-section *Crenatifoliae*. A plant similar to *V. gracilis* from which several good garden violas are directly descended. The lower petal is notched and the reverse side of the flower has a particularly long spur. It is a good garden plant in its own right although its dainty flowers lack the substance of more recent garden hybrids. It is a native of Italy and the Balkan Peninsula.

V. calcarata: A compact, almost stemless plant no more than 4in (10cm) high with violet, yellow or occasionally white flowers about $1\frac{1}{4}$in (3cm) in length with a long, slender spur projecting from the reverse side. It is a native of the alpine regions of Central Europe and falls within the sub-section *Crenatifoliae*.

V. cavillieri: A variety of *V. Bertolonii* from western Italy.

V. cenisia: Another member of the sub-section *Crenatifoliae*. A short-stemmed plant up to 6in (15cm) high with small leaves. The flowers are pale violet, about 1in (2.5cm) long and appear around July. It is a native of the European Alps where it flourishes in limestone areas.

V. clementiana: A pansy native to Asia Minor and very similar to *V. altaica*. Sub-section *Crenatifoliae*.

V. comollia: A pansy very similar to *V. cenisia* with pale purple or almost white, yellow-centred flowers. Another member of the sub-section *Crenatifoliae* and a native plant of the Alps of Northern Italy.

V. cornuta: A plant growing to as much as 12in (30cm) high with particularly tufted habit and violet, lavender, or white flowers approximately $1\frac{1}{4}$in (3cm) long. It is a native of the Pyrenees and flowers profusely throughout the summer. *V. cornuta* has played an important role in the development of garden violas and violettas as a result of cross-breeding with the garden pansy, *V. Wittrockiana.* It is a member of the sub-section *Crenatifoliae.*

V. corsica: A pansy closely akin to *V. Bertolonii.* It is native to Corsica and Sardinia and is recognisable by the fact that the lower petal is not notched as in *V. Bertolonii.* The flowers are blue.

V. declinata: A pansy of sub-section *Crenatifoliae* making a plant from 4 to 7in (10–17.5cm) high. The 1in (2.5cm) long flowers are violet with a yellow throat; the petals are quite broad and the plant bears many similar characteristics to *V. tricolor.* It is a native of Eastern Europe.

V. elegantula: Another of sub-section *Crenatifoliae* and a native of Yugoslavia. It is a plant 4–12in (10–30cm) high and the flowers, which are variable in colour are about 1in (2.5cm) long and appear between May and June.

V. × florariensis: Sub-section *Crenatifoliae.* A chance hybrid between *V. cornuta* and *V. tricolor* with purple and yellow flowers and a long flowering season. An early encouragement to those seeking to effect further improvements for the garden.

V. gracilis: Sub-section *Crenatifoliae.* A dainty plant growing to a height of about 6in (15cm) with compact habit and rich violet flowers about $1\frac{1}{4}$in (3cm) long with a pronounced spur on the reverse side. The true species emanates from the Bithynian Olympus near Bursa in Turkey. Many of the plants distributed as *V. gracilis* are considered to be of a coarser, hydrid nature.

V. graeca: A variety of *V. Bertolonii* from the Balkan Peninsula.

V. grisebachiana: A pansy similar to *V. cenisia.* The plant reaches a height of no more than 3in (7.5cm) and the flowers of violet or blue are about 1in (2.5cm) in length. It is a native plant of the Balkan Peninsula.

V. Herzogii: A variety of *V. allchariensis* with narrower leaves and smaller yellow flowers.

V. heterophylla: A synonym of *V. Bertolonii.*

V. hispida: The Rouen pansy. A member of sub-section *Crenatifoliae* and not unlike our natives *V. tricolor* and *V. lutea.* It is a plant of straggly nature and the flowers which are about $\frac{3}{4}$in (2cm) long are of pale violet and rayed and appear between May and August. In the wild this pansy is restricted to certain areas of north-eastern France where its future well-being is of concern to conservationists.

V. × hortensis: Another name that has been applied to *V. × Wittrockiana,* the collective name for garden pansies. (This name has also been applied to a form of *V. odorata,* the sweet violet).

V. latifolia: A variety of *V. stojanowii,* similar to *V. saxatilis.*

V. lutea: The mountain pansy native to the northern upland areas of the British Isles and Europe. It is a plant with creeping stems beneath the soil surface. The flowers are commonly yellow, sometimes violet or a combination of both colours and rayed. It is a species that has made a major contribution to the programme of development of garden pansies, violas and violettas. Sub-section *Crenatifoliae*.

V. macedonica: A synonym of *V. saxatilis macedonica*.

V. messanensis: A sub-species of *V. Bertolonii* from southern Italy.

V. munbyana: Sub-section *Crenatifoliae*. A long-spurred pansy recorded in North Africa and Greece. The stems, up to 8in (20cm) high, grow from a prostrate base and the yellow or violet flowers are about 1¼in (3cm) long.

V. olympica: Another name for *V. gracilis*.

V. orphanidis: A species native to the Balkan Peninsula, prostrate in habit and with hairy foliage. The flowers are about 1in (2.5cm) long in shades of violet, blue or purple-mauve. It blooms over a long period. Sub-section *Crenatifoliae*.

V. pseudo-munbyana: Another *Crenatifoliae* pansy, similar to *V. munybyana* but differentiated by its incised leaves. The plant grows to a height of about 8in (20cm) and produces violet-purple, rayed flowers about 1½in (4cm) long. It is a plant believed to have originated from North-West Africa.

V. rothomagensis: A synonym of *V. hispida*.

V. saxatilis: A perennial pansy of the sub-section *Crenatifoliae* closely comparable to *V. tricolor*. It forms a plant up to 8in (20cm) high with leafy stems which hug the ground at the base before ascending. The flowers, which are usually yellow are up to ¾in (2cm) long. It is a summer-flowering pansy native to eastern Europe and Turkey. The variety of *V. saxatilis* called *macedonica* is similar but its flowers are usually violet.

V. stojanowii: A plant 3 or 4in (9cm) high with noticeably hairy leaves. Its yellow flowers are about ½in (1cm) long. It is of the sub-section *Crenatifoliae* and originates from the Balkan Peninsula. There is a variety *latifolia* which is very similar to the species *V. saxatilis*.

V. tricolor: The heartsease or wild pansy. The most significant ancestor of our garden pansies. It grows to a height of 12in (30cm) and the flowers are about ¾in (2cm) long; there is considerable variation in colour but the rayed flowers are commonly a combination of mauve or violet, white and yellow. It is relatively common throughout the British Isles, Europe and Asia.

V. valderia: A pansy similar to *V. cenisia* but with more hairy foliage. It grows to a height of 3in (7.5cm) and produces pale lilac flowers. It is native to the maritime Alps of Italy and France and has a reputation for being difficult to cultivate successfully in the garden.

V. × Visseriana: A group name adopted by botanists for all the hybrids having *V. cornuta* and *V. gracilis* as their two parents. This group has also been called *V. cornuta hybrida* and *V. gracilis hybrida*.

V. × Williamsii: The group name for all violas (tufted pansies) and violettas derived from the cross-fertilization of the garden pansies, *V. Wittrockiana* with *V. cornuta*. This group has also been called *V. Stuartii*.

V. x Wittrockiana: The group name by which botanists identify all garden pansies. This is a variable group of hybrid plants derived by rigorous selection and breeding from *V. tricolor, V. lutea* and possibly *V. altaica*. *V. tricolor maxima* and *V. tricolor hortensis* are alternative names that have been used for this group of plants.

V. zoysii: A *Crenatifoliae* group pansy similar to *V. calcarata* but a smaller plant growing to no more than 3in (7.5cm) high. The flowers vary in size from $\frac{3}{4}$in (2cm) to $1\frac{1}{4}$in (3cm) long and are usually yellow, sometimes lilac. It is native to the limestone areas of the eastern Alps and the Balkan Peninsula.

Of all the species and varieties listed above, comparatively few have had any truly significant part to play in the development of the garden pansies, violas and violettas. All the species are a delight to those enthusiasts whose style of gardening is to collect, nurture, cultivate and propagate successfully the wild species, particularly those that present a challenge that may have eluded others. Few occupations can excite the true enthusiast, blessed with sufficient health and strength, more greatly than the adventure of searching out the wild flora in the more remote and inaccessible corners of the world whether the purpose is to acquire a specimen, collect seed, record on film, further botanical knowledge or merely soak up the delights of such an experience. To those whose aim is to acquire plants or seeds it is only right that there should be laws to govern the extent of such activities and, in an age when there is ever increasing concern related to all aspects of nature conservation it cannot be assumed that plant or seed collection are permitted activities. It is most important before embarking on any such exercise to be aware of not only what may seem morally acceptable but also what may in fact be legally forbidden, such laws no doubt varying from one part of the world to another.

Many of the *Viola* species require considerable care and control if they are to be successfully cultivated away from their natural environment. Keen observation of the environment in which they thrive will indicate the conditions which will be necessary to ensure successful cultivation in captivity. Enthusiastic alpine gardeners will employ the alpine house and all other equipment available to reproduce those conditions which require constant monitoring. The results of such efforts can be regularly viewed on the show benches of the Alpine Garden Society, the Scottish Rock Garden Society and other related organisations and the rewards of so much devoted care and attention are there exhibited for the inspiration and admiration of others.

Indiscriminate hybridisation within the genus *Viola* is frequent, especially so amongst members of the section Melanium. All species in this section are believed to hybridise readily with one another irrespective of differing chromosome numbers and the potential, therefore, for the introduction of yet more interesting hybrids in the future is considerable.

2

History and Development of Pansies, Violas and Violettas

The major work concerning the development of pansies, violas and violettas as we now know them began in the early years of the nineteenth century although references in literature to the pansy can be found very much earlier. The common name 'pansy' is believed to be of medieval French origin, being derived from the word 'pensée', meaning thought or remembrance. There is an early reference to the pansy, probably *Viola tricolor*, from Jean Ruel who lived from 1474 to 1537. He calls the plant 'pensea' which is assumed to be a Latinised version of the French *pensée*. In 1536, Otho Brunfel in his *Herbarium Vivae Eicones*, published in Strasbourg, featured a woodcut of *Viola tricolor* beneath a caption which reads '*herba sancte trinitatis*', a name which has been translated as 'herb trinity', suggesting a possible reference to the three colours violet, yellow and white, which are commonly combined in the petals of the common wild pansy or heartsease, *Viola tricolor*. Or perhaps the name referred to the three-segmented seed capsule of the pansy, a prominent feature of the plant which appears after the ripe seeds have been shed. In 1542 a woodcut depicting *herba trinitatis* appears in Leonard Fuchs' Herbal *De Historia Stirpium* printed at Basel. The foliage illustrated suggests either considerable artistic licence or alternatively that the name *herba trinitatis* was applied to perhaps more than one species of viola; in this case perhaps the field pansy *Viola arvensis*. William Shakespeare (1564–1616) makes specific reference to the pansy in *Hamlet* with Ophelia speaking the words 'and there is pansies, thats for thoughts'. This seems to confirm the suggestion that the name is indeed of French origin. The poet Edmund Spenser (1553–1599) in his *Shepherds Calender* of 1580 refers to 'the pretie pawnce' which is assumed to be a reference to *Viola tricolor*, and the poet John Milton (1608–1674) wrote of 'the pansie streaked with jet', undoubtedly a reference to the fine dark lines or rays which radiate from the centre of the flower. In this

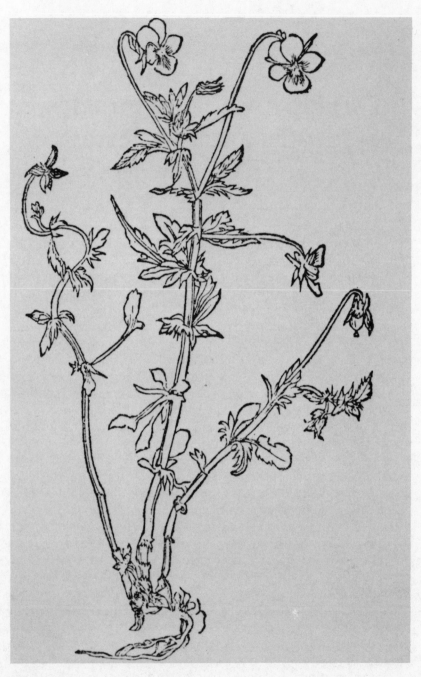

Wild Pansy or heartsease, *Viola tricolor*, 1536

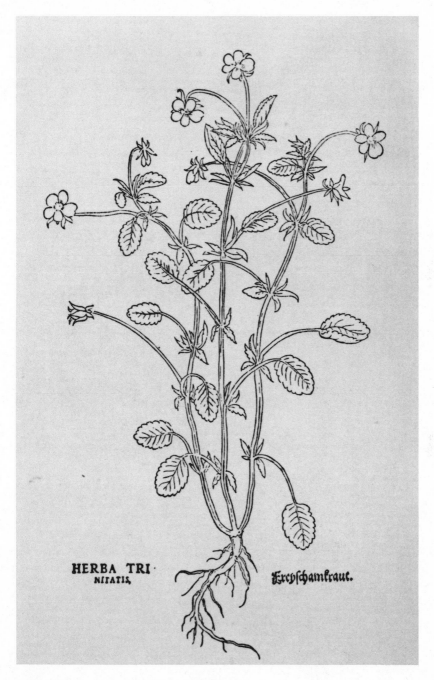

Wild Pansy or heartsease, *Viola tricolor*, 1542

Pansies, 17th Century

particular case the flowers were amongst those to be placed upon the hearse of Lycidas.

Throughout history, the wild pansy has been identified under countless names. In sixteenth-century France it was referred to as '*Menues Pensées*' and '*Herbe de la Pensée*' and amongst other colloquial names were 'pensado', 'pinchada', 'pansado', 'pansego', 'panseyo', 'panseo', 'panse' and 'pansa'. Closer to home the following names have been in use over the years – 'kiss me at the garden gate', 'tickle me fancy', 'three faces under a hood', 'call me to you' and 'jump up and kiss me'. The name 'flamey' has in the past been used in the north of England, the suggestion being that the three-colour combination of the flower of *Viola tricolor* is not unlike the colours produced in the flames of a wood fire. The name 'Johnny Jump Up' is still used extensively across the Atlantic but the name for *Viola tricolor* most commonly encountered in recent years is heartsease, the sixteenth-century spelling of which has heartesease and the seventeenth-century spelling hartsease. The name heartsease can surely effectively render all these other somewhat cumbersome names superfluous.

Initial interest in *Viola tricolor* along with so many other wild flowering plants would undoubtedly have been directed towards its possible medicinal properties rather than to its purely decorative merits. John Parkinson in his *Paradisus Terrestris* of 1629 makes reference to *Viola tricolor* together with another of our native viola species *Viola lutea* having the qualities of a purgative and he offers suggestions for it 'being taken either freshe, or dried having been made into a powder, especially the flowers'. He also mentions a double form of *Viola tricolor*, possibly *Viola tricolor flore duplici* or *duplex*. He refers to *Viola tricolor* as *Viola flammea tricolor* perhaps for the same reasons that those in the north of England were to adopt the name flamey. It was to be many years before any positive steps were taken to materially improve the qualities of *Viola tricolor* although Parkinson observed that heavy manuring had resulted in 'fairer colours and a better scent than where they grow wild'.

There is little, if any, positive evidence of notable improvement to the wild viola species until the early years of the nineteenth century when certain gardeners began to recognise the possibilities of employing them for formal decoration in the flower garden. Amongst early gardeners to show interest in pansies were Lady Mary Bennet, later to become Lady Monke, daughter of the Earl of Tankerville, who encouraged her gardener William Richardson to select, cultivate and improve the native, wild species of viola which had been introduced to her garden at Walton-on-

Thames, where she planted them in the figure of a heart. At the same time, 1812, James Lee, who had inherited from his father the then famous Vineyard Nursery in Hammersmith, West London, had obtained from Holland a particularly large-flowered, blue pansy, and William Richardson was able to acquire this variety and to introduce it to his breeding programme at Walton-on-Thames. Richardson and one of James Lee's foremen named Reed worked in conjunction with one another to produce about twenty varieties, significant ancestors of much that has since followed. At much the same time a Mr Brown, a nurseryman from Slough, Buckinghamshire, was offering for sale what he claimed to be the first true, all blue, self viola which suggests that both Brown and James Lee had quite possibly obtained the same variety from the same source at much the same time.

At around this same time there was activity just a few miles distant at Iver in Buckinghamshire. At Iver Grove lived Lord Gambier, retired from a career in the Royal Navy where amongst other things he had commanded the Baltic fleet. In his retirement he developed an interest in gardening and encouraged his head gardener, Thompson, to gather together the wild pansies that grew in the vicinity and to introduce them into the garden of Iver Grove. It would appear to be more than mere coincidence that Lady Mary Bennet and Lord Gambier should not only be fostering at the same time an interest in cultivating and improving the wild pansy, but also living within just a few miles of one another. It may well have been that a mutual connection was James Lee of the Vineyard Nursery, Hammersmith, who was also within the vicinity or possibly Brown of Slough who was close at hand. As ambitious gardeners both Lady Mary Bennet and Lord Gambier, if not already acquainted, may well have transacted business through their respective head gardeners with James Lee, then one of the most influential nurserymen of the day.

Thompson, at Iver, applied himself diligently to the task of selecting the best specimens that he could find. Record has it that he too obtained the particularly fine blue *Viola tricolor* that was being offered by Brown, the nurseryman of Slough and from elsewhere he obtained what he described as 'a darker sort', believed to have originated from Russia. With these superior varieties Thompson was able to introduce fresh blood into his breeding programme and after a few years, by about 1818, he was beginning to achieve positive improvement in terms of size of flower, and was sufficiently pleased with the progress that he had made that he selected one of his better seedlings, which had attracted the attention of Lord Gambier, and gave it the name

'Lady Gambier'. Thompson propagated a stock of this plant and the Gambiers derived pleasure from presenting them to friends and acquaintances. Thompson was later to find a variety being offered under the name of 'George the Fourth' which was so similar that he expressed the opinion that it was almost certainly a seedling of his 'Lady Gambier'. It is not recorded who was responsible for the introduction of 'George the Fourth' but writing upon the subject some twenty-three years later Thompson acknowledged that such progress had been made since the initial appearance of 'Lady Gambier' and 'George the Fourth' that they had been completely over-shadowed by far better varieties and could now be reckoned 'as little better than a weed'. 'Lady Gambier' had attracted attention if only for the size of its flowers and it was not long before Thompson had produced another flower which he described as 'of such monstrous proportions' that he christened it 'Ajax'. At this stage Thompson had been successful in producing increasingly large blooms but had yet to achieve the circular shape of flower to which he aspired. In later years he was to describe the flower of 'Ajax' as being 'lengthy as a horses head'. He considered that he had 'worked wonders' but with ambition unabated he continued his efforts towards his dream of perfection. He was eventually rewarded for those efforts with a flower of such rich colouring, large size and fine shape that he saw fit to give it the name 'Thompsons King', a sure indication of the degree of satisfaction this achievement had brought to him. For the next fifteen years or so considerable improvements were achieved in both size of flower and colour marking although it is interesting to note from illustrations of the period that the flowers were still elongated in shape and the dark blotch of the pansy, which was later to become so distinctive a feature, had yet to make an appearance. An illustration in *The Gardeners Chronicle* in 1841 suggests the early introduction of the blotch, without which, to many, a pansy is not a true pansy. The blotch is that characteristic dark patch which appears on the lower petals of the pansy. It is derived from the thickening and consolidation of the fine dark lines or rays which radiate from the centre on *Viola tricolor* and other related viola species. It was around this time that our friend Thompson at Iver found, by pure chance, amongst some self-sown seedlings, a flower which he later described as having 'what appeared to me a miniature cat's face steadfastly gazing at me'. Undoubtedly he was seeing for the first time a flower blotched and whiskered in such a way as to appear almost cat-like and it is hardly surprising that it should have caught his eye. Thompson isolated and nurtured this seedling and chose to give it the name 'Madora'. It is therefore reasonable to suppose that 'Madora' was the first of the blotched pansies or at the very least a most important ancestor of all subsequent blotched pansies. As development continued the blotch was gradually taking over from the traditional dark rays that radiate from the centre of the wild pansy. It is interesting to consider that the rays are believed to be nature's way of providing a visual guide to bees and other insects in their search for nectar and the consequent transfer of pollen from flower to flower and this may perhaps explain why blotched pansies are believed to set seed less readily than rayed pansies.

From 'Madora', Thompson was able to harvest seed from which he selected a seedling with a more pronounced blotch which he called 'Victoria' and from 'Victoria' the improvement continued, although the base colours of these early blotched pansies were restricted to shades of blue, yellow and white, not unlike the colours of the original wild pansy, *Viola tricolor*, from which the initial development had begun.

In about 1837 Thompson experienced the excitement of discovering amongst his seedlings a dark bronze flower which he isolated and called 'Flamium' and this was joined by others with the names 'Tartan' and 'Vivid' and finally 'King of Beauties' which by 1841, almost thirty years after breeding had begun, he described as 'the best flower of its kind that has ever been submitted to public inspection'. A proud claim indeed from the man who had made such a worthy contribution to the world of the pansy. Little wonder that in the south of England he became affectionately known as 'the father of the heartsease'.

Between 1827 and 1833 almost 200 new varieties of pansies were raised and by 1835 there are known to have been 400 named varieties of pansy on sale in England. Such was the interest generated amongst the gardening public that it was not surprising that examples of these improved English pansies should find their way to France and eventually Belgium and beyond. Illustrations of the period indicate quite clearly the stage of development which had then been reached: the flowers are relatively small when compared to the pansies of today whilst not appearing materially very different to some of the smaller-flowered bedding violas that we still grow. Back in London J. Sinclair and J. Freeman published in 1835 their *History and Description of the different varieties of Pansey and Heartsease now in cultivation in British Gardens* – an indication of the extent to which pansies were now capturing the imagination of enlightened gardeners. In 1841 was seen the formation of the Hammersmith Heartsease Society, later to be-

Viola tricolor, 1833

Bouquet de Pensées

Bouquet of Pansies, 1833

come the London Pansy and Viola Society, who staged their first exhibition in that year. Colour plates of 1842 show clear evidence of more circular flowers, with fuller, overlapping petals and increasingly bizarre markings and colourings, although the colours are still relatively subdued when compared to some pansies of today.

In 1844 came the formation of the Scottish Pansy Society, now the Scottish Viola and Pansy Association, another indication of the extent of interest that had now been generated. Undoubtedly the Scottish climate with its moist, cooler summer weather had been found to be particularly suited to pansy culture.

THE FLORIST OR SHOW PANSIES

The term 'florist' in this connection should not be confused with the generally accepted meaning of the word today. Florist has come to mean to most of us one who offers for sale to the public not only cut flowers and pot plants for the house and conservatory but also the skills associated with floral arrangement, bouquets, wreaths and an enormous variety of other floral decorations and tributes of one sort or another. In a wider sense a florist is a student of flowers or the author of a flora or account of specific flowers. In our case, when we speak of a florist, we are referring to one who cultivates a flower to a particularly high and agreed standard of perfection, ever striving for still further improvements and who exhibits the flowers in competition with others. It is undoubtedly the regular element of competition that has in the past ensured ever increasing standards of perfection. A florist's priorities are directed more towards producing exquisite blooms for the show bench and less towards the suitability of a particular variety for general garden application. The florists of yesteryear with their concern for ever greater improvement and perfection have done much to popularise not only pansies and violas but many other of our garden flowers.

It was around 1840 that the term Show pansy was adopted to cover the exceptionally fine examples of the flower which were considered worthy of a place on the show bench and it became necessary to lay down some sort of formal definition of what, in the opinion of the florists, constituted an acceptable Show pansy. The basic requirements were that the bloom should be as near as possible circular in outline. The base, or ground colour of the lower three petals should be matching, but not necessarily be the

Viola tricolor and varieties, 1838

Viola lutea, Viola saxatilis, Viola sudetica, Viola grandiflora, 1838

same colour as that of the two upper petals. The ground colour would invariably be white or a shade of cream.

The accompanying diagram demonstrates the proportions to which the perfectionist florist would aspire, the outline circular and the petals disposed in such a manner that they conform to a circle.

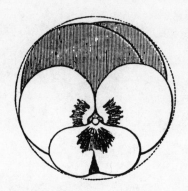

Florist Pansy, 1841

The basic definition of a Show pansy was subsequently expanded to include four basic categories. The first category being the white ground pansy – the permitted ground colour being if not a pure white at least a creamy white. The second category was the yellow ground pansy in which any shade of yellow was permitted provided that the bottom three petals were of a mutually consistent shade and the top pair of petals matched one another, even if this shade differed from that of the bottom petals. The third category of Show pansy was the self, a self-coloured pansy being one in which all five petals are of one consistent colour, whatever that colour might be. The fourth category was the belted pansy in which the ground colour should be consistent throughout the whole flower but where there should be a belt or margin of a consistent colour on the outer edges of the petals so as to form an unbroken margin around the outer circumference of the flower. The margin, of whatever colour, should be uniform in width whether broad or narrow and should be clearly defined so as not to appear to bleed or feather into the ground colour. In the case of the yellow ground pansy, the favoured colours for the belting were shades of bronze crimson, puce, mulberry, claret and other shades of rich, dark crimson. For white ground pansies, the most acceptable colours for belting were shades of blue, violet and purple.

The blotch became an increasingly vital characteristic of the pansy, the requirements being that it should be symmetrical in outline, solid, dark and dense in colour with clearly defined edges and have no suggestion of bleeding into the ground colour of the petals. In all cases the central eye of the flowers should be well defined in outline and be orange or yellow in colour. The petals should be of good substance, flat, and have a texture comparable to fine velvet. So these were the ideals to which the florists aspired, and as interest spread, the competition improved to produce ever finer flowers.

Pansies, 1842 (Reproduced by kind permission of Henriette Clifford)

A TYPE OF A DARK SELF VIOLA

FANCY TYPE OF THE VIOLA
(SOMETIMES KNOWN AS THE
"COUNTESS OF KINTORE" TYPE)

ANOTHER OF THE FANCY TYPE
OF VIOLA. "THE MEARNS"

EDGED TYPE OF FLOWER. VIOLA
"DUCHESS OF FIFE"

Violas, 1898

THE FANCY PANSIES

It was during the 1830s that English Show pansies found their way to Belgium and France where growers saw fit to continue a programme of improvement but along somewhat different lines to those of the English florists. The rigid requirements that had become accepted for English Show pansies were perhaps too restricting in that they allowed for little in the way of fresh ideas.

Pansies, when grown in quantity, will cross-pollinate with their neighbours with considerable abandon and the inevitable result is seedlings, the flowers of which show great variation in colouring, markings, size and shape. Interesting as so many of these fancy, even bizarre flowers are, they were unacceptable to the traditional florists of Great Britain who had perhaps been a touch too pedantic when specifying the essential qualities for Show pansies.

Continental growers, in particular the French and the Belgians, felt no obligation to abide by these rigid British standards. They set to work to produce even larger pansies than had hitherto been seen, but of a more relaxed and informal nature. They were unconcerned that one colour should blend into another or that the flowers should have a precisely circular shape. If the petals did not lie perfectly flat or the edges of the petals were waved or rippled they were still held in esteem provided those petals were large and full and of fine substance. Virtually any colour or combination of colours was acceptable, strong rich colours being amongst the favourites. Above all they selected flowers with larger blotches – the larger the better – so that eventually, in extreme cases, the lower three petals of the flower might be a deep, dark, dense blotch leaving little else other than a narrow outer margin that reflected the colouring of the two top petals. In some cases the blotch might extend to the top two petals also. Illustrative plates of 1844 suggest however that the large, blotched fancy pansy as we know it today had not yet been fully developed.

Amongst those actively involved in the development of these Belgian – later to be renamed Fancy – pansies was a Mr McIntosh who, around the middle of the nineteenth century was gardener to the King of the Belgians. Another significant grower of the day was Mr John Salter of Shepherds Bush, West London. John Salter had emigrated to France in 1843 and set up in business growing, amongst other florist flowers of the day, pansies. His nursery was at Versailles. Due to political upheaval, in 1848 John Salter saw fit to return to London where he re-established his business, under the name of 'Versailles Nursery' at Hammersmith, West London. John Salter had no doubt acquired considerable business connections whilst on the Continent and within a year or so he is known to have visited Belgium. There, he was impressed by the quality of the pansies then being grown by Mr McIntosh for the Belgian King. It is possible that McIntosh had acquired his original stock from John Salter and by prudent selection had now produced significant improvements. John Salter returned to Hammersmith with seed acquired from McIntosh from which he produced some particularly fine flowers with blotches so large as to virtually cover the lower petals. He distributed these pansies for sale under the name of Belgian Pansies.

Around 1858 – by which time John Salter's and perhaps Mc-Intosh's pansies would have been distributed far and wide – some particularly fine pansies were received from M Meillez of Lille, France, by E. G. Henderson and Son of the Pineapple Nurseries, Welling Road, St Johns Wood, North London whose nursery occupied part of what is now the world-famous Lord's Cricket Ground. The pansies were seemingly considered a rather special acquisition in that Andrew Henderson enlisted the help of William Dean of the Bradford Nursery, Shipley in Yorkshire to undertake their culture in the belief that they would stand a greater chance of flourishing in the cooler, moister climate of Yorkshire than in the drier and, in those days, smokey atmosphere of London. Record has it that the traditional florists of the North of England rather frowned upon these new introductions, considering them to be an inferior product which failed to conform to their idea of what constituted a perfect Show pansy, but this in no way detracted from their appeal to the general gardening public and they became increasingly sought after, particularly in Scotland. It was William Dean who, around this time, saw fit to question why these pansies should continue to be called Belgian Pansies and instead adopted the appropriate name Fancy Pansy which was widely accepted and is used to this day. One of the first references to Fancy Pansies had appeared in *The Gardeners Chronicle* in 1849. In *Floral Magazine* of 1862 were illustrated in colour two florists' named varieties of pansy together with two pansies described as 'of a race lately introduced from Belgium and France and in which we foresee great improvements'. The author went on to say:

It is sometimes said of the growers of florist flowers (show pansies) that they lay down rules with regard to the form and marking of their special favourites, which are either impracticable, or, if obtained, are of no advantage to the flower; and of floral delineators (artists), that they make their subjects more perfect than they are in nature. But we have ever found that by placing two flowers side by side, one of which fulfilled the required conditions, the other not and then appealing to those who were not florists, they have always acknowledged that, however apparently conventional the rules, they are founded on good taste and a just appreciation of beauty and if any one considers the drawing of the florist varieties in the present plate too perfect, we can only say that when 'Lady Lucy Dundas' was exhibited by Downie, Laird and Laing it was pronounced to be the nearest approach to a perfect circle that had as yet been obtained in this class.

The author goes on to suggest that all fancy pansies would 'gain were they of the same exquisite rotundity as the florists varieties'.

At this time Fancy or Belgian and French pansies had not been classified, 'their bizarre character making it extremely difficult'. Mr John Downie of the Scottish nursery Downie Laird and Laing was one of those who undertook the cultivation and improvement of the Fancy pansies and he produced a number of named varieties; one of the most famous of which he named 'Dandie Dinmont'. It is significant to realise that up to this time all attention was concentrated entirely on the quality and size of the pansy bloom, no particular reference being made to the habit of the plant on which it grew, which in the case of these early pansies would have been lax and straggly necessitating the use of small sticks to support the growth and pegging down and some form of protection from the elements to ensure that the flowers reached maturity unblemished and fit for the show bench.

In the 1850s John Fleming, gardener at Cliveden Manor near Maidenhead in Buckinghamshire, had already attracted considerable attention with his bedding schemes using pansies; one of the earliest recorded examples of pansies being employed in this way. John Fleming was responsible for introducing some new varieties, amongst which were 'Clivedon Yellow', 'Clivedon Deep purple' and 'Cliveden White' and he introduced into his breeding programme a particularly fine blue pansy – which is believed to have originated from Russia – and a fine white pansy called 'Great Eastern' – which he had acquired from Harry Hooper of Bath. John Fleming is also known to have grown 'Magpie', possibly the oldest of all the named varieties of pansy or viola. 'Magpie' is believed to have originated in a French cornfield where it was found growing wild. It was being offered for sale by John Salter of the Versailles Nursery in Hammersmith, London in 1857. 'Magpie' was subsequently offered for sale under a number of other names; 'Mazeppa', 'Paul Fry' and 'Wonderful' being just some of these.

In 1852 John Downie of Downie, Laird and Laing, the Edinburgh nurserymen, staged an exhibition of six different varieties of Fancy pansy at the Botanic Gardens in Regents Park in London. By the mid-1850s North of England growers were showing particular interest in pansies and from 1860 onwards Scotland was to become the major centre for their development aided by the even more favourable summer climate found there. Pansies always perform best in relatively cool, moist conditions and are at their most vulnerable during hot, dry spells of weather.

Between 1859 and 1860 James Grieve, perhaps more famous for having introduced the ever-popular dessert apple which carries his name, became involved in the pansy saga. Grieve was Nursery Manager of Dicksons of Edinburgh and the story has it that he embarked upon a breeding programme which involved not only existing pansies of the day but also the wild species *V. lutea* and its blue-purple variety *V. lutea amoena* which were native to the Pentland Hills to the south of Edinburgh.

Amongst the early results of his efforts was 'Grievii' which was described as an excellent yellow bedder or bedding pansy. Grieve was also known to have been experimenting in a similar manner by cross-pollinating Show pansies with *V. cornuta*, the horned pansy of the Pyrenees, which had been introduced to Great Britain around 1776. Grieve has recorded that in 1863 he acquired *V. amoena* and cross-pollinated it with purple pansies. He also crossed *V. cornuta* with the Show pansy 'Dux' from which he named a seedling 'Vanguard'. He acquired *V. stricta* – the precise identity of which causes some confusion – from which he raised 'Ariel' and 'Bullion', a rayed yellow still available commercially to this day, as well as a number of other varieties with neither blotches nor rays. The possibilities must have seemed endless as of course they are when embarking on an exercise of this nature.

In 1867 James Grieve stepped up a gear when he acquired *V. cornuta* 'Perfection' and in his own words 'crossed every bloom with everything I could lay hands on'. And why not. The more crossing he could engineer the greater the chance of producing something outstanding, and the result was 700 seedlings which included 'The Tory', 'Lilacina', 'Canary' and 'Holyrood'. Crossings with *V. lutea* produced 'Grievii', 'Pallida' and 'Golden Gem'. These he then crossed with a yellow Show pansy marketed by E. J. Henderson of London called 'Golden Bedder' which gave rise to one of his most successful creations: 'Sovereign'. Other successful varieties introduced by James Grieve included 'Stanley', 'Mary Gilbert', 'Dorothy Tennant', 'Royalty', 'Souvenir', 'Virginalis' and 'Merchiston Castle'. For sheer volume of first-class new violas or tufted pansies, those introduced by James Grieve and his employers Dicksons of Edinburgh were at the time unsurpassed.

At the same time John Baxter of Daldowdie was busily

employed attempting to breed still better pansies and in 1863 John Wills was making use of *V. cornuta* and selected varieties of *V. lutea* with the names *V. lutea grandiflora* and *V. lutea major* in his breeding programme. Both *V. cornuta* and *V. lutea* are of more perennial nature than the wild pansy *V. tricolor*. The short-jointed, tufted habit of *V. cornuta* and the creeping, procumbent habit of *V. lutea*, together with their perennial nature and hardiness, presented qualities which, if they could be introduced into existing pansies, would definitely be to the pansies' advantage, rendering them more suitable and adaptable plants for general garden work. By now Scottish growers were at the forefront of pansy development, their climate having been found preferable to the hotter, drier climate of southern England. Notable growers of that era included William Paul, John Sutherland, Andrew Irvine, Matthew Campbell, Alex Lister and John Smellie.

Many more significant, if somewhat isolated moments in the history of pansy development are on record. In 1863 the true value of the Pyrenean species *V. cornuta* was becoming more fully appreciated due to a great extent to the activities of Mr John Wills.

In *Floral Magazine* of 1864 there was a fine, colour illustration of Fancy pansies grown by William Dean at his nursery at Shipley, near Bradford in Yorkshire. In the accompanying text William Dean wrote: 'The Fancy pansy is now making rapid strides towards perfection of form and is fast becoming popular.' He stressed that the habit of these plants rendered it necessary then, as now, if used for bedding, to peg the longer, more straggly shoots to the ground. This would protect the plant from wind damage and encourage further rooting. In the same publication it was emphasised that the Fancy pansy was originally of English origin before it found its way to France and much of the credit for its improvement was given to M Meillez of Lille who had died around 1861. William Dean, who received the plants from the Pineapple Nurseries of St John's Wood, London, is given much credit for having saved these plants from passing into obscurity as they might well have done upon the death of M Meillez.

By 1864 William Dean was producing several thousand seedlings from these Fancy pansies and he selected a number of the best of them for further trial. At the same time two of the 'Great Metropolitan Floral Societies' had included classes in their schedules for Fancy pansies for which they were now offering special prizes.

Illustrated in the colour section are more varieties of Fancy pansy, this time from the nursery of Messrs Downie & Co in the year 1865. Such illustrations indicate the extent to which the superb standards then achieved have so sadly been allowed to decline in more recent years.

Two years later, in 1867, *Floral Magazine* tells us that the previous few years had produced weather unfavourable to pansies in the south of England. The article appeared alongside a colour plate of Fancy pansies from the nursery of Messrs Downie, Laird & Laing of Scotland. The author reports that Mr Fleming of Clivedon Manor, Buckinghamshire, is proving that with the Fancy pansy it is now possible 'to have the parterre interesting in winter, brilliant in spring and gorgeous in summer'. The particularly fine blue variety at the top of the plate had been raised in spite of the weather by Mr Laing at Stanstead Park, Forest Hill in south-west London.

1869 saw the publication in Paris of a book devoted to pansy culture, written by J. Barillet and entitled *Les Pensées*. It covered the history, cultivation, propagation and uses of the pansy.

THE VIOLAS

Around this period the viola – variously described as the tufted pansy or bedding viola – was beginning to make a positive appearance on the gardening scene, alongside the developing pansies (*V. cornuta* being the species which undoubtedly had the most significant effect in this connection).

In the late 1860s B. S. Williams of Holloway, north London had introduced an improved variety of viola *V. cornuta* with the name *V. cornuta* 'Perfection'. 'Perfection' is believed to have originated in the garden of Rotherfield Park in Hampshire. The same period saw the introduction of one of our most revered violas, 'Maggie Mott', a silvery-mauve flower with superb fragrance which has stood the test of time and is perhaps the most sought-after variety to this day. In 1871 Richard Dean, brother of William, was busy cultivating pansies and violas in his small garden in West Ealing, London. Dean's initial work centred around *V. cornuta* 'Perfection' and *V. lutea grandiflora* to which he introduced 'Clivedon Purple' – doubtless acquired from John Fleming of Clivedon.

As a result of his efforts he was able to offer four new varieties for sale – 'Blue Bell', 'Lothair', 'Princess Teck' and 'Corisande'. 'Blue Bell' became a firm favourite and had soon acquired a reputation for withstanding the heat and drought of southern summers like no other viola. Its bright blue flowers were produced in succession over a particularly long period.

Richard Dean introduced at much the same time a group of violas which he called 'Tom Thumb' bedding violas and which he described as very dwarf and compact in growth, with an abundance of small flowers, similar, one is led to suppose, to the smaller-flowered or Miniature violas that we grow today. These varieties share many but not all the characteristics of the rayless and fragrant violettas which were so soon to be introduced. No mention was made of fragrance and it can be assumed that the 'Tom Thumb' violas would have possessed rayed flowers. Amongst the 'Tom Thumb' varieties offered for sale by Richard Dean in 1871 were 'Blue Gem', 'Lily White', 'Little Gem', 'Painted Lady' and 'Yellow Boy'. There are many admirable small-flowered violas in circulation today which are in all probability comparable to Richard Dean's 'Tom Thumb' varieties. It would therefore not have been inappropriate to adopt this name or some other as a means of differentiating them from the larger-flowered, rather more flamboyant Bedding violas. They are, in many respects, the most attractive and satisfactory of all the violas for general garden work.

Mr Barron, Superintendant of the Chiswick Gardens, made full use of *V. cornuta* at this time as an edging to larger flower beds and as an informal carpet beneath shrubs, two applications for which the plant is ideally suited.

In *Floral Magazine* of 1872 there appears a superb colour plate of Fancy pansies from the nursery of Messrs Downie, Laird and Laing. The accompanying text draws attention to the manifest progress that has been made when comparison is made with earlier varieties. During that year Messrs Downie, Laird and Laing had exhibited large numbers of these Fancy pansies and the writer expresses the opinion that: 'in regularity of form, brilliancy of colour and especially size, they have advanced immensely and may in all these points take rank with those long known as Florists pansies'. In the same year *Floral Magazine* illustrated in colour six Bedding violas and pansies from James Grieve at the nurseries of Dickson & Co of Waterloo Place, Edinburgh. In this plate we can detect a slight change of emphasis which can best be explained by quoting directly from the accompanying text written by Dicksons:

The first varieties were obtained some seven or eight years ago by hybridizing *V. montana*, *V. cornuta*, *V. lutea*, *V. amana* [presumably *V. amoena*] and *V. stricta* [it seems unlikely that this would have been the species which we now recognise as *V. stricta*] with Show pansies and by carefully continuing the hybridizing with the finest seedlings of each season, we have now succeeded in raising a considerable number of valuable sorts, similar to those now figured raising annually from twelve to fifteen thousand seedlings, for the purpose of obtaining eight or twelve varieties superior to those previously sent out. In selecting these we have kept in view:

1   HABIT, which must be branching and compact.

2   FLOWERING PROPERTIES, which must be both profuse and continuous; thus while the native species *V. amana* [*amoena?*] after two years of garden cultivation could not be induced to bloom for more than six or eight weeks in the early part of the summer, we have now got greatly improved seedlings forward which will flower continuously from the beginning of April to October.

3   COLOUR, which to be used extensively must be of one shade and that a distinct and striking one. There are a few exceptions to these such as 'Fairy', 'Fairy Queen' and 'Butterfly' with double upper petals and distinct margin of golden yellow.

4   SIZE, to this quality we attach the least importance, the primary object being to obtain the greatest amount of a certain shade of colour within a given space, and this is probably better effected with a medium sized than a large flower, the former being less likely to be injured by wet weather. These flowers are invaluable in wet seasons, as while geraniums and other bedding plants suffer much, they continue to bloom in great profusion throughout the entire season.

The writer is clearly describing the forerunners of the tufted pansies or violas and violettas of today and his opinions are as apt and valid today as they then were.

Amongst varieties introduced by James Grieve of Dicksons was that of 'The Tory', a deep-blue flower with a dark blotch which was still being offered for sale thirty-eight years after its introduction.

1872 saw the beginning of the breeding work undertaken by Dr Charles Stuart of Chirnside, Berwickshire, whose achievements we shall look at in greater detail later.

In 1873 Hendersons, of St Johns Wood, North London, were offering for sale the varieties 'Imperial' and 'Blue Perfection' – a large, free-flowering viola considered to be a distinct improvement upon *Viola cornuta* 'Perfection'. In 1875 Dicksons of Edinburgh introduced the varieties 'Sovereign' and 'Alpha' – the latter was described as more of a pansy than a viola. It is perhaps inevitable that there will always be violas with pansy characteristics so pronounced as to make absolute classification difficult. If by viola we mean 'tufted viola', the descriptive name by which they were originally known, violas that lack tufted habit should perhaps be classified under another heading. There will always be violas hovering on that dividing line and perhaps it is a mistake to be too fastidious in such definitions.

In 1875 Richard Dean introduced to commerce more varieties of his own raising, 'Crown Jewel', 'Royal Blue', 'Lilacina', 'Mulberry' and 'White Swan'. 'Lilacina' and 'White Swan' are names that appear in nurserymen's lists to this day. Mr B. S. Williams introduced a particularly fine white variety which he named 'Mrs Gray'. By this time, the mass bedding of pansies and violas in public parks and gardens was becoming common practice, giving rise to the name Bedding viola as opposed to the show and exhibition varieties whose lank habit of growth was far less appropriate for presentation in this manner.

Such was the interest now shown towards pansies and violas that the Royal Horticultural Society sponsored trials for Bedding violas at their Chiswick gardens, in this way providing an opportunity for the merits or otherwise of the latest varieties to be assessed away from the inevitable pressures of competitive, commercial practice. Amongst those who submitted plants for trial were Dicksons of Edinburgh, Richard Dean of West Ealing, James Cocker & Sons and Dr Charles Stuart, an amateur grower and breeder from Chirnside, Berwickshire.

In 1872–1873 Dr Charles Stuart began work much along the same lines as those undertaken by Dr John Wills ten years earlier by concentrating on the possibilities of combining the best characteristics of *V. cornuta* with the garden pansy. In 1874 Dr Stuart applied the pollen of a garden pansy called 'Blue King' to the stigma of *V. cornuta* and from the pod of ripe seed that resulted from this crossing he was able to raise twelve plants which he tended with loving care. These twelve seedlings matured into plants with the good tufted habit of *V. cornuta* and the blue flowers inherited from the pansy 'Blue King'. It was these characteristics which gave rise to the adoption of the somewhat short-lived name 'tufted pansy'. The name itself was appropriate for this new group of pansies but it was very soon superseded by the somewhat ambiguous and confusing title 'viola'. Viola is the collective name for all members of the *Violaceae* family which includes violets, pansies, violas and violettas and it is therefore hardly surprising that there has always been a degree of confusion in the minds of both novice and expert as to the precise difference between a pansy and a viola.

Dr Stuart took the development of this tufted pansy a stage further. By applying the pollen of a pink pansy to the stigmas of these first-generation seedlings, he was able to raise a second generation of seedlings which not only had the same admirably tufted habit, but also came in a greater range of colours. He then selected what he considered to be the best of this second generation and propagated from them vegetatively; that is to say he took as many cuttings as possible from each selected variety so that the progeny would be identical to the plant from which the cuttings were taken. He submitted these plants for trial alongside other growers at the Royal Horticultural Society's gardens at Chiswick, London. If nothing else this would show how well the plants might fare in the warmer, drier climate of the south.

The criteria by which the judges were to consider each plant's merit were from the point of view of compactness and dwarfness of habit, profusion and continuity of bloom, and usefulness and effectiveness of colour; characteristics that would combine to make them good bedding plants. Dickson & Co submitted 'Alpha', 'Golden Gem', 'Peach Blossom', 'Queen of Lilacs', 'Sovereign' and 'The Tory'. Richard Dean provided 'Bedfont Yellow', 'Blue Bell', 'Lilacina', 'Lothair', 'Lily White', 'Tom Thumb', 'Magpie', 'Mulberry', 'Princess Teck', 'Royal Blue' and 'White Swan'. From James Cocker & Sons came 'Novelty'; from Mr G. Westland, 'Blue Perfection' and from Dr Charles Stuart varieties of his raising.

In the autumn of 1875 Dr Stuart had the immense satisfaction of learning that six of his seedlings had been awarded first class certificates and that his plants had been judged the overall winners of the trial, beating the highly-respected and long-established Dickson & Co of Edinburgh into second place. Dr Stuart was entirely satisfied with his success and prepared to rest on his laurels. He propagated his winning varieties and broadcast their seed for bedding display but took no particular steps to introduce further improvements. An interested colleague, on seeing one of Dr Stuart's pansies, a fine white self, expressed the opinion that the flower could be improved and refined still further if it could be produced devoid of rays. Dr Stuart took this suggestion to heart but it was to be a further ten years before, in 1887, he found by chance among random seedlings the very thing: a pure white flower entirely without rays, and with the added bonus of a particularly fine fragrance. He took as many cuttings as possible from this plant and had soon built up a sizeable stock. Once again Dr Stuart, who in his own words was no more than a 'humble amateur' must have felt pleased with this achievement. Sufficiently, in fact, to send a box of this variety to Mr William Robinson, the influential and well-respected editor and proprietor of *The Garden*, a major gardening periodical of the day. William Robinson immediately recognised the plant to be a new strain of viola and featured it in a subsequent edition of his magazine; a most effective way of bringing Dr Stuart's achievements to the notice of the gardening public. A tufted, perennial pansy had been developed at the expense of the size of the flower which had up till then been such an obsession. The result, however, was a plant which – whilst a long way removed from the whims of the florists – was of far greater versatility and appeal for ordinary garden work. Dr Stuart's new plant was to all intents and purposes a miniature form of viola. It was given the name 'Violetta' thereby becoming the original member of a whole new class of violas that we now call violettas.

Writing about his achievements in later years Dr Stuart made the interesting observation that he had achieved these tufted pansies or violas by applying pansy pollen to the stigma of *V. cornuta*, thus making *V. cornuta* the seed parent. When the process was reversed, in other words, when he applied the pollen of *V. cornuta* to the stigma of ordinary garden pansies, the resulting progeny were no improvement on those existing pansies to the extent that they had not inherited the tufted habit.

Dr Stuart continued in his efforts to extend his family of violettas but record has it that he was now finding it a less rewarding task. His programme involved the cross-pollination of 'Violetta' with other notable pansies in an effort to extend the range of colour whilst at the same time retaining flowers devoid of rays and the compact habit of 'Violetta'. Although the rays are an integral part of most viola species, there is little doubt that their total absence provides a flower of infinitely more refinement, particularly so in the case of white and pale-coloured flowers on which any rays are so much more accentuated. Dr Stuart, writing in 1898, tells us that by applying the pollen of 'Violetta' to a white pansy with few rays he produced 'Sylvia', a particularly fine rayless creamy-white flower. He subsequently crossed 'Sylvia' with other pansies but registered disappointment that out of 150 seedlings he could only produce one plant without rays, the variety 'Border Witch'. We must bear in mind that Dr Stuart had described himself as no more than a humble amateur – that group of people who have always made such a valuable contribution to the world of gardening – and all lovers of violas and violettas should feel affection and gratitude for his admirable contribution towards the development of these plants.

By 1880 it could truly be said that the Show pansy was in its heyday. Judging by illustrations of the time the perfection in outline, the well-defined blotches and margins, improved petal substance and clearer, richer colour all added up to a quality of flower that has never been surpassed. It must be said that in later years the Show pansy has not been without its critics. As has been previously stated the devotee of the Show pansy was concerned with the quality of flower alone and it is sad that no greater effort was taken to improve the habit of the plant to render it more suitable for general gardening work. The flower was the Show pansy's glory, the plant and its habit of growth having little else to commend it. Like so many of the florists' show flowers, it was grown by those with little if any land in which to operate. The florists' flower was an admirable pursuit, both absorbing and relaxing, for those working in what might be no more than a tiny garden or backyard. Where it is not possible to grow in quantity it is appropriate to concentrate on a particular garden flower, attempting to grow that flower to perfection, bestowing upon it all the care and attention that success will require. Flower shows throughout the season would make the pursuit all the more fun and engender ever fiercer competition for the top prizes.

THE VIOLETTAS AND MINIATURES

The violetta was by now attracting increasing attention and at the 1894 Viola Conference held at the Botanical Gardens, Edgbaston, Birmingham, it was agreed that violettas – aided no doubt by the initial encouragement of William Robinson of *The Garden*, should now be officially recognised as a group distinct from violas. A paper was read at the conference bearing the title of 'The Violetta, or miniature variaties'. Rules were laid down as to what should be the essential properties of a violetta in order to make a clear distinction between violettas and violas: it was acceptable for the flower to be rather more oval or elongated than would be required of a Show pansy or exhibition viola. The petals were to be smooth and of good substance; the colour to be bright and clear; the eye of the flower to be bright yellow or

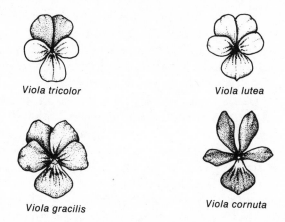

Viola tricolor

Viola lutea

Viola gracilis

Viola cornuta

Four viola species which have played a significant role in the development of pansies, violas and violettas for the garden

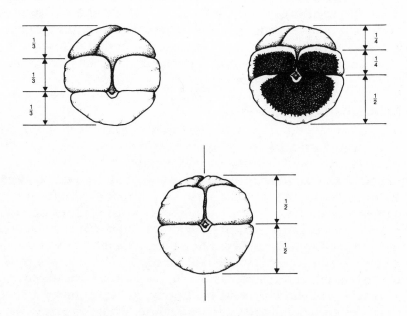

Three examples of pansies and violas with an indication of the proportions which constitute a flower fit for Show or Exhibition

orange, which could run into the lip of the lower petal. No rays or other central markings were to be permitted and the flowers were to have a distinct fragrance and measure no more than $1\frac{1}{2}$ in (3.75 cm) and no less than 1 in (2.5 cm) in width. Of equal importance was the habit of the plant which should be dwarf and procumbent with small, bright, closely-packed leaves giving an overall short-jointed, bushy appearance.

Regrettably some people today do not pay full regard to all these requirements when classifying plants under the heading violetta; a practice which invites confusion. This is by no means a recent anomaly. As far back as 1896, within only two years of violettas receiving formal recognition, a Mr W. Baxter was expressing concern at the Viola Conference of that year that small-flowered violas were masquerading as violettas, when there was reason to suppose that they were nothing more than violas, deliberately undernourished in order that they might pass unnoticed as violettas.

In 1908 Mr Howard Crane, a prominent grower of the day, was suggesting that the size and shape of the violetta flower was to a great extent a matter of taste and personal preference and he remarked that there were many very beautiful violas with flowers less than 1 in (2.5 cm) in width that were excluded by what he called 'these ultra strict rules'. Whilst one cannot doubt the charm of the violetta, its formal definition confuses some and invites criticism from others. Perhaps this inherent problem could be alleviated if agreement could be reached to introduce a separate group to contain all those small-flowered violas – similar to Richard Dean's 'Tom Thumb' violas. Positive steps have in fact been taken in recent years to do so, under the heading, 'Miniature violas'.

The smaller-flowered violettas found favour throughout the 1890s amongst those no longer excited by the sheer size of blossom, but until the turn of the century they were only available in a somewhat restricted range of rather pale colours. Writing in 1908, only twenty-one years after Dr Charles Stuart had produced the first violetta, Howard Crane tells us that the growing of violettas had not 'caught on' and until very recently had almost slipped into oblivion. The apparent reason for this decline was that in spite of all its admirable qualities, nurserymen were too accustomed to the larger, faster-growing and relatively coarser varieties of viola. They failed to appreciate the excellent qualities of the violetta, qualities which in many ways made it a superior little plant for general gardening purposes. However, violettas survived and by the early years of the twentieth century were beginning to command greater interest. Those who had perservered with the violettas had improved the constitution. The plants were stronger and on stouter stems, flowers were of good substance and had a greater range of colours. Howard Crane and his father D. B. Crane had between them introduced some forty new varieties of violetta amongst which were shades of white, blush orange, yellow, blue and even edged colours. Writing in 1908 Howard Crane went so far as to recommend what were, in his opinion, the best eighteen violettas then available – the '*crème de la crème*' as he called them. Many of the older varieties he considered unworthy of inclusion in this list, dismissing them as inferior tufted pansies and not true violettas. It is hardly surprising that he included Dr Charles Stuart's original variety 'Violetta' in his list of eighteen. Crane attached particular importance to the quality of strong fragrance that a true violetta should always possess and which was so evident in all those he selected for this, his list. The eighteen are noted overleaf.

Sadly none of these varieties has survived to be with us today. 'Purity' has been adopted as a name for a white violetta of recent introduction and the viola 'Lavinia' which is currently in circulation should not be confused with the original plant to which Mr Crane referred. By 1910 there appears to have begun a steady decline of interest in violas and violettas which is not easy to explain. Fashions change in gardening as in all things and within a few years the 'War to end all wars' was to have such devastating impact on the lives of so many. The decline in interest was focused initially on the violas and violettas, interest in Show pansies being relatively unaffected.

In 1910 William Cuthbertson, proprietor of Dobbies of Edinburgh, Orpington and Marks Tey, produced a well-illustrated treatise on pansies, violas and violets; a sequel to his earlier book of 1895. Amongst those to the forefront of growing at that time were William Sydenham, Septimus Pye and James Grieve, former nursery manager of Dicksons of Edinburgh who had already made such a valuable contribution to the cause and was now in business on his own account.

1911 saw the formation of the National Viola and Pansy Society with headquarters in Birmingham. At that time the Society had 412 members including thirty-six professional growers who exhibited in the open classes of all the shows and published lists of their varieties. The society was controlled by twenty-two council members under the chairmanship of Mr Harry Woolman

THE BEST EIGHTEEN VIOLETTAS
As recommended by Howard Crane in 1908

Blanche – Clear silvery white, quite distinct; not quite as free flowering as some of the newer kinds, however.

Commodore Nutt – Bright yellow circular flower, very charming. Compact habit.

Cynthia – Pale blush-lilac of oval form, yellow eye; delightful creeping habit, and very long footstalks. New.

Diana – A beautiful primrose-yellow flower suffused yellow, oval in shape; quite a distinct advance. Fine long footstalks. New.

Eileen – Charming deep blue flower, neat yellow eye; extremely free flowering, and very strong constitution. Persistent bloomer. New.

Estelle – One of the smallest of the miniature section. Pure white, slightly suffused yellow on the lower petals. New.

Forget-Me-Not – One of the older Violettas. Rather larger flower than the original 'Violetta' and the newer kinds. Colour – bluish-lilac with white centre; very free.

Lavinia – Beautiful blush-lavender, veined a deeper shade, splendid creeping habit. A lovely acquisition. New.

Gertrude Jekyll – A most dainty little circular-shaped flower; a perfect bi-colour, lower petals rich yellow, upper petals primrose. Very distinct. New.

Olivia – A most dainty flower, colour – white, faintly tinted lavender-blue; yellow suffusion on lower petals. Long footstalks. New.

Purity – An improved form of the original 'Violetta', fine substance in the petals. Colour – pure white, heavily suffused with yellow on lower petals. Long footstalks. New.

Queen of the Year – China blue in colour, sometimes flecked with white. Circular shape. Quite distinct. Scarce.

Rock Blue – Charming little deep blue flower, effective yellow eye; a perfect gem. New and choice.

Robbie Jenkins – A most delightful little flower of perfect form. Another minute-flowered variety; white, very deeply suffused yellow on lower petal. New.

Sweetness – One of the most minute blooms of this type; white, with yellow eye. Long footstalks. New.

Thisbe – Beautiful pale bluish flower, with yellow eye; beautiful compact habit. Long footstalks. Dense tuft. New.

Violetta – The original of the type, pure white, suffused yellow on lower petals. Long footstalks.

Winifred Phillips – Very pretty little flower, edged and tinted blue on white ground; quite distinct. New.

whose family are still well known in the world of chrys-anthemums. Many of the council members were head gardeners employed by the larger houses and estates of the day and up until the outbreak of World War I in 1914, shows were held at various venues throughout the country. Shows were subsequently held at the Birmingham Botanical Gardens and later at Handsworth Park. In more recent years the society's meetings and shows have been and still are held at the Uplands Allotments Association at Handsworth, Birmingham. 1915 saw the formation of the North of England Pansy and Viola Society, which until very recently – along with the National Viola and Pansy Society – was actively engaged in growing, showing, propagating and distributing the best of the Show and Fancy pansies and Exhibition violas. These associations are fulfilling a vital function gathering all the knowledge and experience of the past to hand it down to succeeding generations.

In 1921–1922 D. B. Crane and Howard Crane produced fresh editions of their books on the subject – a valuable contribution towards keeping dwindling interest alive between the wars. In 1933 D. B. Crane staged a display of a dozen or so varieties of violettas in sinks at the Royal Horticultural Society hall and again, in 1939 was responsible for a display of violettas in a formal garden setting at the Chelsea Flower Show. World War II (1939–1945) did little to encourage the further development of pansies and violas and there was minimal progress to record until Howard Crane took up his pen once again to produce in 1951 a comprehensive little book with the title *Pansies and Violas for Exhibition and Garden*. Seven years later Roy Genders was to do much the same thing with his book *Pansies, Violas and Violets*. In 1953 viola trials sponsored by the Royal Horticultural Society's Wisley Gardens in Surrey were an indication that all was not forgotten. In 1960 and 1961 Howard Crane was keeping the memory alive with articles on violettas and viola species in the Royal Horticultural Society Journal. Trials for pansies were held at Wisley in 1961 and 1962 and again in 1971 and the following year saw another trial for violas.

It is hardly appropriate in an account of this nature to list all the many amateur growers and commercial nurserymen of the past together with all the countless named varieties of pansy, viola and violetta now sadly long extinct, but which have played such an integral part in the history of this splendid little flower. If so many of the old named varieties had been ousted by superior introductions, the story would be happier than is the case. Social upheavals, changing fashions and two World Wars are probably just some of the reasons why much dedicated effort on the part of pansy and viola enthusiasts is needed today in order to ensure that all is not lost and that once again we can attain the admirably high standards that prevailed so many years ago. At present, emphasis has been directed more towards pansies and violas for garden bedding work, and it would be sad if the Show pansy, the Fancy pansy and the Exhibition viola were allowed, through complacency and lack of enthusiasm, to become no more than a fading memory.

There are a number of nurseries now catering for the renewed interest in violas and pansies (*see* Appendix I).

Joseph A. Jackson and Son of Kettleshulme were undoubtedly the longest established, having been in business for over 100 years. Between 1938 and 1953 Jacksons received numerous awards for their exhibits of pansies and violas at the Southport Show and their last list consisted of approximately fifty named varieties of Bedding violas, Exhibition violas and violettas, some of which were old established varieties, and other varieties which they themselves had raised and introduced.

Richard Cawthorne of Swanley has done much in the last ten years or so to further interest in violas and violettas as a result of some fine exhibits at the Chelsea Flower Show. His current list shows more than 280 varieties of Bedding violas, violettas and viola species and contains not only old varieties rescued from possible extinction but new introductions of his own raising.

Elizabeth MacGregor of Kircudbright is another viola and violetta specialist. Her current list of ninety varieties includes not only violas and violettas but a number of viola species. Amongst old-established varieties she includes quite a number of varieties of her own raising.

Hazeldene Nurseries of East Farleigh, Kent have done as much as anyone in recent years to encourage and provide for those who share their love for the pansy, viola and violetta. Their current catalogue lists approximately 120 named varieties of Bedding violas, violettas, Exhibition violas and the increasingly rare named varieties of Fancy and Show pansies. They also distribute seedling pansies and violas and seed. In recent years they have staged fine exhibits at shows throughout the country including the prestigious Chelsea Flower Show.

Bouts Cottage Nurseries of Inkberrow are well-established specialist growers of violas and violettas, with an impressive list of approximately eighty-five varieties. They exhibit at Chelsea Flower Show and elsewhere.

The most recent specialist grower of pansies and violas to

have appeared upon the scene is the Tom Thumb Nursery of Spalding, who has published an illustrated list of approximately 150 named varieties.

In addition there are amateur enthusiasts and members of the specialist societies who will freely exchange amongst themselves and others not only plants, cuttings and seed, but also advice based upon practical experience.

It would appear therefore that if sufficient dedicated enthusiasts persevere, the future for violas, violettas and pansies will be secure. The scope for further refinement and improvement and for the introduction of fresh colour combinations is almost endless and it is inconceivable that there will never be at least a few enthusiasts to carry the story of pansies, violas, violettas on into the future.

3

The Soil

Pansies, violas and violettas are not unduly particular as to the nature of the soil in which they will grow, but as with any garden plants, it is well to consider the situation prior to introducing them to the garden. The basis of all successful and pleasurable gardening is a reasonably fertile and workable soil and unless you are fortunate enough to possess the sort of loam of which so many gardeners can only dream, it is worthwhile at the outset to consider if some practical steps can be taken to compensate for any of the shortcomings in your own particular piece of soil. It is the texture and structure of the soil which can make such a difference to the success and pleasure of gardening. Although there is no simple or easy solution there are a number of things that can be done to improve the physical condition of a poor soil.

The first thing to do is to recognise the nature of your soil, always bearing in mind that soils can vary quite considerably even within the confines of a small garden. If a garden is to be developed from previously uncultivated meadow the task will be relatively simple but on the other hand the garden accompanying recent housing developments can produce many initial problems. There will inevitably have been considerable disturbance to the land as a result of which the existing topsoil may well have been buried or to all intents and purposes removed by the action of mechanical excavation and levelling of the site. Potentially fertile loam topsoil may well be buried under subsoil or transferred elsewhere and it is not unusual to find that beneath a seemingly tranquil surface there lies a mixture of bricks, tiles, cement, sand, glass and any amount of the inevitable paraphernalia resulting from building construction. The initial task will be to investigate the whole area, digging in so far as is possible with a fork to examine what may lie beneath the surface. Armed with bucket or barrow and pick or crow bar, all foreign matter must be systematically removed from designated growing areas to a depth in the region of 12in (30cm), and stacked elsewhere. During the course of this operation the nature of the soil will become apparent and it will fall somewhere between the two extremes of on the one hand heavy clay soil and on the other light sandy soil. All soils, whether of heavy or light texture, are composed of just four basic constituents: mineral particles, organic matter, water and air. All these are vital to the well-being of the plants that we wish to grow. The basic difference between the texture of one soil and another varies with the proportions in which these four constituents are present.

The mineral particles form the inactive basis of the soil and consist of particles of rock broken down by generations of weathering into gravels, sands, silts – which are sand so fine as to no longer retain the characteristics of grittiness – and clays in which the particles are so minute as to adhere together in the form of a dense paste when moist.

The organic matter within the soil, commonly referred to by gardeners as the humus content, consists of a mixture of living, decomposing and dead animal and vegetable matter which in conjunction with the action of bacteria, moisture, air and temperature gradually breaks down to release nutrients into the soil, and in the process of doing so improves the texture of the soil, enabling it to retain vital moisture.

The air content of the soil is vital not only to the support of plant life but also to the bacterial and animal life which makes such a valuable contribution to its fertility. It also allows for the escape of any toxic gases produced within the soil by the processes of decay.

The water content of the soil is essential if only because plants can only absorb nutrition in solution. No matter how rich and fertile a soil, without sufficient moisture in which that nutrition is dissolved it is unobtainable to the plants. Moisture is equally vital in order to maintain the rigid cell structure within the plants.

Soil, in whatever condition, will therefore contain mineral particles, organic matter, air and water, but the all-important question is: in what proportions? In simple terms, a light sandy soil will consist of as much as ninety per cent mineral particles. A heavy clay soil may contain as much as fifty per cent pure clay particles but the soil to which we all aspire will fall some way between the two. It is fortunate that most plants – and violas and pansies are certainly no exception – are tolerant as to the composition of the soil in which they grow. The lightest and heaviest soils are to be avoided where possible however, but this does not mean that the prospect of producing good plants on such soils is by any means impossible. Due to their open texture, light sandy soils lose moisture rapidly and nutrients are readily lost to the leaching action of rain. In their favour, light sandy soils are easy to cultivate and due to their free draining nature can be successfully cultivated throughout the year.

Clay soils on the other hand are more fertile, and provided the texture can be improved to render them hospitable to fibrous rooted plants, chances of success are very good. In its raw state however, clay is difficult to cultivate. Little can be achieved when clay is wet, and when dry, a surface crust will form, making the task extremely onerous. The occasions when clay soil can be effectively and successfully tilled are restricted to those mostly short periods when the soil is neither too wet nor too dry.

The soils to which all gardeners aspire are the medium soils which – as the name implies – contain balanced proportions of sand and silt (or clay) thereby combining the qualities of both in such a way as to produce a medium infinitely more attractive to both plant and gardener.

The name which traditionally falls as music on the ear of the gardener is loam. Loam describes a well-balanced soil which can be tilled with comparative ease, will retain moisture and air and only in the most extreme circumstances will become unduly dry or waterlogged. A medium loam soil will consist of a mixture of approximately half sand and half silt or clay. The lightest loams contain a greater proportion of sand and the heavier loams contain a larger proportion of silt and clay. Any of these loam soils will support the majority of garden plants, including violas and pansies.

TEXTURE

Once you have established the type of soil with which you are dealing, it is wise to consider the ways in which you may improve it, always bearing in mind that there are no simple, seemingly magic solutions. Any steps taken will involve considerable physical effort.

If the problem is that of a stony soil, all larger stones should be removed from the surface and it is wise to cultivate no deeper than is necessary otherwise more stone will be brought to the surface and the job will become endless. In a very stony soil it is only practical to remove the largest stones in order to make cultivation comfortable and there is no reason to be concerned with the small ones which will not unduly interfere with the tilling of the soil. Stony soils are often free-draining and their moisture-retaining properties can be substantially improved by incorporating organic matter to increase the humus content.

Peaty soils are exceedingly rich in organic matter. Their ability to hold excessive moisture can be improved by the application of lime. Their texture can also be improved by the addition of a more loamy soil if this is a practical proposition.

Chalky soils are excessively alkaline, a situation that suits many garden plants, although we cannot include pansies and violas amongst them. Although they are light in texture and relatively easy to cultivate they are not as free-draining as a sandy soil and can become too soft and sticky to be satisfactorily workable when wet. If the layer of topsoil is shallow it should not be cultivated deeper than necessary otherwise more of the underlying chalk will be brought to the surface and the alkalinity will become even more pronounced. The texture of a chalky soil can be improved by adding organic matter and – if alkalinity is a major problem – peat.

Sandy soils are free-draining and easily worked. They tend to warm more readily in spring and are therefore suitable for the establishment of crops early in the year at a time when heavier soils would still be cold and wet. Organic matter and sticky moisture-retaining manures should be incorporated in the surface of the soil in an attempt to reduce the leaching effect of rain with its consequential loss of soil nutrients.

Medium soils present few problems, but gardening on a medium loam is a pleasure unfortunately denied to many.

A silty loam may form a surface crust in dry weather following rains but this can be kept open quite easily by regular scarifying of the surface with an appropriate hand tool, thereby enabling moisture to penetrate and the soil to breathe. A loam must not however be neglected and regular applications of organic matter to replace those that are consumed will keep the texture in good heart.

Clay soils are undoubtedly the most soul-destroying of all and call for physical effort which is inevitably beyond the power of some. The first priority is to install adequate drainage in an attempt to keep moisture-content at an acceptable level, and to dig the clay to enable the winter frosts to penetrate. A surface application of lime will improve the texture of clay but the effects of this are not of a long term nature and clay has the unfortunate ability to revert quite quickly to its former inhospitable consistency. Sharp sand and grit, if incorporated in sufficient quantities and thoroughly mixed with clay, will improve its overall texture and stable manure with a high straw content will greatly help to open up the otherwise compacted nature of such a soil. Organic matter will improve the texture of clay provided sufficient attention has been given to drainage. To apply organic matter to an already saturated clay will do little to make life more pleasant for the gardener. Clay soils are potentially quite fertile – more so than hungry, free-draining sandy and chalky soils – but much of that fertility will be unavailable to fibrous-rooted plants unless the texture can be made more friable.

The evidence of poor soil drainage will probably become apparent during winter – when the plants are at their most vulnerable – and following heavy rainfall or prolonged wet weather. If water lies on the surface of the soil for any length of time, it is a matter for serious concern as saturation will not only starve the plants' roots of air but the bacterial activity within the soil will also be seriously impaired. Toxic gases will accumulate, harmful organisms will flourish and plants other than those which relish soggy ground will perish. The excessive drainage of sandy soils, whilst presenting problems, is by no means as serious as the waterlogged condition of land which has inadequate natural drainage.

There are various conditions which give rise to bad drainage. If the underlying rock is of a non-porous nature, water will be trapped and when it reaches a certain level the effect will become all too visible. There is no simple solution for this situation.

Another common cause of drainage problems is sub-surface pan. Repeated digging or ploughing to the same depth encourages a consolidated smooth surface to form beneath the topsoil. The water which has percolated through the topsoil reaches a surface reluctant to absorb it. This problem is commonly encountered where the subsoil – as is often the case – consists of heavy, already compacted clay. A traditional answer to this, and the only practical solution, is an operation called double-digging. This practise is often recommended, although it is not a task for the faint-hearted and requires considerable strength and stamina. The first spit of topsoil is removed to reveal the underlying subsoil. The latter is then cultivated with a spade or fork to break any panning and open the soil to encourage the free passage of water to a greater depth. The effect of such an operation will be comparatively short-lived unless you take the opportunity to incorporate an adequate quantity of sharp grit, gravel, weathered clinker, ash, or any other granular matter which will retain the open structure for many more years. On no account must subsoil be brought to the surface, or precious topsoil be buried, but by approaching the job in a systematic fashion, this can be avoided. However, the hard pan of subsoil may be so compacted that a conventional spade or fork may not be adequate, in which case a pick-axe is perhaps a more appropriate tool for the job. If all else fails, you will have to consider some form of artificial drainage: a trench or interconnecting trenches at the base of which must be laid drainage pipes or bricks or stones. These will collect excess water and carry it away to lower land where it can be dispersed. This is a major exercise but necessary if successful cultivation is envisaged as a long-term venture.

If the cause of bad drainage is non-porous underlying rock, remedies of this nature are impractical and you must then consider raising the level of the beds in which the plants are to be grown. If adjacent topsoil is added to a bed, the level can be raised to a point at which waterlogging of that bed can no longer occur. Excess water will drain from the bed into the marginal soil from which the topsoil has been removed and it can then be channelled away to a lower part of the garden. With adequate initial planning of a garden, topsoil can be removed from those areas designated for paths, patios and driveways, and used to raise the level of those areas chosen for cultivation – thereby making maximum use of available topsoil.

There are three main methods of digging. On light, adequately-drained soils, single-digging is probably sufficient. Single-digging simply means turning over the soil to the depth of the spade or fork in a consistent fashion, and in so doing burying any surface vegetation to such a depth that it will die and eventually rot down to improve the organic content of the soil. Any perennial vegetation – particularly roots – should be thoroughly removed at this stage. A spade may be necessary for compacted soil but for the majority of light soils a fork will probably prove to be the most satisfactory tool for the job. If any manures, composts or base fertilisers are to be added, this can be done in conjunction with the digging on heavier soils. On previously uncultivated ground, or on land which has become unduly compacted and where inadequate drainage is apparent, double-digging as pre-viously described is the most appropriate procedure. A third alternative to consider is ridging, a method of autumn digging in which strips of soil the width of three spades are formed into pronounced ridges by turning the two outer strips in upon the centre. The object of the exercise is to expose the maximum surface area to the action of winter frosts: frost action will have the effect of breaking up the surface soil. If your soil is of reason-able texture, and you wish to grow violas and pansies there is no need to consider anything more elaborate than straightforward single-digging.

FERTILITY

Having improved, in so far as is possible, the texture of the soil, you should then pay attention to its potential fertility. It is important to be aware of any excess alkalinity or acidity in the soil. Comparatively few plants are happy in an excessively acid soil, and violas and pansies are no exception. The same situation applies with a soil of excessive alkalinity. The best way of establishing the facts is to test the soil to identify its PH value. The PH value is measured using a scale of numbers which run approximately from zero to fourteen. The lower numbers signify acidity, the higher numbers alkalinity, and a PH number of 7 implies neutrality. Soils usually fall within the range 3.5 to 8.5 with the average garden soil restricted to a range no greater than 4.5 to 8. A PH reading of 4.5 or thereabouts is cause for concern and action unless the plan is to grow azaleas, camellias, rhododendrons, heathers and other plants which show preference for acid soils. Similarly a PH value of 8 is excessively alkaline, a situation to the liking of carnations and pinks, wallflowers, delphiniums, the cabbage family and many of the alpine plants introduced from such conditions in the wild. Many plants show considerable tolerance but a PH figure in the region of 6.5 is appropriate for the gardener who wishes to cultivate a variety of plants. The traditional antidote to acidity is lime – a relatively cheap material which is easy to apply provided care is taken not to do so in excess. Lime should not be applied in conjunction with other fertilisers. If manure has been incorporated with winter digging, postpone liming until February. After liming, allow a month before repeating the dose. If lime has already been applied during winter to a heavy soil (to help the formation of a crumb structure) this should already have had a marked effect on any acidity present but it should be borne in mind that lime is readily soluble and therefore leaches from the soil comparatively easily.

It is rather more difficult to render an alkaline soil less so, but it is unlikely that you will encounter a soil so alkaline as to not satisfactorily support pansies and violas.

Having attended to the acidity or alkalinity of the soil, attention can now be directed towards its nutrient or fertiliser content. Fertilisers are readily available as organic or inorganic matter, or as a blend of the two. Like lime, the initial attraction of inorganic fertilisers is the ease with which they can be applied. They are blended in the manufacturing process either to compensate for deficiencies in the soil or as balanced mixtures to replace nutrients taken from the soil by way of harvested crops. Some fertilisers are supplied in relatively crude form which will only break down slowly into solution over an extended period. These fertilisers are usually applied to the soil as a base dressing to be taken up by the roots of maturing plants as they reach deeper into the soil. Quick-acting, more soluble fertilisers are useful when applied as a surface dressing to the plants as they grow. Subsequent rain or irrigation will carry the nutrients down to those areas of the soil where young root growth is at its most active. No fertiliser will act more quickly than those already in solution and applied in liquid form to the soil around a growing plant. All fertilisers in con-centrated form must be kept from direct contact with stems, foliage and flowers; the only exception being foliar feeds in which the soluble fertiliser is applied to the leaves in a sufficiently dilute form as to be absorbed as an instant nutritional boost.

The basis of most garden fertilisers are the three major plant nutrients – nitrogen, phosphates and potash; commonly abbrevi-ated to the initials N, P and K. A reputable fertiliser will be clearly labelled to indicate the percentage content of these three ingredients. The nitrogen, or N component, the phosphate, or P component, and the potassium, or K component, will be accompanied by three figures. The figures correspond to the percentage of each component in the order N, P and K. It therefore becomes possible, armed with a little knowledge of the part played by each of these ingredients, to compare proprietory fertilisers and to decide on the one most appropriate for a par-ticular purpose. In the case of the phosphates a well-labelled fertiliser will indicate what proportion of that phosphate is soluble in water – in other words how much of that phosphate will become almost immediately available to the plant. The remainder of the phosphates will only be soluble in mineral salts, which means that they are only slowly made available to the plant and are therefore of more long-term value.

Nitrogen is commonly considered to be the leaf provider of plants and it is used to boost those crops where foliage is of paramount importance such as grass and leaf vegetables. Stunted growth, pale leaves and weak stems are the signs of a shortage of nitrogen. Nitrogen applied as a top dressing in spring and summer can provide rapid improvements but like most quick-acting fer-tilisers it is rapidly leached, particularly in light soils, and should not be applied in excess of a plant's immediate requirements.

Phosphate's are commonly called the root producer. They are instrumental in encouraging the formation of a vigorous root system, so vital to a plant's ability to absorb nutrient and moisture from the soil. Light soils will lose phosphates more readily than heavier soils. A base dressing of bone meal is one of the traditional ways to ensure that there is a supply of slowly released phosphate available to perennial plants. Poor root development, a purplish tinge on leaves and poor yield of fruit, are all signs of a possible phosphate deficiency. Root vegetables will never perform to their best where there is a lack of phosphate.

The third of the major plant nutrients is potash commonly considered to be the flower producer. A deficiency of potash can be suspected when flowers lack strength of colour. Yellow and brown leaves may well be the result of potash deficiency and plants may well exhibit less resistance to disease. The obvious solution is to apply a base or top dressing, as appropriate, of a fertiliser with a high potash content.

The next most important plant nutrient after nitrogen, phosphates and potash are the three substances calcium, magnesium and sulphur. Calcium is important in that it renders acid soils more neutral and it is instrumental in maintaining the carbon dioxide content of the soil. Flowers, fruit and vegetables all benefit from an adequate presence of calcium in the soil. Calcium deficiency exhibits similar symptoms to nitrogen deficiency: stunted growth and pale leaves. Lime can be applied where calcium shortage is suspected but if the soil is already alkaline an alternative material, gypsum, should be used instead. Soils rich in potash are improved by the addition of calcium where it is lacking.

Magnesium deficiency may be suspected when yellow or brown patches form between the veins of mature leaves and when young leaves fall for no other apparent reason. If the diagnosis proves correct, a compound fertiliser with a magnesium content applied as a base dressing or top dressing should counter this deficiency.

Sulphur may sound like an unlikely plant nutrient. It is unusual for sulphur deficiency to manifest itself other than in areas well away from industrial pollution. The symptoms are similar to those of nitrogen deficiency and the balance can be redressed by applying any fertiliser containing a balanced proportion of sulphur.

In addition to the major nutrients nitrogen, phosphates and potash and the secondary nutrients calcium, magnesium and sulphur we must consider another six substances, minute quantities of which are necessary in a soil for optimum fertility. These are the trace elements iron, manganese, molybdenum, boron, zinc and copper. We now live in an age where we can readily purchase a wide, sometimes bewildering, choice of inorganic fertilisers all packaged in forms that are convenient and easy to apply. The inherent danger is that fertilisers can be applied in excess of a crop's ability to consume them and the consequent build-up can leach from the soil into our streams and rivers where other forms of life suffer as a result. Fertilisers have, however, become an important element in maintaining the fertility of intensively cultivated soil and unless the nutrient value of the soil is maintained, any subsequent crops whether vegetables, fruit or flowers will become progressively lighter.

Fertilisers fall basically into two categories, organic and inorganic. Organic fertilisers are, as the name implies, of animal or vegetable origin which, as a result of bacterial action within the soil, break down to provide, amongst other things, a significant amount of the nitrogen requirement of plants. Bacteria are relatively ineffective in cold, acid or waterlogged soils and the composition of the soil is therefore contributory towards the speed at which an organic fertiliser will work. Organic fertilisers are slow acting, releasing nutrients over an extended period.

Inorganic fertilisers are manufactured from purely inorganic chemical components and although considered synthetic or artificial – names suggesting that they are in some way inferior – it is recognised that once broken down into the feeding solution, it is unlikely that a plant will detect any difference between a fertiliser derived inorganically and that derived organically. Inorganic fertilisers do not rely upon bacterial action in order to render them freely available to plants and are consequently faster acting. Organic fertilisers are better applied as a base dressing, and the faster acting inorganic fertilisers are useful when applied as a boost to a rapidly-growing crop. Care must be taken when applying the more concentrated inorganic fertilisers that residue does not touch leaves and young stems where it can have a harmful, scorching effect. Fertilisers are readily available in solid and liquid form: powders will dissolve rapidly, granules break down more slowly and are therefore of more long-term value, and slow release fertilisers are specifically formulated to release nutrients over a period of many months. Liquid fertilisers are fast acting and ideal for applying during the growing season in conjunction with irrigation. Liquid fertilisers can be purchased either in concentrated liquid form to be diluted in accordance with instructions, or as powders which should be readily soluble in the specified quantity of water.

Fertilisers are commonly divided into two further sections. Straight fertilisers – which contain one major nutrient and are, therefore, to be employed where a distinct requirement has been isolated – and compound fertilisers – which contain a mixture of plant nutrients, primarily nitrogen and phosphates and usually potash.

Finally there are foliar fertilisers formulated for spraying onto the leaves of a plant through which they can be gradually absorbed into the sap stream. They boost the growth of a plant where the root action is perhaps restricted by poor soil conditions. Foliar feeding provides an instant boost and should be applied as an evening spray when rain is not forecast. It should remain moist on the leaf surface allowing sufficient time to be absorbed.

For certain plants, there are specifically formulated fertilisers. Rose and tomato fertilisers for example are high in potash, and lawn fertilisers are high in nitrogen, but for a general purpose application to cater for the needs of most plants – violas and pansies among them – it is prudent to apply a balanced fertiliser in which the nitrogen, phosphate and potash components are in roughly equal proportion to one another. Above all, you should apply all fertilisers sparingly, in accordance with manufacturers' instructions and resist the temptation to exceed the stated dose which may well prove detrimental to the well-being of the plant. Take the trouble to measure the surface area to be treated and accurately measure the quantity of fertiliser to be applied to that area for optimum effect. Pay heed to any manufacturer's advice as to the recommended frequency of applications. In this way you should avoid any harmful build-up of excessive, and therefore possibly harmful levels of salts in the soil.

Fertilisers

There are many proprietory fertilisers available in liquid, granular and powder form and the following list represents just some of them:

Basic Slag   A slow-acting fertiliser, high in phosphates, which can be applied 4–8oz per sq yd (112–224g per sq m) in autumn and winter. A suitable dressing for wet, acid soils.
Bone Flour   A fertiliser high in phosphates to be applied any time at 2–4oz per sq yd (56–112g per sq m). Faster acting than the traditional bone meal.
Bone Meal   A coarser grade of the above for more gradual, long-lasting effect.
Chilean Potash Nitrate   A quick-acting fertiliser. High in both nitrogen and potash to be applied at 1–2oz per sq yd (28–56g per sq m) in spring and early summer as a top dressing.

Dried Blood   High in nitrogen. A top dressing for spring and summer at 1–2oz per sq yd (28–56g per sq m)

Fish Meal   High in nitrogen and phosphates and an appropriate base dressing when applied at 2–4oz per sq yd (56–112g per sq m) in winter and spring.

Growmore   A well-balanced inorganic fertiliser with equal proportions of nitrogen, phosphates and potash. Fast acting and convenient to apply.

Hoof & Horn Meal   High in nitrogen. Apply at the rate of 2–4oz per sq yd (56–112g per sq m). The speed of action is dependent upon the fineness of the meal.

Nitrate of Potash   Particularly high in potash with nitrogen also. Quick-acting when applied at 1–2oz per sq yd (28–56g per sq m). Usually in liquid form.

Nitrate of Soda   High in nitrogen and very quick to act. Apply at no more than 1oz per sq yd (28g per sq m) avoiding stems and leaves. Not recommended for clay soils.

Nitro–Chalk   High in nitrogen. The chalk component will help to neutralize an acid soil. Apply at 1–2oz per sq yd (28–56g per sq m).

Poultry Manure   A balanced organic material to be applied at no more than 2oz per sq yd (56g per sq m) as a top dressing. It can be applied in heavier doses as a base dressing.

Rock Phosphate   A phosphate fertiliser for autumn and winter. Apply at 4oz per sq yd (112g per sq m).

Soot   Contains nitrogen. It should be allowed to weather before applying as a base or top dressing.

Sulphate of Ammonia   A nitrogen fertiliser. Fast-acting when applied at no more than 1oz per sq yd (28g per sq m). It turns the soil more acid.

Sulphate of Potash   High potash feed. A base or top dressing to be applied at no more than 1oz per sq yd (28g per sq m).

Superphosphate of Lime   High in phosphates. A base dressing to be applied at the rate of 2–4oz per sq yd (56–112g per sq m).

Urea   A common component of liquid fertilisers. It is high in nitrogen and is fast acting. Apply at $\frac{1}{2}$oz per sq yd (14g per sq m) in spring.

Urea Formaldehyde   Similar to the above but can be applied at any time of year at the rate of 1–2oz per sq yd (28–56g per sq m). The nitrogen is released more slowly and gradually over a long period.

Wood Ash   High in potash. Quick acting. Apply at 4–8oz per sq yd (112–224g per sq m) and store under cover to retain the nutrient.

Specific fertilisers should only be applied to soil which has been sufficiently analysed to establish what it does or does not already contain or in which any deficiency is clearly indicated by the condition of plant growth. If in doubt it is wiser to maintain fertility by applying a balanced formula fertiliser strictly in accordance with the manufacturer's instructions.

Humus

It must be remembered that fertilisers will do little if anything to improve the physical structure and texture of a poor soil and it is not only the drainage but perhaps most important of all the humus content of the soil we should strive to maintain. Humus is that part of a soil which consists of partially decomposed organic matter. All dead vegetable and animal matter of whatever kind is gradually broken down by the perpetual activities of the many millions of bacteria and other microscopic organisms to which the soil is home. Soil without humus is nothing more than finely ground rock and as such is unable to support the vast majority of plant life. The action of the bacteria creates heat – commonly witnessed by the decaying process of manures and grass clippings. When the process has reached a stage at which the manure or compost has settled to a more normal temperature, has broken down into a less fibrous and more crumbly structure and ceased to smell offensive, it is said to be well rotted. It is then ready for application as a base dressing, top dressing or mulch, the value of which can never be over-stated. The advantage of conventional stable or farmyard manures and composts is that whilst they are unscientific preparations of variable content, they are a combination of nutrient and humus matter, a most natural and balanced way of maintaining the structure, texture and nutrient level of cultivated soil. If unrotted organic matter such as grass clippings, fresh dung, live weeds or seaweed are cultivated into the soil it must be understood that the increased activity of bacteria which will result can rob the soil temporarily of nitrogen. It is therefore important that nitrogen in some form should be added when applying fresh unrotted manures. Heat will be generated to such an extent as to harm plant growth and unrotted manures should therefore only be incorporated in fallow ground or away from the roots of plants until the rotting process has subsided. Well-rotted manures on the other hand cannot damage roots and they will not consume nitrogen to the detriment of the plants.

Peat, pulverised bark and sawdust are all additional organic materials which can improve the texture of soil. They can be used effectively for mulching the surface of the soil to conserve moisture and stifle weed growth but they provide little if any nutrition. Their chief value lies in their ability to open up the texture of heavy soils and to retain moisture in light soils. Amongst the materials employed as humus-makers for the soil are the following:

Bark   Bark is available in various consistencies both coarse and fine. It is useful as a surface mulch and a 1in (2.5cm) thick layer will stifle weeds over a long period if left undisturbed. The soil beneath will remain cool and moist; conditions favoured by many plants.

Compost   No two recipes for compost are the same. Build up 6in (15cm) layers of organic matter separated by 1in (2.5cm) layers of soil. Keep excessive water out and insulate the container to keep the heat in. Leave for a few months.

This natural process should produce some valuable compost for surface mulching of the soil. A bucket per square yard is the quantity to aim for but it is unlikely that an average household can produce sufficient.

Farmyard Manure   Protect from rain until the straw is rotted and the smell has subsided and apply as a surface mulch or dig it in. Farmyard manure is moisture retentive and particularly useful on light soils.

Green Manure   A green manure is a crop grown specifically to dig into the soil or to be composted and returned in its entirety to the soil. Land that would otherwise be fallow can have a crop grown in order to fix the nitrogen within the soil – the nitrogen might otherwise be lost to leaching or to the atmosphere. There are many plants that can be used for green manuring – mustard and leguminous plants such as vetches, clovers, peas and lupins are such examples. Red clover is suitable for summer cropping and a mixture of rye grass and vetch is more suitable for winter cropping.

Leafmould   Leaves can be composted in 6in (15cm) layers divided by 1in (2.5cm) layers of soil. Oak and Beech leaves are particularly suitable. The process is slow and a vast bulk of leaves will, when composted, produce comparatively little mould which can be dug in or applied as surface mulch. It may have the effect of rendering the soil more acid.

Peat   Sedge peat breaks down more readily in the soil than moss peat which opens up a compacted soil and helps to retain moisture. Clean and easy to handle and a good surface mulching material.

Poultry Manure   Rather too rich for direct application to the soil except in very small quantities but an ideal activator for the compost heap.

Sawdust   To be used with discretion. It can be responsible for depleting the level of nitrogen in the soil and should therefore be used in conjunction with a nitrogenous fertiliser.

Seaweed   Provided all traces of salt are washed away, seaweed can be dug directly into the soil without composting.

Sewage sludge (dried, activated)   Rich in nutrient but will add very little humus.

Spent Hops   Allowed to weather and then applied at the rate of a bucket per sq yd will raise the humus content a little.

Stable Manure   Usually contains a high proportion of straw or wood shavings. Allow to rot well before applying. Particularly beneficial when mixed with a clay soil.

Straw   Compost the straw well with other green organic matter before applying to the soil.

Provided that the soil is of a reasonably open and crumb-like structure and yet contains sufficient organic matter to conserve moisture throughout periods of dry weather and provided also that it is neither excessively acid nor alkaline and contains a reasonable level of balanced nutrients, there is no reason why it should not be perfectly possible to cultivate fine, healthy violas, violettas and pansies.

4

Site and Cultivation

When deciding where in the garden to site violas, violettas and pansies, two basic principles should be borne in mind. We are concerned with plants which perform best when their roots are in cool, moist soil and, like so many other flowering plants, they blossom with the greatest profusion when subjected to the maximum amount of sunlight. A potential problem will therefore arise: in those areas exposed to the full force of the sun, the soil will become the hottest and driest, and conversely those areas that receive most shade will have the coolest and moistest soil. The object of the exercise is therefore to arrive at an acceptable compromise falling somewhere between these two extremes. If we are compelled to live with one of these circumstances, the exposed situation is preferable in that steps can always be taken to retain the cool moist conditions that the roots will prefer. Where the soil is becoming too dry, the obvious reaction is to supply more moisture through some form of irrigation, the most usual being to employ a hose or watering can.

IRRIGATION

No matter which method is used it is important that the moisture should be supplied gently and over an extended period which will allow the soil and plants to absorb that moisture. Absorption is a slow gentle process and to apply water in a forceful, abrupt manner can not only splash the flowers with soil but even damage the plants. If water is applied at a rate in excess of the soil's ability to absorb it, it will cause the surface of the soil to form a crust. This crust will then have the effect of making the soil less receptive to subsequent applications of water.

The ideal manner in which to apply water is as a fine gentle spray or mist, if wind conditions permit, and the process should take place over a period of time sufficient to ensure that the soil is moistened to such depth as to reach the deepest roots of the plants. A sufficiently moist soil can be encouraged to retain that moisture by regular light waterings. If the soil has become dry to any great depth it is vital to apply sufficient moisture to ensure that not only the surface area but also deeper ground are wetted. The root tips are sensitive to moisture and will attempt to search it out wherever it might be. Deep moisture will encourage deep root penetration which will then help the plant to resist any subsequent conditions of drought. If dry soil is wetted insufficiently it will have the effect of attracting the moisture-sensitive root tips towards the surface and the plant will then become much more vulnerable to any subsequent periods of dry weather. Watering, for maximum effect, should be done at the end of the day when the sun will no longer be competing by causing immediate evaporation and transpiration. Gentle watering at eventide will allow the plants the cool of night to absorb and utilise that moisture before the process of evaporation begins once again at daybreak. Violas, violettas and pansies will always react as if to prefer rain water to tap water but it is probable that it is the manner in which that water is applied rather than its physical properties that is the deciding factor. More often than not nature provides relatively gentle moisture over an extended period. The occasional torrential downpour is no more welcomed than a comparably forceful application by artificial means. When dealing with only small numbers of plants the water should be drawn into a container and then allowed to stand until such time as it has warmed a little. Plants are unlikely to react kindly to the sudden drop of temperature that results from applying water directly from a main supply but when watering larger areas by hose pipe this is, of course, unavoidable.

It should be borne in mind that all irrigation or rainfall will leach a certain amount of the nutrients from the cultivated soil, and applications of fertilizing materials should be related to the amount of rainfall or irrigation that is taking place. In the ideal season the balance of rainfall to sunshine will call for little or no supplementary watering but we must always be prepared for those many occasions, all too soon forgotten, when the weather turns hot and dry and the maintainance of soil moisture becomes the major preoccupation of the moment.

In this connection the value of mulching the soil cannot be over-emphasised. A mulch of composted organic matter applied to the surface of the soil will do much to retain the moisture within it and protect it from the dessicating effect of the sun. Mulch will also smother potential weed growth and encourage an environment in which worms will be active and play their part in keeping the surface soil open and of friable texture. There is often a price to pay in that the cool moist conditions provided by the mulching material will be a popular rendezvous for slugs and other less welcome visitors.

It is unfortunate that the average household may have difficulty in producing enough organic waste matter to provide as much compost or mulch as could profitably be employed in the garden. There are however various alternative materials on the market such as peat, bark, mushroom compost and spent hops which can be purchased to supplement the home-produced material. Lawn clippings are perhaps the most readily available mulching material for the average gardener. They can not only be composted with soil and other materials but can also be employed as an immediate mulch, provided that two important warnings are heeded. Clippings from grass which has been recently dressed with any preparation containing a weed killer must never be used in this way. They must be applied in a layer sufficiently thin that there will be no noticeable build-up of heat caused by their process of rotting. A handful of fresh lawn mowings applied in a thin covering around the soil of violas, violettas or pansies will do much to keep the roots of the plants cool and moist in summer. No mulch should be applied in such a way as to come into direct contact with the stems and foliage of the plant. If mulch is considered as no more than something with which to shade the roots and stifle weed growth, then it is one of the most useful 'tools' at the gardener's disposal.

SITUATION

Having discussed methods with which to retain moisture, we can also consider the ways in which we can influence the effect of the heat of the sun. Irrespective of a plant's overall preference for sun or shade, the flowers of that plant are largely affected by direct sunlight. Anemones, Celandines and other plants which flourish in the damp, shaded conditions of deciduous woodland exhibit their flowers to best effect only when they are in direct contact with the sun's rays and in this respect so do violas, violettas and pansies. In a reasonably moisture-retentive soil there is no reason why they should not be grown in fully exposed, unshaded soil. I have never witnessed more spectacularly floriferous violas and violettas than those which I grow in considerable quantity on a totally exposed south-east-facing Somerset hillside where the only shade is from late afternoon onwards. This means that in the summer they can be exposed to the full force of the sun's rays for eight hours or more a day, and in such conditions flower with abandon virtually continuously from April until the first frost of Autumn – indeed there is rarely a day in the year when it would not be possible to pick at least a buttonhole or a small posy of flowers. It should be emphasised however that to grow violas, violettas and pansies under such conditions it would be wise to have a supply of water readily available if only as an insurance against a period of drought.

If you only have a limited amount of time to tend to the garden, it is perhaps wiser to lessen the risks by choosing a site for violas, violettas and pansies where they will receive respite for at least part of the day from full exposure to direct sunshine. In the majority of gardens, there will be areas which throughout various periods of the day will be shielded partially or totally from direct sunlight. An east-facing wall, fence or hedge will of course receive only morning sun and conversely a west-facing one will receive only afternoon sun. A totally exposed south-facing fence or wall is potentially a problem area for violas, violettas and pansies unless the level of moisture in the soil can be sufficiently maintained to compensate for the excessively hot, dry, baking conditions which might otherwise prevail. A north-facing wall will probably not be conducive to the cultivation of the best plants. Any benefits from the cool, damp soil will be overshadowed by the tendency of the plants to become drawn and ungainly in their efforts to reach more light and this may well lead to a lack of flower production. Perhaps the ideal conditions are those in which the dappled shade of larger shrubs or trees filters a percentage of sunlight sufficient to encourage flowers. What may appear as dappled shade in May and June may of course become heavy shade by July and August and there is therefore no simple solution. In a hot, dry summer, we shall inevitably wish for some shade, but in a dull wet summer an exposed situation is always preferable, and all that we can do is to hedge bets in the face of our unpredictable weather.

Violas, violettas and pansies will grow well and look good when used as a base carpet beneath roses and other small shrubs which can afford them some summer shade without ever casting too much shadow. They can be incorporated in the planning of an herbaceous border in such a manner as to receive some shade from other taller neighbouring plants. Alternatively, if grown sufficiently close to one another, a mass feature of violas, violettas or pansies will form. They will knit together, thereby completely covering what would otherwise be soil exposed to the drying effect of sun and wind. Grown in such a way, they will maintain for themselves the cool, moist soil conditions that they so like.

They will also suffocate competing weeds, and to all intents and purposes perform the function of a surface mulch. Violettas and smaller violas, if planted no more than 10in (25cm) apart, should by June have put on sufficient growth to link one with the other. The larger violas should perhaps be planted a foot or more apart to achieve a comparable effect.

Employed informally, violas, violettas and pansies blend naturally with other garden plants. If they are to be planted in a shady area of the garden it is wise to anticipate that the plants may well grow appreciably taller than they would in a more exposed, sunny spot. Grown alone in this manner they may well become lax and fail to display their blossoms to best advantage. This can be alleviated if they are planted in conjunction with other plants which will provide some support through which the violas are able to grow upwards. The *Cornuta* violas, when grown in the environment of a mixed herbaceous border, will often react in this attractive manner. In competing for attention with surrounding plants they will scramble upwards and in so doing attain a height that they would never reach without such support. In this respect they are an ideal plant to incorporate in the forefront of a mixed herbaceous border. There, their accommodating nature can be used to great advantage to fill the odd spaces between other plants of more predictable habit.

In the traditional informality of a cottage garden there are few situations, if any, where pansies, violas and violettas whether, deliberately planted or perhaps self-sown, will look incongruous. Individual plants can be used indiscriminately to fill any small space which might otherwise lack colour and interest and their inoffensive colourings blend sympathetically with almost all the flowers of the cottage garden. If you decide to give them greater emphasis, whole areas can be given over entirely to violas, violettas or pansies. The greatest impact will be achieved when sufficient plants of a particular colour or variety are grouped together. As with all garden plants, an isolated specimen can very often be lost when competing for attention with too many others. A mass display of one single colour, even when planted in an informal manner, is invariably more spectacular and effective than the 'one of everything' style of gardening.

Having decided upon a variety or a colour scheme it is well to consider a group or drift of that variety. You should resist the temptation to lessen the potential impact by introducing too many other distractions. Violas and violettas are particularly valuable in this respect, in view of their exceptionally long and continuous flowering period. Violas, violettas and pansies can be used in a slightly more formal manner as edgings or borders to beds, paths and driveways. The compact, uniform habit of violas, and violettas in particular, lends itself towards defining such outlines. The smaller violas and violettas are particularly suitable for smaller, more intimate bedding schemes and narrow footpaths, and the bolder, taller-growing varieties for edging shrubberies, driveways and wider walkways.

For those of you wishing to take formal styles of gardening to their extreme, violas, violettas and pansies should be considered in conjunction with geometric bedding schemes, parterres and knot gardens. Solid blankets of colour – a style so often seen in the context of public parks and gardens – are an ideal subject for violas, violettas and pansies. If they are bedded out sufficiently closely together, they can be relied upon to provide colour throughout summer and to a lesser extent during spring and autumn and even winter when employing varieties of winter-flowering pansies.

Parterres and knot gardens are traditionally delineated by out-lines of dwarf box edging and it is the pockets and spaces within the overall design which can provide the ideal home for violas, violettas and pansies. If the edgings are of no more than a few inches in height, the violettas and small compact violas are the ideal plant for infilling. Where the edging is perhaps a foot or more in height, larger, taller varieties of viola or pansy would of course be more appropriate. This traditional style of gardening is presently attracting renewed interest – a style which although associated with gardening and landscaping on a grand scale is eminently adaptable to much smaller gardens.

CONTAINER GROWING

Associated with both formal and informal gardening styles are those methods of culture best described as container growing. The quantity, quality and variety of available containers for growing plants today is perhaps greater than ever before. At the less expensive end of the market you will find plastic containers which are very suitable for accompanying modern environments. At the top end of the market there are some truly magnificent examples of traditional craft and design which are a joy to behold in themselves. Between these two extremes, a multitude of pots, pans, urns and troughs in various combinations of terracotta and stone-like material can be found, which allow those who possess no more than a patio, courtyard, roof top or porch, to create an attractive small area of garden. Timber tubs, barrels and window boxes are equally suitable for such application and every bit as satisfactory, provided steps are taken to preserve the timber from the deterioration that will inevitably result from direct contact with damp soil over a long period of time. If investing in timber containers, it is worth considering a separate insert to fit within the tub or container so that the soil is free from direct contact with the timber. A secondary effect of such an inner lining will be to provide cavity insulation. This will prevent the contents of the container becoming unduly hot when sunshine falls on its outer walls. All but the thickest of containers will tend to become very hot when exposed to full sunshine and if no shade is afforded, you must constantly replenish the moisture which will be lost very rapidly in a containerised soil.

When watering containers, it is wise to water not only the contents but the container itself. Terracotta and similar materials have considerable powers of absorption and a dry container will in itself absorb much of the moisture from the soil. Gardening in containers gives greater flexibility in that all but the heaviest vessels can be moved and rearranged with ease and if potted plants are plunged within a larger container they can quite easily be replaced with others when their main contribution has ended.

The ultimate in 'containerisation' is perhaps the hanging basket – a somewhat unnatural method by which plants are suspended above ground in baskets containing a suitable growing medium. Undoubtedly, there are many plants which can be grown most attractively in this manner but it is open to question whether violas, violettas and pansies should be numbered amongst them. Invariably, a hanging basket will be viewed from below and it is therefore at its most effective when the plants it contains are of a weeping, trailing habit. Where the situation is such, however, that the basket is viewed beneath eye level – such as in a basement or sunken area of the garden – there is no reason to suppose that violas, violettas and pansies would not be very effective so arranged. The all-important cool, moist soil conditions must be adequately maintained.

All these matters are no more than a combination of individual taste and preference and the adventurous gardener should never feel reluctant to experiment in all the many ways in which plants might satisfactorily grow. Much of the fun of gardening lies in being innovative and, by trial and error, establishing a system which suits both the gardener and the plant.

5

Propagation of Violas and Violettas

Whilst there are a number of methods by which violas and violettas can be propagated, the choice when considering pansies is more limited. Pansies are invariably grown from seed and treated as annuals or biennials according to the season in which the seed is sown. Named varieties of pansy must however be propagated vegetatively.

There is much advantage to be gained by propagating fresh violas and violettas on an annual basis. Young plants on fresh young roots are likely to perform more reliably than older plants which have been left *in situ*. Mature plants may not survive a severe winter unscathed although their vigour can be enhanced by transplanting them to fresh soil in each successive season.

Violas and violettas invariably provide most positive and dynamic effect when grown in groups or drifts of more than one plant of a particular favourite. More than one method can be employed for increasing stock. As with many other herbaceous garden plants there are four basic methods of propagation, namely division, cuttings, seed and to a lesser extent, layering. The method you choose will to a great extent depend on what is ultimately required and in what quantity.

DIVISION

It should be understood from the outset that not all violas and violettas possess such habit of growth as to make division of the plant a practical proposition – unless only a very small number of plants are required. A noticeable exception to this rule are the varieties of *V. cornuta* whose habit of growth is to produce a mass of rooting underground stems which can quite easily be detached from the parent plant with the minimum of disturbance. They can then be transferred directly to wherever they are required to grow. These outer growths can be carefully lifted and severed from the parent plant at any convenient time during autumn or winter, when in all probability they are already in the process of

Separate clump with hand fork

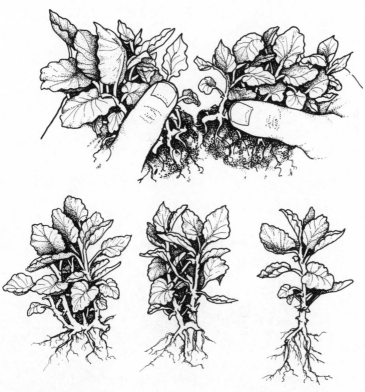

Propagation by division: division of a mature plant into rooted portions of various sizes

Mature plant

Mature plant trimmed and top-dressed

Subsequent growth of basal shoots ideal as cuttings

Propagation by cuttings

forming roots of their own. If these roots are carefully transplanted into well-prepared soil and gently watered in, they should develop into fine flowering plants for the following season. Some simple form of protection against excessive winter wet is a wise precaution, but other than this no coddling is necessary. An alternative method of increasing stocks of the *cornuta* varieties is to lift the whole plant in autumn or spring and simply divide it or cut it carefully into as many portions as is possible, ensuring that each portion has a share of the root of the plant. A sharp knife with a serrated cutting edge is the ideal tool for the purpose. If new young root growth is in evidence, old, woody roots can be trimmed away and the divisions can then be transplanted into well-prepared soil elsewhere. Plant slightly deeper than before, water well in order to consolidate the soil around the roots, and such divisions should require no further attention.

Violas and violettas of truly tufted habit can be divided in much the same way as the cornutas if not with quite such ease. If the plant is to be divided in autumn it is advisable in late July or early August to draw the surrounding soil towards the plants, thereby raising the level of the soil round the base of the shoots and encouraging these basal shoots to form fresh young roots. If the soil texture prevents this operation, the same result can be achieved by top dressing the plant with a fine friable compost which can be gently worked around the stems of the plant and watered in. Provided that the plant is then kept reasonably moist you will find, when lifting to divide in autumn, that the root system is somewhat larger and more healthy than it might otherwise have been, and it will be that much easier to make divisions. Once again the actual division must be undertaken with great care, so that each portion of plant has sufficient root growth to ensure its survival when transplanted into fresh ground. To attempt to divide a plant into too many small plants is not recommended. Bedding violas of more straggling, pansy-like growth do not lend themselves to division in this way and are best multiplied from cuttings or even perhaps layers.

Division is a relatively crude but none the less simple and effective method of increasing stock of violas and violettas in modest numbers.

CUTTINGS

To those who master the technique, cuttings are without a doubt the most satisfactory method of propagating the vast majority of

Severed basal shoot

Basal shoot with blanched underground stem

Basal shoot with rudimentary root system

Stem cutting

Cutting prepared for insertion

Cutting inserted in sharp sand'

Propagation by cuttings

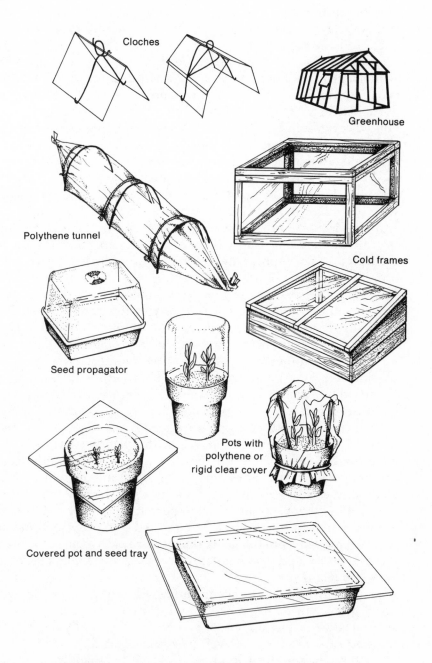

Cloches

Greenhouse

Polythene tunnel

Cold frames

Seed propagator

Pots with polythene or rigid clear cover

Covered pot and seed tray

A selection of structures all suitable for the propagation of pansies, violas and violettas; no artificial heating required

violas and violettas. The cuttings require no artificial heat and only the most simple form of protection against adverse weather conditions is necessary during the first few months of their existence. It is in fact quite possible to strike cuttings in suitably prepared soil in an appropriate position without any form of artificial protection whatsoever, provided the operation is undertaken during the milder, more hospitable seasons of the year.

Any stems which have matured to the stage at which they are hollow are unsuitable for cuttings and should only be used in the absence of more healthy cuttings with vigorous and firm stems. It is unlikely that hollow cuttings will root or that if they were to do so they would produce a plant of quality and vigour. Likewise, flowered or flowering stems should be avoided. Stems with buds should be disbudded when preparing the cuttings.

If you decide to propagate by means of cuttings, it is important that the parent plant from which the cuttings are taken should be cultivated in an appropriate manner. The ultimate object is to provide an adequate supply of healthy, vigorous, non-flowering shoots from the base of the plant; this situation can be encouraged by trimming away, quite severely, any of the flower-producing top growth in late July or early August. In a normal season the plant will have been flowering with considerable abandon virtually continuously for two or three months. As a result, a considerable amount of extended top growth will have been produced by late July or early August. This growth, having been left unattended, will be supporting a mass of seed capsules, fading flowers, flowers and yet more flower buds, all of which are best sacrificed in the interest of allowing the plant's energies to be concentrated into producing healthy new basal growth from ground level. At the same time, more light and air will be able to reach the crown of the plant and this will be instrumental in preventing these basal shoots from becoming unduly tall or lank in their search for more light. The severed top growth should be totally removed from the site in the interests of hygiene, otherwise there is a likelihood that as it decays it will encourage and harbour pests and diseases.

Having trimmed the plant sufficiently to remove the top growth without damaging the basal growths beneath, it is now an appropriate time, if considered necessary, to apply a light top dressing of some form of well-balanced plant food. Any weed growth can be removed and if the soil is of suitable texture it can be drawn very gently inwards towards the crown of the plant, although this operation is by no means essential. The final operation is to water gently in order to settle the soil around the plant.

Provided that the soil remains reasonably moist, the basal shoots should now put on sufficient growth during the next month or so to enable the process of taking cuttings to start in September or early October. The operation can in fact be undertaken at any suitable time between then and the end of the year, but in a normal year an early start is preferable lest winter weather should arrive unduly early. Manipulating cuttings with chilled frozen fingers is neither satisfactory nor enjoyable.

Preparation

Prior to the actual removal of the growth for cuttings, full preparation for their reception and further treatment is vital. Undoubtedly the most important decision is to establish where the cuttings are to be housed during the weeks or months during which they will be forming roots. As previously mentioned, the structure in which they are to be housed can be quite simple and unsophisticated. Protection from strong winds, heavy rain and snow is important and anything used will serve the additional purpose of protecting the cuttings from excessive cold. Cuttings taken in September will in all probability be left undisturbed until March or April of the following year and it is therefore important that the structure be sufficiently robust to withstand rough weather.

Basic Materials and Methods

If you possess a glass house, this will be a perfectly acceptable home for cuttings, either on or even beneath the staging if the glass extends to ground level. An alternative is the polythene tunnel. For propagating violas there is no need for a structure into which you can walk and stand up. Low polythene tunnels supported on wire hoops with an internal width of 18–30in (45–76cm) are quite adequate for accommodating trays or pots of cuttings. They are relatively cheap to purchase, simple to erect, easy to ventilate – by simply lifting and lowering the sides – and easy to shade. Opaque white polythene, if used in place of the more usual clear translucent sheeting, will provide an ideal environment in which to root cuttings and will not require additional shading material. Whichever polythene you use, it should preferably be a type of sheeting designed for horticultural use. These materials contain something which counters the ultra-violet rays of the sun – which are otherwise instrumental in reducing the overall life of the polythene.

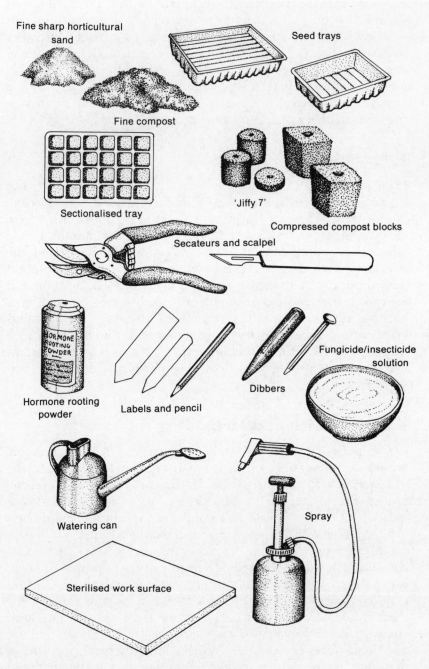

Fine sharp horticultural sand

Seed trays

Fine compost

Sectionalised tray

'Jiffy 7'

Compressed compost blocks

Secateurs and scalpel

Hormone rooting powder

Labels and pencil

Dibbers

Fungicide/insecticide solution

Watering can

Spray

Sterilised work surface

Basic equipment and materials for propagation

Equally suitable is the traditional garden frame which is available in many forms with either solid or translucent sides and a translucent sloping top which will shed rain. If you require no more than a handful of cuttings, a box or large pot with a sheet of glass or clear plastic to cover it is all that you need. In all cases, there must be adequate facilities for ventilation and some form of shading. This should ensure that the atmosphere within remains buoyant and the sunshine can never generate excessive heat or scorch the cuttings. Shade can be provided by applying a proprietory liquid to the glass but perhaps the most satisfactory solution is to use one of the plastic, woven shading materials that are now readily available. Such materials filter out as much as fifty per cent of the light and can, if needs be, be left permanently in place above the cuttings to guard against unexpected winter sunshine. It is of vital importance that the cuttings are housed in a reasonably moist, humid atmosphere until they can be judged to have formed a viable root system.

After the first few weeks, however, it is very important that they should be ventilated freely in all but the most severe weather. A close, static atmosphere will encourage fungal disease, but you must remember that ventilation will cause the cuttings and their compost to dry more readily, in which case they must be sprayed with a mist of water when necessary, in order to prevent flagging.

You must then decide what rooting medium or compost is to be employed and what containers are to be used. No great depth of compost is required, 3in (7.5cm) being quite sufficient. Cuttings can be inserted in pots of clay or plastic, seed trays of timber, plastic or expanded polystyrene, in compressed compost blocks or in suitably prepared soil forming the base of a bottomless garden frame.

If the latter method is employed, the soil should be adequately prepared. It must be thoroughly forked over and all extraneous matter such as sticks, stones, weeds and any roots of perennial weeds removed. The soil must be pulverised into a very fine tilth to a depth of about 6in (15cm). If the soil is heavy, sharp sand should be thoroughly incorporated, and if the soil is of a dry, powdery nature, fine moss peat should be added to improve its ability to retain moisture. The soil should be raked very level and allowed to settle, or consolidated by applying pressure to a suitable board laid upon the surface. If space permits, cuttings should be inserted approximately 3in (7.5cm) apart in rows approximately 3in (7.5cm) one from another. Some labels and a pencil are vital pieces of equipment at this stage, as are a supply of dry, free-running sharp silver horticultural sand, and a dibber some way between an $\frac{1}{8}$ and a $\frac{1}{4}$in (5mm) in diameter with which to make holes to receive the cuttings. A 4 or 6in (10 or 15cm) nail makes an ideal dibber, the flat head when reversed being perfect for firming the soil or compost around the base of the cutting. A vertical hole is made with the dibber to a depth of 1in (2.5cm) or so and a pinch of the dry silver sand is fed into the hole. Most cuttings benefit from having their base embedded in moist sharp sand – a situation which encourages them to rapidly form new roots. The sand is inert but the roots will rapidly extend beyond it into the soil or compost from which they are able to draw nutrient. The rooting will however be taking place during a period when the viola is virtually dormant and will therefore require very little nutrition from the soil. The only other equipment required will be a hormone rooting powder, some fungicide and insecticide, a spray with adjustable nozzle and a watering can with a fine, top-quality, brass rose.

If, therefore, you decide to propagate in a frame, the actual preparation of the cuttings can start. Concentrate on one variety at a time otherwise confusion will ultimately abound. Using very sharp, pointed scissors or an equally sharp pointed knife, remove healthy and robust basal growth very carefully from the parent plant – severing it from the plant as low down as possible. Varieties of viola and violetta vary considerably in their habit and manner of growth and it will become readily apparent that no two varieties are precisely the same in this respect. A violetta or truly tufted pansy will present few problems and will probably offer a choice of cuttings far in excess of requirements, in which case the strongest and healthiest should be chosen. If the soil is gently removed from around the base of the intended cutting, you may well find that the shoot is already forming young root growth – an ideal situation, although a shoot with root already attached should perhaps not be referred to as a cutting. Such cuttings are usually referred to as 'Slips' or 'Irishman's cuttings.' It is well to remember that a proportion of the cuttings may for one reason or another fail to root. Take more cuttings than you need, so that the strongest, most vigorous of them can be chosen when planting out in spring. Other shoots may show no sign of rooting but will have a white or blanched area of stem below ground level and these will make equally ideal cuttings. If you prefer, the entire plant can be lifted from the soil, making the detachment of cuttings that much easier. In bad weather the detailed work can be undertaken at a bench under cover. It is not a bad idea to keep to one side a bucket or bowl of fungicidal solution in which to place the cuttings. This will keep them fresh and at the same time give them a thorough dosing to guard against any fungal attacks – an ever-present risk in the closed and damp environment of the propagation frame. The base of each cutting can then be tidied up by trimming cleanly with a razor-sharp implement just beneath a leaf joint – except in the case of those with blanched stems which will possess no such leaf joints. Carefully remove any leaves and leaf stalks that would otherwise be buried beneath ground level. Dip the base of the cutting in a little hormone rooting powder, insert the cutting into the prepared soil ensuring that the base is enbedded in the sand. Firm the compost around the cutting and the job is to all intents and purposes over. Some 100 or more years ago, when the culture of violas and violettas was of a standard that has yet to be surpassed, hormone rooting powder was unheard of and it is therefore by no means a vital tool of the plant propagator. It is however cheap to purchase and so simple to apply that it makes sense to use it for all cuttings. Many of the proprietory brands contain a fungicide and should be used fresh, since effectiveness seems somewhat dependent upon it not having remained too long on the shelf. There are also liquid and gel forms of rooting hormone which are equally simple to apply.

If you decide to root the cuttings in pots, trays or compressed blocks the basic operations are of course much the same. An immediately apparent advantage however is that the actual operation of inserting cuttings can be undertaken on the potting bench with protection from adverse weather before the containers are then placed in the propagating frame. Inserting cuttings directly into a garden frame is an awkward, back-breaking task when handling other than small quantities. If a standard seed tray is employed, forty cuttings per tray is a comfortable quantity to aim for, or twenty if using the even more convenient half-size seed trays. Sectionalised seed trays have the added advantage of preventing the roots of adjacent cuttings becoming entangled one with another – a distinct advantage when they are ultimately potted up or planted out. Any of the good quality proprietory seed and potting composts are suitable for the job and the tray should be filled to capacity and gently firmed to consolidate the compost.

If using pots, the operation is no different except that by using large pots – leaving sufficient room between the top of the compost and the top of the pot – the pot itself can be made to form a miniature propagating frame by placing a sheet of glass or clear plastic on top. There are innumerable propagators available, consisting of a seed tray with fitting, translucent cover. The best of these also incorporate some form of adjustable ventilation and there are even individual flower pots with clear plastic fitting covers if you only require one or two cuttings.

Perhaps the most simple propagator of all is the pot into which a few sticks or hoops of wire are inserted to support an inverted polythene bag used to cover the rooting cuttings. Ventilation should be introduced gradually, as the cuttings show indication of rooting, and removed entirely as soon as they have become self-supporting.

If you decide to use compressed compost blocks for cuttings, the operation is of course somewhat different. Blocks can only be made satisfactorily immediately prior to requirement. A special compost formulated for blocking is needed and some form of tool with which to make the blocks. Various tools are available with which to mould the blocking compost into blocks. An ingenious handyman (or woman) can construct a mould of appropriate dimensions incorporating a plunger to eject the block from the mould. (The blocks can be cubic or cylindrical in shape.) Water is added to the compost to bring it to the recommended consistency, so that a correctly compressed block will retain its shape and not crumble or shatter, provided that it is handled with appropriate care. The process of inserting the cuttings into the blocks is no different to that of other methods. Blocks are best housed in seed trays for ease of handling and a distinct advantage of this propagation method is that the roots of each cutting are unlikely to become entangled with those of neighbouring cuttings.

This will cause less disturbance to the plants when the time comes for potting up or planting out. If you are planning to propagate in greater quantity you will find tools with which to make blocks in multiples – as many as twenty – and of course, in a variety of sizes.

An alternative to the compressed block is the 'Jiffy 7': a medallion of dry, compressed compost contained within fine netting. If the Jiffy 7 is allowed to absorb sufficient moisture it will expand to fill the netting, forming a cylindrical or barrel shape not unlike that of a compressed peat block. Cuttings can be inserted in the normal manner and when roots are in evidence, the whole thing can be potted up or planted out. It is advisable, though not essential, to release or partially release the outer netting before doing so.

SEED

Seed is perhaps the most simple and natural method of multi-plying violas and violettas but it must be clearly understood from the outset that when growing from seed, there can never be any absolute guarantee that the resulting plants will be similar to the parent plant. All too often, the plants produced from home-harvested seed will be inferior in one or more respects to the parent. It is however equally significant to remember that every garden variety of viola and violetta that has been considered worthy of being named and vegetatively reproduced for wide-spread distribution has started life as nothing more than a seedling itself. Where a particular variety is grown in isolation from any other variety of pansy, viola or violetta, it is reasonable to suppose that any seed formed will, if not the result of self-pollination, be the result of cross-pollination from a neighbouring plant of the same variety. (Self-pollination in this context describes a flower in which the stigma has been fertilised by pollen from the stamens of that same flower or other flowers on the self-same plant.) If we accept that any seedlings subsequently arising from seed fer-tilised in this manner will inherit characteristics from the parent or parents, it is reasonable to suppose that the progeny will exhibit certain basic characteristics of the parent. However, these will often manifest themselves in what can only be considered as an inferior form. If, for instance, seed from a large-flowered, frag-rant, rayless, yellow tufted viola, which has been grown in total isolation from other varieties, is harvested and germinated, it is reasonable to expect the majority of those plants to produce yellow flowers. It can be little more than wishful thinking on the other hand to expect the majority of them to have inherited in full measure every other characteristic of the parent. Inevitably a proportion of the seedlings will have smaller flowers, possibly of inferior shade, shape and substance. Fragrance may be diminished, rays may have reappeared and the tufted habit of growth may well be less in evidence. Also – once you have decided upon the type and colour required – if you intend to reproduce from self-grown seed alone, you will need to rogue out ruthlessly those seedlings that do not reach acceptable standards. You should retain only those that attain the standard required. In this way, a measure of control will be introduced, and provided that only those plants of acceptable standard are permitted to pollinate one another (and also provided that no pollen from a conflicting variety is allowed to make contact with them) any resulting seed should produce a strain of plants of reasonable conformity one to another. If at any time foreign pollen gains access, or if the elimination of inferior seedlings is neglected, a deterioration of quality in that particular seed strain will rapidly become evident.

In the normal course of events, basic wild species of plants will reproduce true to type or reasonably so, if only because in nature they will tend to grow in colonies in which a particular colour and variety of plant predominates. Named garden varieties can never be relied upon to reproduce true to form from seed although some varieties are more reliable and predictable in this respect than others. In the artificial environment of the garden the opportunities for promiscuity between different compatible varieties are considerable, especially when grown in close contact to one another. Where pollen is transferred by insects or the wind, a plant which may appear isolated may well receive pollen from a considerable distance away. Under truly controlled conditions, any visiting insects or wind-borne pollen must be positively excluded by totally enclosing the flower that is to bear seed, only allowing access to pollen that has been specifically chosen for pollination. It is possible in these circumstances to transfer ripe pollen from a specific flower and to apply it to the receptive stigma of the flower that is chosen to bear the seed. The usual tool for collecting and transferring pollen is a fine, clean, camel-hair paint brush. If self-pollination is to be avoided, you will need to remove the pollen-bearing stamens from the seed-bearing flower before they have reached the stage at which the pollen is ripe and ready to fall. Controlled pollination of the pansy, viola or violetta is, as you can imagine, a task calling for infinite patience, a steady hand and in all probability a magnifying glass. Methods of controlled pollination are worthwhile when the specific aim is to attempt to combine certain characteristics of the plants into one. The chance of success, however, is not very high, and in the search for perfection there will be much disappointment.

If you have neither the patience nor the inclination to become involved in such practices as hand-pollination there are fortunately far less complicated alternatives. Pansies, violas and violettas show an enthusiastic tendency to cross-pollinate one with another with no help whatsoever from the gardener. It therefore stands to reason that where a number of different varieties are grown in close proximity to one another there will be considerable variety in the resulting progeny. Seeds can be harvested for sowing in controlled conditions but if allowed to fall naturally they will germinate readily without further attention.

When the seed is ripe, the capsule will split into three segments and the seed will be ejected with quite considerable force to fall some distance from the parent plant. The cracking sound of a seed being ejected from ripe seed pods is a familiar sound amongst pansies, violas and violettas in the warm, dry days of later summer. Self-sown seedlings produced in this natural manner are worth preserving if only for trial. If practical they can be left in position to mature to the point of flowering when the colour of the flower alone may encourage further nurturing of the seedling so that its progress and characteristics can be assessed before it is discarded. Seed maturing early in the season will produce flowering seedlings by later summer. Seedlings germinating later in the summer should not be expected to flower the same season but can be carefully potted up and transferred to a frame or nursery bed which will afford sufficient protection from winter weather. They can then be planted out for assessment the following spring.

Seed Harvesting and Storage

If you prefer to start a collection of violas from seed rather than purchasing plants, you can find a number of commercial seed strains, and a selection of those currently available is listed in Chapter 12.

If, however, you are planning to use self-harvested seed, it is important that the seed should be harvested at the correct time and stored in a suitable manner. If a viola or violetta flower has been pollinated – whether by hand or by natural means – the flower petals will wither and eventually fall. The green sepals, which originally enclosed the flower bud, remain to provide protection for the fertilised ovary. The ovary will slowly expand in size over a period of a few weeks as the seeds develop and enlarge within. At this stage in its development the seed capsule will be of a fresh green colour and it will hang down protected from above by the sepals. As the capsule reaches maturity two things will become apparent. The capsule, now quite large and rounded in shape will become increasingly pale in colour turning through pale green to an almost straw-like colour. At the same time, the capsule will raise its head towards the sunlight enabling the sunshine to gain maximum access to the seed pod and to ripen and dry the structure still further. Provided that there is adequate sunshine and conditions are not unduly wet the capsule will ultimately divide into three segments revealing the seeds within, which should, if ripe and healthy, appear smooth, rich, brown and of shiny texture. Some varieties produce a seed of a somewhat

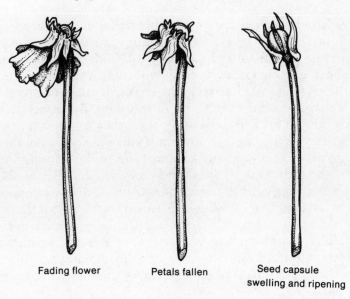

Fading flower   Petals fallen   Seed capsule
                                          swelling and ripening

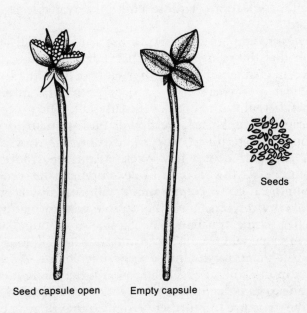

Seeds

Seed capsule open   Empty capsule

Stages in seed production

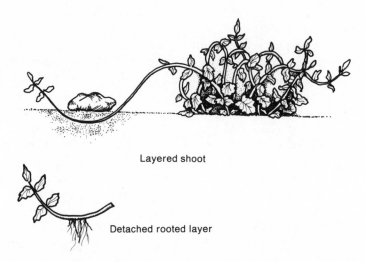

Layered shoot

Detached rooted layer

Propagation by layering for a plant lacking suitable basal shoots

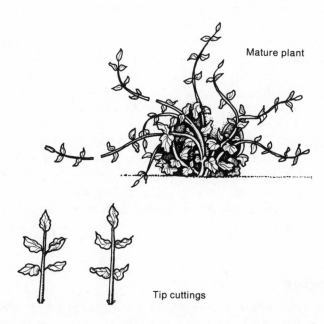

Mature plant

Tip cuttings

Propagation by tip cuttings for a plant lacking suitable basal shoots

paler colour than others but the majority will be of a shining rich mahogany colour.

If a seed pod has split into its three segments whilst still on the plant, some seeds may well have been lost and it is important that such pods should be harvested without delay, picking the pod complete with stem and placing the entire thing into a seed-proof paper bag. Fold the top of the bag to prevent seeds subsequently ejected from the seed pod from being lost. The bag or bags of seed should then be placed somewhere cool but well ventilated whilst the remaining seeds are released from the capsule. If seed is in short supply or for some reason considered particularly precious it is a risk to leave the pod on the plant until it opens. The appropriate harvest time is when the stem has straightened and the ripe pod is facing upwards or outwards from the plant and no longer hanging downwards. Gentle pressure with finger and thumb applied to the tip of the pod will cause it to crack into its three segments sufficiently to reveal the contents within and you can see if the seeds are ripe or almost so. If pods are harvested at this stage no seed will be lost but it is advisable to remove them with a full length of stem which will enable the final stage of maturing and ripening to take place in a natural manner. It is all the more important, if the seeds are to be harvested at this stage, that they be stored under dry, well-ventilated conditions. Paper bags are preferable to polythene allowing for a full circulation of air. The bags can be suspended close to an open door or window or placed outside in fine weather to enable them to dry in a gradual and natural manner.

Within a few weeks or perhaps even days the ejected seed will have congregated in the bottom of the bag. Stems, seed capsules and any other debris can be disposed of and the clean seed is now ready for either sowing or storing. If you plan to store the seed over winter, the preferred method is to put the paper packets in a tightly sealed container such as a biscuit tin or screw-top jar which can then be placed anywhere which will remain dry and free from extreme fluctuations of temperature – particularly heat.

Seed Sowing

Seed can be sown immediately, this of course being nature's way of things but remember that seed sown in late summer or early autumn will have little time to reach maturity before the onset of winter and some form of protection will be advisable or necessary if the small seedlings are to survive winter unscathed.

The advantage of autumn sowing is that seedlings so grown will be that much more advanced when planted out in the following spring than those grown from spring-sown seed. Whether the additional trouble required to provide winter protection for later summer-sown seed is worthwhile is open to question, unless the object is specifically to produce early spring flowers. Extending the flowering season of a plant – which in the normal course of events can be expected to bloom from April to October – is perhaps unnecessary.

Sowing of seed is a relatively simple exercise but is worth undertaking with care and precision. If sowing in pots or seed trays, fill the containers with a good quality proprietory seed compost and gently consolidate the compost to ensure a level surface with no air pockets. Sprinkle the seed evenly over the surface of the compost, resisting the temptation to set the seed too thickly – $\frac{1}{2}$in (1cm) between seeds being an appropriate distance. Cover the seed evenly with the very thinnest layer of sharp sand, fine grit or compost. The object of the exercise is to do no more than hold the seed in place and to exclude light from direct contact with the seed. Some people advocate leaving the seed uncovered on the surface of the compost. Water with extreme care by immersing the base of the seed tray or pot in water. Allow time for that water to be absorbed upward to the surface of the compost, or alternatively spray lightly with water from above. At all costs avoid abrupt watering which can so easily induce the seeds to float to the surface and to congregate in a mass thereby rendering the spacing of the seeds a wasted exercise. Protect the pots or trays from direct sunshine, heavy rain and any birds or beasts. Take steps if necessary to discourage slugs, mice etc, and the process of germinating viola seed is over – apart from ensuring that the compost is at all times moist but never saturated, and that the temperature remains within the range of 64–68°F (18–20°C). Within a few weeks, if all is well, germination will be in evidence and the seedlings can be pricked out, potted up or planted out just as soon as they have produced a recognisable little plant 1in (2.5cm) or so in height. The seedlings should be lifted with extreme care lest their roots be in any way damaged. It is safest to hold the plant by a leaf with one hand whilst the other hand provides support for the root whilst in transit. Plant the seedling to at least the same depth as that to which it has already been growing. To lessen the shock of transfer from compost to soil – if planting into open ground – sprinkle a handful of the potting compost around the roots of the young plant and water gently but thoroughly to settle the compost around the fibrous root system. Be aware of the possibility of attack from slugs or aphids and if necessary react accordingly.

LAYERING

The layering technique is worth considering when other forms of propagation appear impractical. For varieties of violetta of tufted habit, the necessity of layering the plant should not arise. For violas of lank habit whose growth is more comparable to that of a pansy it may well be that if you desire to propagate vegetatively – which is the only method that can ensure that all characteristics are retained within the new plant – there will be no practical alternative.

A mature pansy, or a viola of pansy-like growth, will offer little if any basal growth from which cuttings can be taken in the normal manner. In the most fortunate circumstances, a plant of lank habit will have produced a number of lateral shoots from the lower regions of the main stem or stems. If these young lateral growths are carefully detached from the stem, and the lower leaves and leaf stipules are removed, they can be treated in the same manner as would be normal cuttings. Under less fortunate circumstances, there may well be none of these lateral shoots, leaving the propagator with only two alternatives. Either the tip of the stem must be used as cutting material or alternatively the whole stem can be layered.

Layering is the technique by which the entire stem is held in some way in contact with the soil or even buried shallowly beneath the surface of the soil. The stem must not be detached from the plant during this process. If the soil is fine and friable the operation is simple. Form a slight indentation in the soil, lay the stem along the indentation, and then either infill with soil and peg down with a piece of bent wire, or simply weigh down with a stone of suitable size to ensure that the stem will be held in close contact with the soil. The green growth at the end of the shoot must remain free and above ground level. The object of this exercise is to encourage the shoot to form an independent root system, so that it can eventually be separated from the old plant and transferred to fresh soil elsewhere. Unlike cuttings, layers will receive sustenance from the main plant until such time as they have rooted and are detached. If the soil is coarse or heavy in texture it is advisable to replace the area around the layer with a moist but free-draining compost of fine texture. The layer can even be put into a pot or tray of compost, sunk beneath it; a distinct advantage when severing a successful layer in order to transfer it elsewhere.

It must be emphasised that the propagation of violas by way of layering is a last resort method to be employed when the division of the plant or the striking of cuttings is not a practical proposition. Layering will not allow the multiplication of plants in any great quantity and this explains the scarcity and decline in numbers of named varieties of pansy – in particular the Show and Fancy pansy, grown specifically for floral competition. The growth habit of these plants makes vegetative propagation by means other than layering difficult if not almost impossible.

PROPAGATION OF PANSIES

The propagation of pansies other than by way of seed, is by no means as reliable and easy as that of violas and violettas. It is the tufted habit of the bedding viola and violetta that makes propagation from cuttings a relatively simple matter with division a possible alternative.

The habit of the pansy is such that it will offer few opportunities for the taking of cuttings and it may be necessary to resort to root lateral shoots and tip growth, or to layer. The pansy does not lend itself to division. The majority of pansies are therefore grown from seed.

6

Raising New Varieties

There is no doubt that many, perhaps most, of the finest named varieties of pansies and violas have arisen from seedlings that are no more than the result of random or open pollination. Open pollination is the term used to describe the natural cross-pollination, effected by the transfer of pollen from stamen to stigma by insects or air movement without the intervention of man. It is wise to have some understanding of the reproductive processes involved in order that we can, if we wish, bring influence to bear upon the results – as opposed to leaving the whole operation to chance. As mentioned in Chapter 5, self-pollination or cross-pollination does not often bring the desired results, and invariably the progeny is inferior in many ways to the parent. If we wish to influence the situation in order to perhaps increase our chance of success in achieving a particular goal it is useful to have at least a little working knowledge of the laws of inheritance.

If a self-pollinated plant produces seedlings identical to itself, and they in turn produce identical progeny, that plant is deemed to be 'breeding true'. Whilst the term 'breeding true' may refer to the plant as a whole, it may also be used to refer to just one or more of the plant's particular characteristics. A plant may, for instance, breed true for colour, true for fragrance or for habit of growth. If a plant breeds true for colour, it can be said that all its pollen grains carry something which controls the colour of the flowers. It takes only one pollen grain to fertilise each ovule of the seed-bearing parent and we would therefore perhaps expect the seed resulting from such a union to produce, if nothing else, the colour of the true breeding pollinator. For this the seed-bearing plant must also contain the same colour characteristic within its own ovule. Indeed, if a plant breeds true for colour, it is an indication that both the male, or pollen-bearing parent, and the female, or seed-bearing parent, share the same inherited colour characteristic.

In spite of this assertion it will become readily apparent that self-pollinated plants can by no means be relied upon *always* to breed true, such plants being said to have segregated. A selection of seedlings from a self-pollinated plant that segregates will show considerable variety, most noticeably in colour. For example, some of the seedlings may have blue flowers and some may have white flowers, which indicates that some but not all the pollen grains or ovules share the colour characteristic of the parent. If, subsequently, any of the varying seedlings, when self-pollinated should give rise to seedlings which all had inherited the colour of their parent, it could then be said that we once more have a plant which is 'breeding true' for colour.

It is the genes within the germ cells of the plant which determine or control the many characteristics of which, colour, leaf shape, stature, habit, flowering season are just a few, there being perhaps thousands more which combine to give a plant its individual identity. The gene is just one small unit of inheritance which is passed from generation to generation to impart its characteristic effect. In recent years, the development of genetic engineering techniques has opened the way for plant breeders to influence still further aspects of inheritance that have hitherto been beyond the control of man.

If a 'true breeding' blue viola is cross-pollinated with a true breeding white viola as pollinator, the theory is that the resulting seedlings will be of an intermediate colour – pale blue. If this pale blue viola is then self-pollinated we can expect to produce seedlings amongst which a quarter will be blue, a quarter white and a half an intermediate shade of pale blue. It is however beyond the scope of this book – and of its author – to become involved in all the details and ramifications of the quite complex laws of inheritance, and the reader wishing to pursue the matter further is advised to refer to more specialist literature on the subject of plant breeding. It is however true to emphasise that the principles governing inheritance are precise and orderly. Characteristics are inherited from one generation to another in accordance with definite rules. These can be employed to advantage by those who wish to attempt to achieve a pre-conceived idea.

It is perhaps of more initial practical interest to the reader to explain the construction of the viola or pansy flower and its breeding mechanism. Close examination of a pansy or viola flower will reveal that apart from the five petals, the green sepals and the characteristic spur at the back of the flower, there is the all-important mechanism of reproduction. By carefully dismantling the flower, and with the aid of a magnifying lens, virtually all will become apparent. Both male and female components are contained within the one flower. In the central eye of the flower, you can see the stigma, with its cavity evolved to receive the pollen grains at the first stage of fertilisation. The stigma, as in many other flowers, is connected to the ovary – in which the seeds will subsequently develop – by a tubular extension called the style. The anthers in which the pollen grains are formed are clustered around the ovary at the base of the flower. The flower is further equipped with a beard or collection of fine hairs in the groove, formed by the base of the lower petal. There are also hair-like structures at the base of the two side petals. These hairs collect pollen which is carried to the flower by visiting pollinating insects. Opinions differ as to precisely what happens to bring about the actual process of pollination. One theory suggests that insects, particularly the bee, are the chief instigators. When the insect extends its proboscis into the depth of the flower to obtain nectar from the spur at the back, it disturbs the anthers and pollen adheres to its body. The foregoing explanation can be made a little easier to understand by referring to the diagram showing a vertical cross-section of a typical pansy or viola bloom which appears on page 16.

The insect is unable to reach the nectar in the spur without exerting upward pressure on the style and stigma. It is this lever action which induces the stamens to release their pollen, which then adheres to the proboscis or head of the insect. At the same time, the stigma is pushed into contact with the pollen which the visiting insect has brought from elsewhere and which has now been transferred to the hairs above. The insect then departs laden with fresh pollen to repeat the process elsewhere.

An alternative to this theory is that when a flower sheds its pollen, the pollen grains fall and become collected in the beard of fine hairs that are found in the groove at the base of the lower petal. Subscribers to this theory can practise a form of hand-pollination by carefully detaching the lower, pollen-laden petal and introducing it to another chosen flower in such a way as to bring it into direct contact with its stigma.

If this theory is correct, the flower would be particularly prone to self-pollination but for the fact that the pollen-laden stamens and the stigma of a flower do not necessarily reach maturity simultaneously. When an insect visits a flower to partake of its nectar, it is inevitable that some of this pollen will adhere to its body. When the insect departs to visit another flower, as it surely will, some of that pollen will be transferred from the body of the insect to the viscid tip of the ripe stigma of that flower, resulting in pollination. And so the process is repeated from flower to flower. This would therefore appear to be an equally plausible explanation as to how pollen is transferred from one pansy or viola flower to another.

Much has been written on the important role played by the

bumble bee in transferring the pollen of pansies and violas from flower to flower, but there is in fact considerable doubt as to the extent to which the bumble bee – or for that matter any insect – is the main instigator of pollination.

In my experience, it is a rare sight indeed to see such insects at work – particularly the bumble bee. Where pansies and violas are grown in company with other plants it may well be that bumble bees will be more in evidence but where violas and violettas are grown in isolation, the bumble bee and his close relations are rare visitors. The occasional butterfly will be seen sipping nectar when alternative sources of food and moisture are scarce, and it is by no means unusual to see the tiny black midges, so familiar on common bind-weed, scurrying in and out of the eye of the pansy and viola flower, no doubt attracted by the nectar, but also by the protection afforded by the flower. It is unlikely that pollen would adhere to the tiny body of the midge to any great extent and it is therefore hard to believe that it plays any major part in the process of cross-pollination. I am therefore of the opinion that air-borne pollen may well play a far greater role than has hitherto been realised. It is common knowledge, particularly to hay fever sufferers, that pollen grains are readily disturbed and transported suspended in the slightest movement of air. The ease with which such air-borne pollen can contact and adhere to the viscid stigma of another adjacent, compatible flower must surely be a reasonable explanation for the fact that violas and violettas will seed profusely, without any particularly apparent intervention from visiting insects – unless of course such insects restrict their activities to the hours of darkness.

Shortly after successful pollination, the petals of the flower will wither and fall and the ovary will start to swell as the seeds develop within. Warm, dry weather will speed the whole process. Shortly before maturity, the swollen ovary – or seed capsule, as it has now become – will lift towards the sunshine and as it ripens, will fade from green to the colour of straw. It will then separate into three segments which will, within a few hours, eject their seed contents with considerable force to land elsewhere. If the seed is then not consumed by birds, rodents or other creatures, it can remain dormant for many weeks, even months in the soil, before suitable conditions induce it to germinate.

If you decide to exert more control over the process of pollination, it is essential first and foremost to ensure that no sort of natural cross-pollination or self-pollination is able to take place. The flowers that are chosen to be the seed bearers must be emasculated before the pollen has ripened or been shed, and this can only be done by removing, with extreme care, all the stamens of these flowers before they reach maturity. This is of course an extremely delicate operation requiring great patience, a steady hand, a magnifying lens, keen eyesight and a pair of precision tweezers with which the stamen can be amputated. At this stage, it is equally important to ensure that pollen from elsewhere cannot come into contact with the stigma. A porous material such as fine muslin can be tied around the flower head to enclose it and exclude any visiting insects or foreign pollen. Alternatively, the plant must be housed somewhere from which insects and pollen can be excluded. Having decided upon the flower which is to provide pollen for the crossing, the pollen must be transferred in some way to the receptive stigma of the seed bearer. It is essential that the pollen should not only be ripe but also that the stigma should be in receptive condition. Pollen is ripe when the stamens open and readily release the extremely fine yellow-green powder of pollen grains. Assuming that the pollen has a limited effective life it is advisable to make use of it without undue delay. A receptive stigma is usually slightly sticky when ripe making the application of pollen that much easier.

In order to gain access to the pollen of the pollen-bearing parent plant, you need to dismantle the flower by gently pulling apart the petals to fully reveal the stamens. Any pollen resting in the beard of the flower may well come from elsewhere and should therefore be avoided. An appropriate tool with which to collect the pollen grains is a fine, dry, camel-hair, artist's paint brush on which they can be transferred immediately to the awaiting stigma of the seed-bearing parent. If more than one crossing is to be made the brush must be thoroughly cleaned or sterilised between each one. Alcohol is considered appropriate for the purpose. The delicate operation is now complete and all you have to do is keep the plant in good health and exclude any possible entry of pollen from elsewhere until a swelling ovary indicates that the operation has been successful. The plant should be protected from rain and allowed to become quite dry at the root. Maximum sunshine will hasten ripening of the seed and the resulting seedlings will then prove the success or otherwise of this whole exercise.

Such is the abandon with which pansies and violas cross-pollinate and seed amongst themselves without intervention from man, that seedlings of almost infinite variety are bound to arise. The majority of these, if not all, will be in some way or another inferior. Left to their own devices, they will tend to deteriorate and revert to plants more akin to the species from which our garden hybrids were originally derived. It is therefore advisable that when embarking upon a programme of hybridisation you should have some specific object in view. There are those to whom the size of a bloom is of paramount importance and others who consider that smaller flowers have more charm. Those who wish to exhibit or display in vases may be concerned to produce flowers on longer, straighter and stronger stems. Colour and marking will undoubtedly figure high on a list of priorities and fragrance may be of significant importance. Amongst other important characteristics will be its floriferous nature, hardiness, stature and habit, disease-resistance and even drought-resistance. A plant may have one particularly admirable characteristic and no others, but efforts can be made – by way of controlled cross-pollination – to impart its one admirable characteristic to a plant that lacks it. Where two plants each possess one characteristic which we wish to combine in one, a simple but totally unscientific approach is to plant those two varieties close to one another but in isolation from others. Cross-pollination will hopefully occur and amongst any resulting seedlings there may be evidence of the desired improvement.

The variety chosen to bear seed should be an already vigorous, attractive variety, of good constitution but lacking, for instance, in colour. The variety chosen to pollinate may have the desired colour but be an otherwise poor specimen, with no other merit than that of the desired colour. It is the seed harvested from the vigorous variety that we would expect to yield seedlings of greater interest than those derived from seed of the reverse crossing. Assuming some measure of success, it then becomes necessary to eliminate any inferior seedlings, only retaining for further possible breeding those, if any, that exhibit any of the desired improvements. By vigorous roguing and repeated efforts in successive seasons it may prove possible in this way to achieve gradual improvement towards the desired result.

NAMING OF NEW VARIETIES

The temptation to give a new variety status by giving to it a name should be firmly resisted until its performance in every respect has been fully assessed throughout a period of at least two seasons and preferably longer. The initial excitement of raising a variety that appears to exhibit improved characteristics should be contained until the plant has proved itself to be fully competent in other desired respects. Many are the frustrating and disappointing occasions when a seedling may show, for instance, a particularly fresh and new colour or colour combination only to be found seriously lacking in other respects. There are so many important characteristics that combine to produce our individual vision of the ideal that we are lucky indeed if we find them all contained within a single plant. Taking a plant with particularly fine blossom, many questions will need to be answered before that plant can be considered worthy of elevation to the status of 'named variety'. For example:

- Is the plant floriferous? (By which we mean will it produce flowers in profusion or will it perhaps ration us to just two or three flowers at any one time?)
- Does it show continuity of flowering, does it cease flowering after its initial flush of blossom, or does it flower only inter- mittently?
- Are the flowers of good shape and the petals of fine substance?
- Do the flowers hold themselves with pride or perhaps hang their heads as if in shame?
- Do the flowers possess a noticeable fragrance?
- Are subsequent flowers of consistent colour and marking throughout the entire season?
- Are the flower stems of good substance holding the flowers clear of the foliage?
- Does the plant show overall vigour?
- Are the flowers resistant to fading from sunshine or marking from rain?
- Is the foliage neat, bright and the plant of compact, tidy growth?
- Does the plant withstand excessive cold, excessive wet, excessive wind or excessive heat and to what extent does it exhibit perennial qualities?
- Does it perhaps appear more prone to disease than others?
- Does it have a habit of growth that will render vegetative propagation easy?

These are just some of the questions to be answered before promoting a promising seedling for further trial. It may well be that there is already in circulation a variety exhibiting all the qualities and to a superior degree. Awareness of the field is essential before valued judgement can be made. It is all too easy to name new varieties indiscriminately, thereby laying claim to a collection in which quantity may well be at the expense of quality.

The actual naming of the plant, whilst of significance to the raiser who bestows it, is little more than a method of distinguishing one variety from another and it is therefore important, in so far as is possible, to avoid duplication of names.

The fashion in recent years to adopt for some new varieties the names of supposedly extinct varieties is not to be encouraged – being not only unnecessary but also inviting confusion. Steps should be taken to establish that a chosen name has never before been in circulation.

7

Show and Exhibition

To many of us, the chief interest in garden pansies and violas is
their undoubted value as versatile plants that can be employed to
decorate the flower garden. There have always been people,
however, who, throughout the whole history and development
of these plants from the early nineteenth century, have been
preoccupied in producing flowers for exhibition and competition
at the traditional flower shows held throughout the country
during the summer months. Under show conditions a pansy or
viola is judged purely and simply on the quality of its bloom, no
consideration being given or marks awarded for anything other
than blooms exhibited in total isolation from the plants which
have borne them.

The whole approach, therefore – from choosing appropriate
varieties, cultivating them to the required standard and then
exhibiting them in a traditionally acceptable manner – is totally
different from that of growing pansies and violas for no more
than informal garden decoration.

Inevitably, as with all types of formal competition, certain
standards have evolved and become accepted as definitions under
which the flowers can be fairly assessed and judged against one
another.

Flowers for competitive exhibition fall traditionally into three
basic categories: Show pansies, Fancy pansies and Exhibition
violas, to which could now be added Bedding violas, Miniature
violas and Violettas; six distinct groups of pansy and viola worthy
of their rightful place on the show bench. The showing and
exhibiting of pansies and violas has, over the years, for one
good reason or another, experienced fluctuating support. It is
comforting to know that there have always been, and still are,
growers dedicated to keeping the tradition not only alive but
active – ever striving to save old-established varieties from extinction and to introduce new and improved varieties to swell the
ranks.

The growth habit of pansies and violas grown for exhibition
is of far less consequence than the quality of their individual
flowers (although habit is of course the all-important characteristic
that will determine the ease with which a plant can subsequently

be propagated). Varieties grown for exhibition will invariably be rambling plants of a loose, untidy habit which provides little suitable growth for vegetative propagation. This explains why Exhibition pansy and viola plants have always and probably always will be in relatively short supply. If the tufted habit of Bedding violas and violettas could be bred into the exhibition varieties without detriment to the quality of their flowers much would have been achieved and propagation would then be considerably easier. On the other hand it is the relative scarcity of the exhibition varieties, coupled with the exceptional skill practised by those who cultivate and show them that is undoubtedly instrumental in preserving the air of mystique which is an integral part of the show scene. Certain standards have been agreed over the years as to what constitutes an acceptable flower in any category. It is the Show pansy which, historically, first appeared upon the scene and gave rise to the formation of the various pansy societies – of which the Hammersmith Heartsease Society, founded in 1841, was undoubtedly the earliest.

SHOW PANSIES

Colour plates of 1833 depict Show pansies as little more than selected and improved varieties of heartsease or wild pansy with particularly interesting colour markings, elongated in shape, rayed and with no suggestion of the eye which was subsequently to become the blotch.

In the *Gardener's Chronicle* of 1841 there appeared an illustration of a pansy superimposed upon a geometric circle with an accompanying exhortation that:

> Having in a former number given a list of some first-rate Pansies, we proceed to lay before our readers the rules by which the form of this favourite flower is determined, and the qualifications it should possess to entitle it to rank as a show–flower. The first and most essential quality to examine is its form, which will be found in the greatest perfection in that flower, round which a circle be drawn, each petal will exactly touch the circle not projecting beyond it, nor stopping short of it. (The diagram overleaf will illustrate the point.)
>
> The petals should be large and broad, because in that case the indentations must be shallow, where the outline of one petal meets another. Bearing these rules in mind,

and examining a few first-rate flowers, the eye will soon become accustomed to judge of its most perfect form and proportion, and will be quickly able to detect any deviation from it.

The other qualities which are combined with form in order to render a Pansy perfect, consist in the petals being of a firm texture, flat, even at the edge, and free from notches. The eye must be clean and well defined; the colours should be rich and vivid, and the markings must have a clear edge. A uniform tint as a ground colour is much esteemed; but the variations and combination of colour are so numerous and beautiful that no precise rules can be formed to govern this point.

The pansy is so universal a favourite, and excites so much attention and interest, that we are anxious to see flowers possessing all the qualities we have enumerated common, and gracing every garden. It is no doubt susceptible of further improvement, if we consider what has already been done by the skill, perseverance, and industry of florists.

Within a few years there is evidence of much progress and we see flowers of circular outline with fuller, more rounded petals and clearly defined belting to the outer edges of the petals.

In *The Florist* of 1848 an attempt was made to define what was then described as 'the points of perfection in the pansy'. Great emphasis was placed upon the flower being circular in outline, with the petals lying perfectly flat and with smooth edges and no crumpling. In achieving this circular outline, with the eye of the flower positioned centrally, the botton petals and two side petals

Edged and belted florist pansies, 1848.

would to a very great extent obscure the two top petals. The bottom petal formed almost half of the visible flower, its upper edge being as near as possible horizontal, the two side petals meeting one another with a vertical line above the centre eye. At this stage in its development the eye of the pansy was little more than a consolidation of the rays of the flower and had yet to evolve by subsequent selection and breeding into the very much larger blotch which became the hall mark of the Fancy pansy.

A writer at this time suggested that the Florist or Show pansy should, for competition purposes, be subdivided into seven distinct categories:

(1) white grounds, edged with a contrasting colour
(2) yellow grounds, edged with a contrasting colour
(3) white grounds, belted with a contrasting colour
(4) yellow grounds, belted with a contrasting colour
(5) dark selfs
(6) yellow selfs
(7) white selfs

'Ground' is the term used to identify the basic colour of the petals which must be utterly consistent to the bottom three petals of the flower.

'Edging' is the term used to describe the fine margin or contrasting colour which may appear on the outer edges of the bottom three petals. The colour of the edging should match that of the top two petals.

'Belting' is the term used to describe the broader band of contrasting colour which may form an outer margin to the three bottom petals and should match the two top petals for colour. The two top petals will invariably be of one consistent colour, any edging or belting being confined to the lower three petals.

The 'eye' is the solid area of dark, rich, almost black colouring at the centre of the flower, formed by the thickening and consolidation of the rays. The eye should ideally be circular in shape and have a clean, smooth, outer edge that does not feather or bleed into the ground colour. The ground colour itself should clearly separate the eye from the edging or belting. The eye of the Show pansy is by no means as large as the blotch of the later Fancy pansy.

A 'self pansy' is one in which all five petals are of one consistent colour, there being no edging or belting. Dark coloured selfs should show no eye or blotch, but white or yellow ground pansies should possess the same eye or blotch as that of edged and belted varieties.

The figure on page 112 is based upon an illustration of 1848 showing both an edged and a belted Show pansy. The overall shape is circular and the edging and belting are of consistent width and clearly defined from the ground colour. But it will be seen that the eye leaves a little to be desired in terms of shape and definition.

In relation to Show pansies there are certain stipulations relating to belting. The colours considered permissible vary between yellow ground pansies and white ground pansies. For yellow ground pansies, the preferred colours for any belting are shades of bronze-crimson, puce, mulberry, claret and shades of dark crimson. For white ground pansies, the preferred colours are blue, violet and purple. The centre of the eye of a Show pansy should be yellow or orange and well-defined and there should be no rays whatsoever on the face of a good Show pansy. The overall visual effect of that flower should be as though the colours had been applied to the petals with the greatest precision by the most skilled of artists resulting in an image of almost unbelievable perfection. The colours should be clear, clean and of utterly consistent strength but of positive contrast one with another, and the whole flower should possess a richness of texture comparable to the finest velvet.

The heyday of the English Show pansy – which had begun in the mid-nineteenth century – appeared to be waning by the turn of the century when the more recent introduction of what was to be called the Fancy pansy captured the imagination of those who found the stipulated requirements concerning Show pansies somewhat irksome. Colour plates inherited from the latter part of the nineteenth century of Show pansies of the day give the impression that the standards of excellence achieved then have never been eclipsed or even matched since. However, if nothing else, they provide inspiration for anyone wishing to dedicate the necessary time needed to re-introduce varieties and to equal all those that have now so sadly fallen into extinction.

The traditional assessment of a Show pansy on the exhibition bench is done by awarding marks of which the total maximum attainable is twenty. The flower will be assessed in seven ways and marks awarded as indicated by the table opposite:

Other characteristics of the pansy are assessed in accordance with aspects considered meritorious and aspects considered defective and these have been interpreted in more recent years as follows:

Condition	3	points maximum	
Form and texture	5	,,	,,
Size	3	,,	,,
Colour	3	,,	,,
Belting	2	,,	,,
Blotch	2	,,	,,
Eye	2	,,	,,
Total	20	,,	

Meritorious Characteristics:

– A flower which is from $1\frac{1}{2}$–2in (4–5cm) in diameter, fresh, clean, circular in outline with smooth, thick, velvety petals without serrations lying evenly on each other and either flat or slightly reflexed so that the surface of the flower is slightly convexed.
– Centre petals which meet above the eye and reach well up on the top petals, and a bottom petal which is sufficiently deep and broad to balance the others.
– A bicolour flower with a ground colour of the same shade throughout, circular, broad, of uniform width and well-defined at its edge.
– Belting of uniform width, of exactly the same colour as the top petals, distinct from the ground colour and well defined at its junction with the ground colour.
– A blotch of good size (though smaller than in a Fancy pansy), dense, solid and approximately circular. In a dark self flower the same shade throughout with no trace of a blotch. In any other self flower – the same shade throughout except for a blotch as in a bicolour.

Defective Characteristics:

– A flower which is less than $1\frac{1}{2}$in (4cm) or over 2in (5cm) in diameter, past its best, soil-marked, concave or lacking a circular outline.
– Petals which are fish-tailed, thin, or of poor substance or serrated.
– Belting which is either very narrow or very wide, of uneven width or ill-defined.

– Belting which is not of the same colour as the top petals, or not distinct from the ground colour.
– Except in a dark self flower, a blotch which is small, thin, or ragged-edged.
– An eye which is dull or ill-defined.

The 'perfect' shape of a Show pansy – as some people would consider it – can best be explained with the aid of a diagram (*see* page 112). If a circle is bisected vertically into two equal halves and divided horizontally into three sectors of equal depth, it can be seen how the five petals (if correctly developed) relate to one another. The lower petals will ideally fill the lower third, the two side petals will fill the centre third, meeting without overlapping at a line as near as possible vertical. The two top petals overlap one another, with the left-hand petal over the right-hand petal. The eye of the flower is centred on the line, one-third above the bottom, and the whole flower is in so far as is possible a full circle. Equally acceptable for Show and Exhibition purposes would be a flower whose lower petal and two side petals occupy a considerably larger proportion of the total area, leaving very much less of the two top petals visible.

You may find all the foregoing overpoweringly pedantic, but to the true florist, the whole pleasure lies purely in the desire to produce a flower which conforms to the agreed standards of perfection. For the dedicated florist too, competition is a prime motivation; and the whole business would become unworkable without clearly defined and accepted rules. It is understandable if florists and gardeners find their attitudes and aspirations somewhat alien one to the other, but where the object of their interest is common, florists and gardeners have much to learn from one another.

Sadly, the true Show pansy has almost slipped into oblivion in recent years and but for the concerted efforts of a dedicated few, it would have been lost for ever. Few, if any, Show pansies are now offered commercially and stocks are invariably limited. Those that survive as Show pansies today bear little comparison to those recorded by artists of the nineteenth century, leaning more towards the Fancy pansy than the fabulous creations which gave the Show pansy such status in its heyday. Without doubt, there is scope for growers to at least attempt to reinstate the Show pansy to its former glory.

FANCY PANSIES

Around 1848–1849, the Belgian pansy, or Fancy pansy as it was subsequently called, appeared upon the scene. To all accounts, it was greeted with great enthusiasm by all, except by those dedicated to the Show pansy – who, not surprisingly, held the Fancy pansy in some contempt, regarding it as an inferior product. Pansies acquired in France in the 1870s by John Salter were referred to by the English Show pansy growers as 'French rubbish'!, if only because they did not conform to the only standards that they considered acceptable. Those who were responsible for the development of the Fancy pansy had no doubt used Show pansies amongst others in their breeding programme but they did not share the unswerving allegiance of the Show pansy florists to the severely restricting rules that they had brought upon themselves. Most members of the garden pansy and viola family interbreed indiscriminately with one another. It is therefore hardly surprising that this natural phenomenon should have invited full exploitation by those who had no reason to accept that Show pansies were the ultimate in terms of perfection. It had become apparent that flowers of considerably larger size with a far greater range of colour or combinations of colour and with larger, more spectacular blotches were obtainable and to the general gardening public these attracted immediate attention at the expense of the smaller Show pansies with their more subdued colourings. The Fancy pansies had a rich, sumptuous quality that commanded instant appeal and the plants' habit rendered them more suitable for bedding and general garden use. In no time at all, the Fancy pansies were finding their way onto the exhibition benches, and competition became as fierce between the Fancy pansies as it had been between the Show pansies. Definitions and rules were required for judging to take place on a fair and honourable basis, but fortunately, flexibility was allowed. This encouraged development of the Fancy pansy, as opposed to the somewhat awesome restrictions which had almost brought further improvement of the Show pansy to a standstill.

The Fancy pansy could be propagated with relative ease from seed and cuttings, and it became widely available to the public at large and has now to all intents and purposes replaced the Show pansies on the show bench, a development which is no doubt due to their ease of cultivation when compared to that of the Show pansy. One of the initial attractions of the Fancy pansy – to those with ambition to enter into competitive exhibition – is the considerably more flexible requirements demanded by the floral societies when compared to those laid down for Show pansies. Any flower of sufficient size, form, texture, colour and marking would in all probability be considered acceptable for competition. Whereas the Show pansy was exclusively a product of Great Britain, and the northern counties and Scotland in particular, the Fancy pansy was to a great extent the result of selection and breeding carried out on the European continent. Belgian and French nurserymen undoubtedly had a large part to play in the early years of the Fancy pansy although the basis for their original breeding programmes owed much to the English Show pansy. By the mid-nineteenth century, Fancy pansies were firmly established. They were mostly large blotched flowers of richly contrasting colours with a sumptuous, velvet-like texture.

As competition became more widespread, guidelines inevitably had to be drawn up as to what in the eyes of the judges would constitute a fine and acceptable Fancy pansy. Early examples of the Fancy pansy were of elongated or oval shape with narrower and more ragged petals than would have been acceptable to the connoisseurs of the Show pansy. Before long, however, further breeding and selection brought greater refinement in these respects. They should share the same basic characteristics as those stipulated for the Show pansy. Unlike the Show pansy, there are no specific stipulations regarding colour or the combinations of colour. The blotch should be large and of a dark, very rich colour of black, violet or chocolate falling symmetrically on the three lowest petals. The same method of scoring as for Show pansies is employed by the judges, the maximum attainable mark being twenty.

Writing on the Fancy pansy in 1889 James Simkins described its form and texture in terms similar to those used for the Show pansy, but emphasised the difference regarding its colour, markings and blotch:

The colours should be harmonious but are not necessarily confined within set limits, as in the Show pansy. It was on account of the fanciful disposition of colours in many of the early varieties, that this section received the name 'Fancy' pansy. The blotch should be dense and solid, and large enough to occupy the whole surface (except a narrow margin) of the three lower petals, but it may flush into the margin, or be suffused with other colour or colours without detriment. The top petals may be either the same colour as the blotch or the margin; in the later case the top petals are usually veined with colour from the centre or flushed with some other colour, such as rose, near their edges. The size of the bloom should not for competition be less than 2in in diameter.

In more recent years the meritorious and defective qualities of the Fancy pansy have been summarised in the following manner:

Meritorious Characteristics:
– A flower which is large, fresh, clean, circular in outline, with smooth, thick, velvety petals without serrations, lying evenly on each other and either flat or slightly reflexed so that the surface of the flower is slightly convexed.
– Centre petals which meet above the eye and reach well up on the top petals, and a bottom petal which is sufficiently deep and broad to balance the others.
– Colours which are harmonious.
– Belting (margin) of uniform width.
– Blotches which are large, solid, rounded and clearly defined.
– An eye which is bright yellow, solid, circular and well defined.

Defective Characteristics:
– A flower which is less than $2\frac{1}{2}$in (6cm) in diameter, is past its best, soil-marked, concave or lacking a circular outline.
– Petals which are fish-tailed, thin, of poor substance or serrated.
– Belting which is very narrow or more than $\frac{1}{3}$in (1cm) wide or of uneven width or ill-defined.
– Blotches which are small, thin or ragged-edged.
– An eye which is dull or ill-defined.

It will be seen from the above that a most significant difference between the Show pansy and the Fancy pansy is that whereas a Fancy pansy of less than $2\frac{1}{2}$in (6cm) diameter is considered defective, a Show pansy of more than 2in (5cm) in diameter would be unexpected and even unacceptable.

EXHIBITION VIOLAS

The Exhibition viola is a show flower of more recent introduction. It has all the characteristics which make it an equally suitable flower for exhibition in competition alongside Show and Fancy pansies. As with the pansies, the qualities of what constitutes an acceptable Exhibition viola must be defined in a reasonably positive manner in order to produce a fair basis upon which one flower can be compared with another. The flower of an Exhibition viola should conform to the same basic proportions as those for pansies. When defined in greater detail, certain differences appear which contrast with the pansies. The colour of an Exhibition viola can be self, mottled, suffused, striped or margined but most important of all it should possess no ray nor blotch. Whilst rays and blotches are acceptable amongst the smaller-flowered Bedding and Miniature violas an Exhibition viola sporting the merest hint of rays or blotch would stand no chance of success in top class competition. Judges assess the value of an Exhibition viola along similar lines to those for pansies; awarding marks for which the maximum attainable is twenty. However, belting and blotch being inapplicable to violas, a total of seven marks are awarded for colour, the total points being apportioned as follows:

Condition	3	points maximum
Form and texture	5	,, ,,
Size	3	,, ,,
Colour	7	,, ,,
Eye	2	,, ,,
Total	20	,,

Once again the characteristics both meritorious and defective can be summarised as follows:

Meritorious Characteristics:
– A flower which is large, fresh, clean, circular in outline, with smooth, thick, velvety petals without serrations, lying evenly on each other and either flat or slightly reflexed so that the surface of the flower is slightly convex.
– Centre petals which meet above the eye and reach well up on the top petals, and a bottom petal which is sufficiently deep and broad to balance the others.
– While the colour may be self, striped, mottled, suffused, or belted there must be no semblance of a blotch or any rays.
– The eye must be bright, solid, circular and well-defined.

Defective Characteristics:
– A flower which is less than 2½in (6cm) in diameter, past its best, soil-marked, concave or lacking a circular outline.
– Petals which are fish-tailed or have V-shaped gaps between them or are thin, of poor substance or serrated.
– Any semblance of a blotch or of rays.
– An eye which is very large or is square or ill-defined.

A significant omission from the list is the question of fragrance, which is such an attractive characteristic of many violas and of such significance, particularly to the blind.

It is important to realise that many of the Show and Fancy pansies and Exhibition violas – whilst producing the most spectacular flower examples for the show bench – are not by any means the most satisfactory plants for bedding and general garden work. The exceptionally large flowers of the Fancy pansy and Exhibition viola are very often far less tolerant of excessive wind and rain than smaller-flowered, more compact varieties and the lank habit of many, in particular the Show pansy, can result in plants that do not display their flowers in the best manner without a certain amount of attention to staking and tying. Serious exhibitors will in all probability practise disbudding in their efforts not only to produce exceptional flowers, but also to induce the chosen buds to reach perfection on the appointed day for showing.

BEDDING VIOLAS

A Bedding viola worthy of exhibition and show should meet the following requirements. The plant should be free-flowering and possess dwarf, compact and spreading habit of growth. The flower stems should be stiff and erect and be of sufficient length to hold the flowers clear of the foliage. The flowers should be of good substance, circular or oval in form, without blotch or rays and with a neat yellow or orange eye. The flowers should be no more than 2in (5cm) and no less than 1in (2.5cm) in width.

VIOLETTAS

If a Violetta is to be considered for exhibition, the flowers must be of good substance and circular or oval in form. The colour should be bright and clear, whatever the shade. When more than one colour is present the colours should be well contrasted. The eye, which should be bright yellow or orange, may run into the lip of the lower petal but no other central marking or rays are acceptable. The Violetta should be free-flowering and the flowers should have a distinct fragrance. They should be no less than 1in (2.5cm) and no more than 1½in (3.75cm) in width. The habit should be dwarf, bushy and procumbent, the foliage compact and small and the flowers should be held clear of the foliage on erect stalks.

MINIATURE VIOLAS

In 1967, by agreement between the British Pansy and Viola Floral Society and the North of England Pansy and Viola Society, standards for the Miniature viola were adopted, thereby opening the way for this valuable group of plants to take its place on the show bench. The requirements for the Miniature viola are similar in all respects to those for the Violetta, except that the flowers should be circular in form and the eye of the flower should always be small and clean-cut. These requirements are in contrast to those for the Violetta, in which flowers of oval form are acceptable and the gold or orange eye is permitted to bleed into the lip of the lower petal. Fragrance is not an essential requirement for a Miniature viola. The dividing lines between a Violetta and a Miniature viola are slight indeed and it is understandable that confusion can arise when attempting to differentiate one from the other.

When it comes to the actual staging of exhibits there are various traditional methods from which to choose. For any major flower show there will be a schedule, published well ahead of the event, in which the various classes will be described in some detail and it is of course important to interpret these correctly.

The following is an extract of the relevant section of the schedule of the 1989 Southport Flower Show:

OPEN TO ALL

Pansies and Violas

General conditions: (Classes 17 to 21) – (a) All stems of blooms in these Classes must be in water. (b) Varieties in commerce and/or seedlings may be shown. (c) All blooms must be named as far as practicable (Class 18 excluded). In close competition, the Judges will take this into account. (d) Classes 17 and 18. A maximum of 100 points may be awarded as follows:

Quality of blooms, 67 points;
Decorative effect, 33 points.

Class

17 **DISPLAY OF VIOLAS AND/OR PANSIES,** to occupy a staging 8 feet in length by 3 feet in width. Any foliage and/or ornamental grasses may be used for decoration. Flat staging 2 feet 6 inches from the ground level will be provided, together with a backrail not higher than 4 feet above the staging. Each display will be allotted separate staging. A small space probably about 18 inches, will be left between the staging for each display.
Prizes: 1st, 'Clay' Trophy (A.13) and £20.00; 2nd, £16.00; 3rd, £12.00.
Prizes (Classes 18 to 20): 1st, £5.00; 2nd, £3.50; 3rd, £2.00.

18 **BASKET OF VIOLAS AND/OR PANSIES,** any variety and/or varieties.

19 **SIX VASES OF BEDDING VIOLAS,** 6 distinct varieties, both fully open blooms (and buds if possible), to be shown with own foliage as grown, 6 stems of one variety only in each vase. Moss, reed, etc, may be used in arranging the exhibits in the vases. Wiring of blooms will disqualify.

The North of England Pansy and Viola Society will award a Special Prize of an inscribed pewter tankard to the first prize winner in Class 19.

20 **TWENTY-FOUR VIOLAS,** not less than 12 varieties, on a board.

21 **THREE VASES FANCY PANSIES,** 3 distinct varieties, 6 blooms of one variety in a vase.
Prizes: 1st, National Viola and Pansy Society Bronze Medal and £3.50; 2nd, £2.50; 3rd, £2.00.

22 **SEEDLING CLASS,** 3 blooms of Violas, 3 blooms Fancy Pansies, 3 stems bedding Viola or Pansy.
North of England Pansy and Viola Society First Class Certificates and Award of Merit Certificates will be awarded. Non-competitive class.

AMATEURS AND GARDENERS

Pansies and Violas

General Conditions: (Classes 112 to 125) − (a) In vase classes, one variety only may be shown in a vase. (b) Varieties in commerce and/or seedlings may be shown in Classes Nos 112 to 125. (c) All stems of blooms must be in water. (d) In the vase classes, only Viola or Pansy foliage allowed. (e) So far as practicable, each bloom in board and vase classes to be named.

The 'Odd Fellows Centenary' Trophy (A.79) will be awarded for the highest points in Classes Nos 112 to 125. See Competitive Regulation No 10(b).

Class

112 **SIX VASES OF VIOLAS,** in 6 distinct varieties, 6 blooms of one variety only in one vase.
Prizes: 1st, £6.00; 2nd, £4.50; 3rd, £2.50.
Prizes (Classes 113 to 127): 1st, £3.00; 2nd, £2.00; 3rd, £1.00.

113 **TWELVE FANCY PANSIES,** in 6 distinct varieties to be shown on a board.

114 **TWELVE VIOLAS,** in 6 distinct varieties to be shown on a board.

115 **SIX FANCY PANSIES OR VIOLAS,** in 3 distinct varieties to be shown on a board.

116 **ONE VASE OF SIX BLOOMS OF A FANCY PANSY.** One variety.
A National Viola and Pansy Society Large Silver Medal will be awarded to the Competitor gaining the highest total number of points in Classes Nos 117 to 123 (M.13). See Competitive Regulation No 10(b).

117 **ONE VASE OF SIX BLOOMS, WHITE SELF VIOLA.** One variety.

118 **ONE VASE OF SIX BLOOMS, CREAM OR LEMON SELF VIOLA.** One variety.

119 **ONE VASE OF SIX BLOOMS OF WHITE OR CREAM GROUND SUFFUSE-EDGED VIOLA.** One variety.

120 **ONE VASE OF SIX BLOOMS, WHITE OR CREAM GROUND EDGED VIOLA.** One variety.

121 **ONE VASE OF SIX BLOOMS, YELLOW GROUND VIOLA.** One variety.

122 ONE VASE OF SIX BLOOMS, FANCY SHADED OR STRIPED VIOLA. One variety.

123 ONE VASE OF DARK SELF VIOLA. One variety.

124 ONE VASE OF SIX STEMS VIOLA (BEDDER).

125 ONE VASE OF SIX STEMS PANSIES (BEDDER).

126 ONE VASE OF SIX BLOOMS VIOLA, any variety or varieties.

127 ONE VASE OF SIX BLOOMS PANSIES, any variety or varieties.

As shown in the Southport Show schedule, points are allocated somewhat differently to the method previously described, a total of 100 being the maximum attainable. These consist of a maximum sixty-seven points for quality of blooms and a maximum thirty-three points for decorative effect.

No matter what method is used to assess the score, the flowers and their staging must be correct in every respect if an exhibit is to deserve a top award.

METHODS OF EXHIBITING

When it comes to the actual method by which the flowers are displayed, there are a number of alternative options. The blooms can be exhibited on boards or trays, in vases or baskets, as sprays or as a growing, flowering plant in a pot or pan. Traditionally, the board or tray was the method by which the Show pansy was displayed.

Boards, Trays and Stands

Whilst there have always been a variety of designs for boards, trays and stands, they all basically consist of an inclined board in which holes are drilled or apertures cut, through which the stem of an individual bloom is passed, leaving the flower alone to lay flat against the plain surface of the board. Boards or trays are designed to accommodate six, twelve, eighteen or as many as twenty-four blooms. The holes are drilled equidistant to one another so that the effect is one of overall harmony. Beneath each hole there is some form of receptacle – filled with water – into which the flower stem extends. If the receptacle is replenished when necessary, it should keep the flower fresh throughout the duration of the flower show. A handyman of no more than average competence would have little difficulty in constructing a board or tray. The most simple need be little more than a metal, plastic or timber sheet, drilled, with some form of adequate water reservoir placed beneath to accommodate the flower stems, and a strut to incline the board at a suitable angle for viewing the blooms at the show bench.

For a show of short duration, the flowers can be kept adequately moist by encircling the stem with saturated cotton wool or soft tissue which can then be overwrapped with polythene sheeting or cling film. Whatever method you use, it is advisable to conceal it from view by means of a suitable skirting beneath the board. Traditionally the board or tray would be painted leaf-green although charcoal grey or black makes an appropriate backdrop for all other than the darkest-coloured flowers. Perhaps the most practical board or tray will have provision for a lid and be constructed in such a fashion that the exhibits can be staged elsewhere and transported to the show bench without fear of damage. A sealed board will help to maintain humidity and protect the blooms from dust, wind and sunshine.

An illustration of an early pansy stand appears in *The Florist and Garden Miscellany* of 1850 along with some interesting observations concerning its construction provided in this case by an exhibitor of the day from Whitby, Yorkshire. The exhibitor suggests that it should be constructed of zinc as opposed to tin, the top painted white and the sides green. For a stand to display twelve blooms, an overall size of 13 × 10in (33 × 25cm) with a depth of 4in (10cm) at the back and 2½in (6cm) at the front is recommended. The base over which this is laid contains tubes designed to hold water and into which the flower stems will project. An obvious improvement to this design could be effected by having the tubes positioned either vertically or preferably leaning towards the back of the stand as this would make it that much easier to position the petals of the pansy flat against the surface of the board. The angle of the flower stem to the plane of the flower explains why this arrangement is advisable. The white surface would display a flower with petals or margins of strong colour to perfection but would be less effective for white or paler flowers, when a green, grey or black surface might provide better contrast.

An attractive design for a 'pansy stand' is offered in the same publication. For this version, the author suggests a neat timber box with a removable lid, painted a dark rosewood and highly varnished. Inside the box, supported by beading (to allow the lid to close without making contact with the blooms) is a fitted plate of ⅛in (3mm) thick zinc painted a yellow-green. If, as suggested,

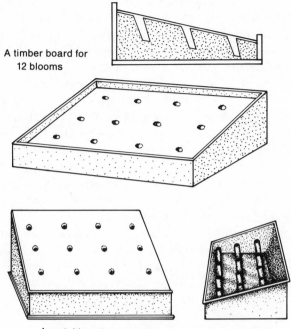

A timber board for 12 blooms

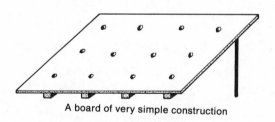

A metal board separated into its two component parts

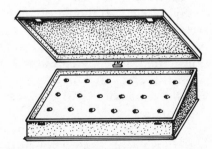

A board of very simple construction

A more elaborate display board with removable, protective cover

Boards for Exhibition and Show

the stand is to accommodate twenty-four blooms, these should be arranged in four horizontal rows of six blooms each. The holes in the zinc plate should be $\frac{3}{4}$in (2cm) in depth and $\frac{1}{2}$in (12mm) in width. The lower or front row of holes should be $1\frac{1}{8}$in (3cm) in from the edge of the plate and $1\frac{1}{2}$in (4cm) in from each side of the plate; and the four horizontal rows should be 2in (5cm) apart. Twenty-four metal tubes to hold the water should be soldered beneath the holes. If these tubes are well angled towards the front of the stand they will ease the job of positioning each bloom in flat contact with the plate. The stand should either be constructed to slope downwards or arranged to slope at an appropriate angle by placing something underneath it at the back. The overall dimensions of this pansy stand are: length 1ft 6in (46cm), width $12\frac{1}{2}$in (32cm) and depth 3in (7.5cm).

James Simkins, writing in 1889, suggested a very similar design of 'pansy tray' with full details relating to its construction. In this case the whole structure was made of lacquered green zinc, and described as very durable. Three sizes were recommended:

No of blooms	length	width	height (back)	(front)
18	19in (48cm)	$10\frac{1}{4}$in (26cm)	$4\frac{1}{2}$in (11cm)	$2\frac{1}{4}$in (5.5cm)
12	$13\frac{1}{4}$in (34cm)	$10\frac{1}{4}$in (26cm)	$4\frac{1}{2}$in (11cm)	$2\frac{1}{4}$in (5.5cm)
6	$10\frac{1}{2}$in (26.5cm)	$7\frac{1}{4}$in (18cm)	4in (10cm)	2in (5cm)

For the large Fancy pansies of the day the holes were to be 3in (7.5cm) apart centre to centre and for the smaller Show pansies $2\frac{1}{2}$in (6cm) was considered sufficient. It would therefore have been prudent to have interchangeable plates for each tray. The zinc tubes to hold water were 3in (7.5cm) in length and angled from back to front as previously described. There should be about $\frac{1}{2}$in (1cm) clearance between the plate and the top of the box and Simkins recommended that a sheet of glass be cut to fit exactly and that this be laid over the prepared blooms to hold them and protect them in transit. The glass would undoubtedly prevent loss of moisture and help to prevent petals from curling. If at any time condensation forms on the under-surface of the glass or the petals, the glass should be removed to allow the moisture to evaporate. It should then be thoroughly dried and replaced as protection. Where difficulty is experienced in persuading a flower to lay flat against the board it is customary to allow the flower

Show Pansies 1833

French Pansies 1844

Show and Fancy Pansies 1864

Fancy Pansies 1862

Fancy Pansies 1865

Fancy Pansies 1867

Violas and Pansies 1872

Viola 'Mary Ellen'

BEDDING VIOLAS & PANSIES.
1. Eyebright   2. Canary   3. In Memoriam
4. White Perfection   5. Advancer   6. Dickson's King

FLORAL MAGAZINE NEW SERIES

Viola 'Agnes Susannah'

Viola 'Huntercombe Purple'   *Viola* 'Daisy Smith'

Violetta 'Leora'   *Viola* 'Lilac Rose'

Viola 'Aspasia'

Viola 'Palmers White'

Viola 'Dusk'

Viola 'Admiration'

Viola 'Letitia'

Viola 'Barbara'   *Viola* 'Mysie'

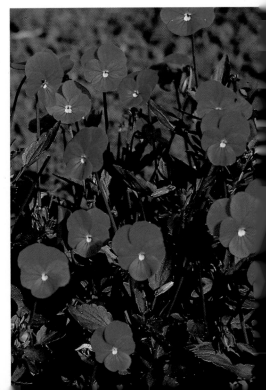

Viola 'Magenta Maid'

Viola 'Ardross Gem'

Viola 'Ivory Queen'   *Viola* 'Mauve Radiance'

Viola 'Thalia'

Viola 'Haslemere'

Violetta 'Rebecca'

Viola 'Chantryland' type

Viola 'Irish Molly'   *Viola* 'Maggie Mott'

Viola 'Jackanapes'

Viola tricolor, garden strain

Viola 'Sarah'

Viola lutea, garden strain

Viola cornuta 'Alba'

Viola cornuta 'Rosea'

Viola cornuta 'Belmont Blue'

Viola 'Irina'

Viola 'Cinderella'

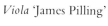

Viola 'James Pilling'

Viola aetolica

Viola 'David Wheldon'

A mixture of small-flowered violas

A mixture of small-flowered violas

Violetta 'Little David'

Violas 'Gladys Finlay' and 'Bonnie Heather'

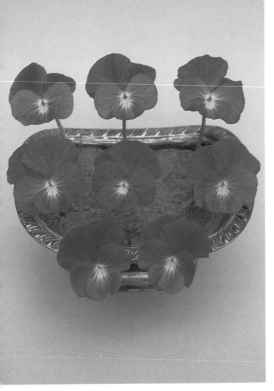

Viola 'Nora May'   A promising new introduction

Hazeldene Nursery, Royal Bath and West Show, 1989

to flag a little by denying it sufficient water and in this way it can be carefully manipulated in the way required. To allow excessive flagging is to invite disaster but provided a flower has only relaxed it can be revived once again by watering gently.

Today, materials other than timber or sheet metal are considered suitable for the construction of a board, stand or tray but no effort should be spared in constructing an attractive product since a display of fine flowers may lose favour in the eyes of the judges due to shoddy overall presentation. It is well to remember that an inferior bloom well presented may steal the title from a better bloom poorly displayed and it is only the finest blooms displayed in the finest manner that truly deserve to win.

As recently as 1968 the North of England Pansy and Viola Society published some detailed instructions for those wishing to construct a simple pansy board. In this case the board was no more than a rectangular plate of 20 or 22 gauge tinned plate, the raw edges hammered around $\frac{1}{8}$in (3mm) diameter wire to achieve a neat, attractive finish. Holes of $\frac{1}{2}$in (12mm) diameter were punched or drilled at a distance of 3in (7.5cm) centre to centre and rectangular cups were constructed of the same tinned plate and soldered behind each hole to hold the water in which each flower stalk will rest. A single-hinged strut is then soldered to the top back face of the plate so that the display can be staged at an appropriate angle to be viewed comfortably by the judges and others. The finished board is then painted the ever popular green.

The three usual sizes for such boards are as follows:

6 blooms	$6\frac{1}{2}$in × $9\frac{1}{2}$in (16.5cm × 24cm)
12 blooms	$12\frac{1}{2}$in × $9\frac{1}{2}$in (31cm × 24cm)
24 blooms	$18\frac{1}{2}$in × $12\frac{1}{2}$in (47cm × 31cm)

For show classes calling for 48 blooms, two 24 boards would simply be staged side by side in contact with one another.

A 6 board consists of 3 horizontal rows of 2, a 12 board consists of 3 horizontal rows of 4, and a 24 board consists of 4 horizontal rows of 6. Simple trays of this nature will fold almost flat and if a box of suitable dimensions is constructed with tiered runners, a number of trays can be accommodated one above the other and in this way transported to the show in a convenient manner. The box must be totally enclosed to protect the contents in transit and steps must be taken to ensure that the water reserves in which the flower stems are inserted do not spill their contents.

Many years ago the National Viola and Pansy Society decreed that a board for 12 blooms should not exceed an overall size of 14 × 11in (35 × 28cm) and a board for 6 blooms should not exceed 7 × 11in (18 × 28cm). They also stipulated that a board should be raised no higher than 5in (12.5cm) at the back.

Paper Collars

It is common practice amongst those who exhibit pansies and violas on trays or boards to use circular collars of stiff white card behind each flower. The stem of each blossom is threaded through a hole cut in the centre of each collar before the flower is mounted on the board. Whether the collar evolved as no more than an aid to support the petals (as it no doubt does) or whether perhaps it was used to emphasise the extent to which a bloom described a full circle (as was the ultimate aim) is not certain. Whatever the intention, there is evidence to suggest that there were and still are people who consider the use of collars unacceptable. There may be people today who even find the traditional display of severed pansy and viola heads on boards distasteful when compared with alternative methods of presentation. Some felt sufficiently strongly about the matter as to voice their opinions in no uncertain terms.

In 1908 Howard Crane in *The Book of the Pansy, Viola and Violet* referred to 'blooms grotesquely arranged on trays'. Attitudes were changing and a movement was afoot to encourage the exhibiting of pansies and violas in an altogether more natural manner. Gertrude Jekyll, writing in her book *Wood and Garden* first published in 1899, expressed the forthright opinion that:

> Shows of carnations and pansies, where the older rules prevail, are ... misleading, where the single flowers are arranged in a flat circle of paper. As with the chrysanthemum, every sort of trickery is allowed in arranging the petals of the carnation blooms: petals are pulled out or stuck in, and they are twisted about, and groomed and combed, and manipulated with special tools – 'dressed', as the show-word has it – dressed so elaborately that the dressing only stops short of applying actual paint and perfumery. Already in the case of carnations a better influence is being felt, and at the London shows there are now classes for border carnations set up in long-stalked bunches just as they

grow. It is only like this that their value as out-door plants can be tested; for many of the show sorts have miserably weak stalks, and a very poor, lanky habit of growth.

Then the poor pansies have single blooms laid flat on white papers, and are only approved if they will lie quite flat and show an outline of a perfect circle. All that is most beautiful in a Pansy, the wing-like curves, the waved or slightly fluted radiations, the scarcely perceptible undulation of surface that displays to perfection the admirable delicacy of velvety texture; all the little tender tricks and ways that make the Pansy one of the best-loved of garden flowers; all this overlooked, and not only passively overlooked, but overtly contemned. The show-pansy judge appears to have no eye, or brain, or heart, but to have in their place a pair of compasses with which to describe a circle! All idea of garden delight seems to be excluded, as this kind of judging appeals to no recognition of beauty for beauty's sake, but to hard systems of measurement and rigid arrangement and computation that one would think more applicable to astronomy or geometry than to any matter relating to horticulture.

I do most strongly urge that beauty of the highest class should be the aim, and not anything of the nature of fashion or 'fancy', and that every effort should be made towards the raising rather than the lowering of the standard of taste.

The Societies which exist throughout the country are well organised; many have existed for a great number of years; they are the local sources of horticultural education, to which large circles of people naturally look for guidance; and though they produce – especially at the Rose shows – quantities of beautiful things, it cannot but be perceived by all who have had the benefit of some refinement of education, that in very many cases they either deliberately teach, or at any rate allow to be seen with their sanction, what cannot fail to be debasing to public taste.

For those who disagree with Miss Jekyll – and there is no reason to suppose that paper collars do not still find favour with some – circles of stiff white card approximately $2\frac{3}{4}$in (7cm) in diameter are required. In the centre of the circle must be a hole large enough to accept not only the stalk but all the structure of the flower except the petals. The collar is held in place by a pin which must of course remain invisible.

If the collar is small enough to remain totally hidden from

view, and if it serves only to provide support to tne flower and its petals, then those who might otherwise share Miss Jekyll's opinion should surely have no cause for complaint. Only where the collar is visible need there be cause for concern. If the sole purpose for using a collar at all is to compensate for shortcomings in the constitution of a flower, then surely we may wonder whether such a bloom is truly fit for exhibition at all.

In its natural state, a fresh pansy or viola flower will appear, if not flat, to be concave. When displaying the flowers on boards it is widely accepted that a flower of slightly convex shape will present itself most effectively and paper collars can be a help in achieving this end. If a bloom with concave petals is permitted to flag through lack of moisture it will be comparatively easy, with great care, to induce the petals to take on the convex shape. With the support of a hidden collar the petals will, when mounted on the board, appear flat. Many years ago the National Pansy and Viola Society stipulated that 'collars may be used on all board classes' implying that it was not apparently obligatory that all blooms displayed on boards should have collars. The decision was left to the exhibitor.

Irrespective of any opposition to the exhibiting of pansies and violas on trays and boards it would be sad indeed if these trad-itional skills and practices were allowed to disappear. It is now left to comparatively few of the older generation of pansy and viola exhibitors to keep the tradition alive, and it is to be hoped that a younger generation will become sufficiently involved to ensure that this aspect of true floristry is not lost for ever.

Sprays

An alternative traditional method of displaying pansies and par-ticularly violas for exhibition and competition in a less formal manner is the spray. This process has seen the evolution of what is considered to be the correct method of construction. Considerable practice and much patience are required before a spray can be effectively produced with confidence. To construct a spray in the traditional way you will need wire and coarse wool. Thin, pliable, but sufficiently rigid wire must be cut into lengths a little longer than the length of the flower stem and the end bent to form a shape not unlike a crook. The bent end of the wire is positioned over the top of the stalk where it joins the back of the flower. In this way, it can subsequently be used to position the flower head to the precise angle that will exhibit it to best effect. The wire can also be used to support a wayward petal or two. The coarse wool, preferably of a green colour to match the flower stalks, is then bound around the flower stem and its wire support to hold both together. A more natural effect is achieved if a piece of the plant's foliage is also bound to each flower stalk and if this is not incorporated in one operation it can be bound on afterwards with more fine wire. Having treated sufficient flowers in this manner, a spray of six or ten flowers can be bound together with raffia, ribbon, or some other suitable material to form a symmetrical pyramid as illustrated on page 139.

The spray can be displayed on an inclined board with a water reservoir, not unlike the boards already mentioned, or in small vases of subdued colour which will not distract attention from the blooms. Sprays of this nature, like board displays, will not appeal to those who prefer to see the flowers exhibited in a less formal manner and it is by no means certain that the true spray is a method still employed today.

Bunches

If you consider the construction of sprays to be unduly and unnecessarily complicated, exhibiting in what is called bunches has its obvious appeal. Bunches are arranged in wide-mouthed vases or shallow bowls in which the flowers can be exhibited in a far more natural manner. Instead of individual flower stalks being used, a whole shoot complete with buds and possibly more than one flower are used. A number of these stalks can be arranged with comparative ease to produce a display very much in-keeping with the true character of the plant as it grows in the garden. A display of this nature will often have greater appeal to the general public.

Vases

There are two basic methods recommended for displaying exhibition blooms in vases. The most simple method is to take a suitable vessel of 8 or 10in (20 or 25cm) in diameter and 2 or 3in (5 or 7.5cm) in depth, depending on the variety to be shown, and to fill it with silver sand which should then have water added to saturation point. The saturated sand will provide adequate moisture to maintain fresh blooms and additional water can easily be added when required. The sand should be thoroughly damp but not so wet as to be too unstable to hold the flower stems in position when they are inserted. The flower stems can then be trimmed to the required length and inserted into the sand at appropriate angles to give a harmonious and well-balanced image to the eye of the beholder.

The alternative to this simple method is to use glass or rigid plastic tubing which when inserted in the sand will form a receptacle into which the flower stems and perhaps some accompanying foliage can be inserted. The usual material for tubes is 10mm soda glass which can be readily melted in a gas flame. The tube can be reduced to the required length by rotating it in the gas flame until it glows red, at which stage it can be pulled apart. Glass tubes can also be carefully broken to the required length if a nick is filed into the glass at the measured breaking point and pressure gently applied from the opposite side. Any sharp or ragged edges to the cut or broken end can be rendered smooth by rotating carefully in a gas flame.

For the most usual exhibition class, which is for a vase display of 6 blooms, tubes of varying lengths will be required: one 10in (25cm), two 8in (20cm), one 7in (18cm) and two 5in (13cm). With tubes of these approximate lengths it will be possible to arrange the 6 blooms in the symmetrical fashion indicated in the illustration on page 139.

It is usual practice to insert pansy or viola foliage in each tube behind the bloom. The foliage will not only help to support the bloom but will also contribute towards a more attractive and less stark display hiding much of the tube work. The tubes can be charged with water which can with care be replenished if necessary. There is an air of artificiality associated with glass tubes which may not appeal to those concerned to exhibit in the most natural manner.

As an alternative to the conventional vase, a small wicker basket makes an equally attractive container in which to display the flowers. If using saturated sand it will of course be necessary to line the basket within to retain the moisture.

No matter what quantity of blooms are specified for a vase, they should be displayed in a symmetrical and harmonious manner.

Pots

Last but by no means least amongst the methods of exhibiting the pansy or viola is the potted plant. A fine specimen plant, roots and all, either transplanted or already growing in a conventional pot of appropriate size is surely the one method which above all can offend no one. The pot itself can be plunged into a bed of peat, bark, chippings or some similar material and the most natural and attractive display of all will have been achieved. Display in this manner is commonly employed for pure commercial show and exhibition whereas for competitive exhibiting amongst fellow florists, permitted methods of display will be dictated by the terms laid down in the schedule of classes for each particular flower show.

It is vital to digest in detail the schedule and the required conditions before embarking upon serious competition of this nature.

Whatever method is employed for exhibiting the flowers, the names of the varieties should be clearly indicated in a neat and attractive manner on white card adjacent to the display.

If cut flowers for exhibition are to be transported any great distance it is important to keep them cool and shaded but ventilated. If it is impractical for their stems to be in water, their freshness can be maintained by laying them on damp fabric sheeting, spraying then with a fine mist of cold water or even wrapping their individual stems in fine 'clingfilm' polythene containing a little water. The cool box in a refrigerator may well preserve flowers that reach perfection rather too soon for the show in which they are to be exhibited.

In all forms of exhibiting, from board and tube display, right the way through to the contrived bedding schemes such as those to be found at the annual Chelsea Flower Show, there is a degree of artificiality. For the serious exhibitor, much planning, cossetting and subtlety of staging will have gone into such displays. The motivation, if it is not simply pride of achievement, will be to impress the judges or to entice the general public into purchasing, and under such circumstances it is most unlikely that the flowers will have been subjected entirely to the unpredictable elements of a totally unprotected environment.

GROWING FOR SHOW

When growing for show the emphasis will, of course, be directed towards producing a sufficient number of top quality blooms. It is therefore important that the plants ate sited in such a way as to allow easy access for the regular attention that they will require. When young plants for subsequent use in show and exhibition work are first planted out into final quarters, any flower buds and flowers should be removed together with their stalks. The object is to develop a strong framework before the plant is permitted to flower. Around the middle of June it is advisable to remove the growing tip of a plant that shows signs of producing only one stem. This will encourage the development of side shoots and if the object of the exercise is to attempt to produce the finest blooms for exhibition, no more than three shoots per plant should be allowed to develop. As these shoots extend, it will be necessary to support each with a split cane to which the shoot, as it grows, is tied. When tying, it is important to allow for subsequent expansion of the stem. By supporting the stems in this way the buds and flowers will be held clear of the soil and be less likely to be splashed with soil during heavy rain.

By late June, flower buds should be in evidence and within a week, depending upon the weather conditions, these should produce mature flowers, hopefully fit for exhibition. During the bud stage, a gentle application of a high potash feed of liquid manure may be advantageous – but great care must be exercised in its application to prevent the plant from being splashed. Once the flower buds have started to open, constant monitoring will be necessary to ensure that all is well. Excessively hot sunshine can shrivel or fade the petals; rain, even a heavy morning dew, can mark and damage the blossoms. Unless steps are taken to discourage them, slugs will feed on the petals at night time.

An integral part of the skill of successful showing is to induce or encourage the flowers to reach maturity and perfection on the day of the show. The weather being ever unpredictable the decision as to when to disbud is not an easy one. When stocks of plants are adequate it is wise to stagger the operation of disbudding in order to hedge bets and hopefully have at least a proportion of plants and flowers at maximum perfection on the appointed day. Some form of simple protection will be vital to guard the plants from adverse weather. Wind can inflict considerable damage and unless the growing area is enclosed by a natural windbreak of hedging or other plants, it is advisable to construct some form of protection using one of the woven fabric materials designed for this purpose. These materials will reduce the force of the wind to an acceptable level whilst maintaining the free circulation of air that is so necessary. Solid walls and fences can produce turbulent conditions which are not conducive to healthy growth. The woven windbreak materials are equally suitable for filtering excessive sunshine. For protecting a plant from above, the most simple structure can be made by securely fixing a board of some sort to a small stake inserted into the ground adjacent to each plant. A well-positioned board of appropriate size, fixed at the correct height will not only protect the plant and its flowers

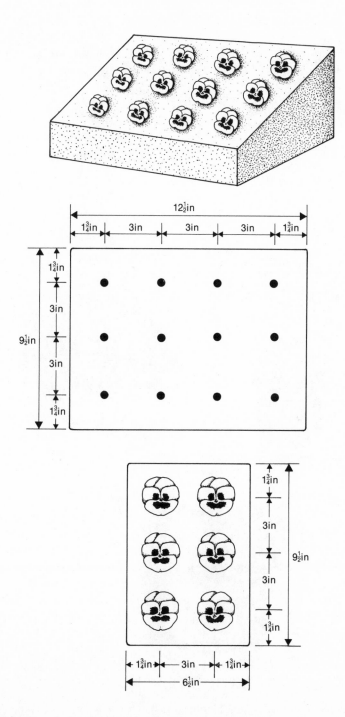

Display boards for Exhibition and Show indicating the recommended dimensions for a 12- and a 6-board

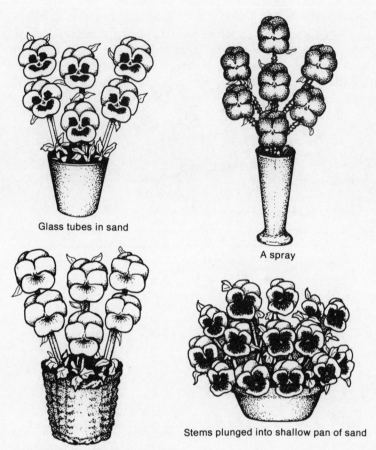

Glass tubes in sand

A spray

Stems plunged into basket of sand

Stems plunged into shallow pan of sand

Mature growing plant in pot or tub

Alternative methods of staging blooms for Exhibition and Show

from rain or hail but it will also provide sufficient shade to protect the flower, without inhibiting its performance. Well-staked pansies and violas will be relatively easy to protect in this manner.

Remember that any application of fertiliser, insecticide or fungicide can disfigure the flowers and foliage and should be applied, if at all, with extreme caution. If you need to use any of these preparations, it is advisable to dilute in excess of manufacturers' instructions and to rinse any residue off the plant just as soon as it is deemed to have performed its function.

Flowers intended for show should be picked with maximum length of stalk, either late on the eve of the show or preferably on the morning of the event, and immediately placed in a vessel of water. They should then be kept in a cool, shaded, well-ventilated area until such time as staging the exhibits begins.

Above all, no matter what method is employed, when showing in competition with others you should be intimately aware of the show schedule, lest the judges award the dreaded decision 'not according to schedule'.

8

Calendar

The suggestions throughout this calendar relate mainly to violas and violettas. It is assumed that the majority of pansies will be raised from seed, other than named varieties of Show and Fancy Pansies.

In providing any form of logical calendar of the basic operations involved in pansy, viola and violetta cultivation, we have several months from which to choose where to begin the growing year. If you start a collection of varieties with the purchase of young plants from a specialist nursery then spring is undoubtedly the time when things begin to happen in earnest. Varieties will have been chosen and orders placed during the quieter days of winter and April or May is the best time of year to bed the young plants out into the garden. If, however, you start by acquiring cuttings or divisions from a fellow gardener, then late summer and autumn is the most appropriate time to make a start. If you wish to grow from seed, then either late summer or spring are suitable starting points. Freshly ripened seed will germinate readily in late summer and some form of simple protection will ensure that the resultant seedlings survive winter unscathed. Spring-sown seed will require little if any cossetting but the resulting seedlings may not reach their full flowering potential until the following spring. Viola cultivation can in fact be started in some shape or form at any season but for the sake of clarity I shall abide by convention and start our year with January.

JANUARY

January is an important month for the gardener, if only as a relatively relaxed period for the all-important pleasure of dreaming and planning for the future. It is the time to obtain all the up-to-date catalogues from the specialist growers, to study any relevant literature, and to acquire as much knowledge as possible in order to ensure a successful year in the garden. Orders for specific varieties are best placed at the earliest opportunity. Growers can only guess future demand and orders for new varieties (or those which may have received exceptional publicity) may well exceed supply. A reputable grower will process any requests in order of receipt and an early order will increase the chances of not being disappointed or of having to await delivery for a further season.

The soil should have been prepared in so far as weather will allow. If the ground has been roughly dug in the autumn, any frosts at this time of year will be welcome – they will play an important part in breaking down the surface soil to the crumbly structure that will be the ideal environment for young plants in the spring. Do not attempt to cultivate wet or frozen soil but, when conditions permit, take the opportunity to clear away any persistent perennial weed growth. If the soil registers excessive acidity, January is a good time for adding a surface dressing of chalk or lime. Winter rains will carry it down in solution into the soil. There is no reason why manure, compost, leafmould or other organic matter should not be applied as a surface dressing during January. It will encourage the beneficial activities of earthworms in the surface soil.

If cuttings have been taken the previous autumn, do not overlook their welfare. Inspect them at regular intervals to ensure that they are unmolested by pests and are not becoming diseased. Occasional light sprays of fungicide and pesticide will not only keep the situation under control but will at the same time maintain humidity and the moisture content of the rooting medium. Bear in mind that under severe winter weather the cuttings may be attacked not only by the more common insect garden pests but also by rodents whose normal, more preferred source of food may no longer be accessible to them. Cuttings should be regularly inspected to ensure that frost action has not loosened the soil around them. If it has, the soil should be carefully firmed around them again. Do not apply excessive moisture at this time of the year, the plants are virtually dormant and their requirements are very small. Even at this time of year the heat of the sun, transmitted through glass or polythene, can become too great for the comfort of the cuttings and it is wise to control the situation, if necessary, by the use of shading which should however be removed as soon as it is no longer required.

FEBRUARY

February, weather-wise, is in many ways no more than an extension of January. It provides the opportunity to undertake any task that has been impossible to perform in the preceding month as a result of any particularly adverse weather. It is a time to anticipate the future. Imagine the very real possibility of drought in mid-summer and ensure that water supply and storage facilities will be adequate in case of an emergency later in the season. Inspect cuttings and over-wintering seedlings closely at regular intervals. Plants, if too dry, will attract aphids. Plants that are too wet will attract fungal rot. Aim for the somewhat elusive balance between the two extremes and all should be well. Remember that at this time of year sunshine through glass or polythene can produce quite high temperatures and consequent stress to a cutting or seedling with insufficient moisture and an under-developed root system. Pests that would normally be dormant will be brought to life by the increase in temperature. Ventilate the cuttings freely in all but severe weather.

MARCH

Invariably, the most unwelcome characteristic of March is cold winds. Ensure that cuttings and seedlings are adequately protected from its effects. Polythene may well be damaged by strong winds. Continue to inspect at regular intervals and give light sprays of fungicide and insecticide as a preventative but also as a means of maintaining adequate humidity. Carefully remove any seriously affected or obviously dead seedlings and cuttings which may otherwise lead to the further spread of disease. If conditions permit, fork the outside soil in preparation for planting next month. Cover the area with polythene sheeting held securely in position by stones and this will not only warm the soil but protect it from excessive rain which may prevent work when the time comes for planting out.

APRIL

The traditional April of heavy showers alternating with warm sunny intervals can in no way be guaranteed. Snow accompanied by cold north and east winds or even virtual drought conditions can all be expected to contribute towards the fun of gardening in April. Be patient. Do not attempt to plant out the young violas until conditions are right. Acclimatise the young plants and rooted cuttings to the outside world by gradually subjecting them to more and more ventilation until they are to all intents and purposes unprotected, and only then begin the process of planting into the open garden. When receiving plants from a nurseryman by mail there is no sure way of knowing to what extent they have been hardened off. It is not a bad idea to afford the new arrivals some protection for the first week or so on the assumption that they may well have been taken straight from some sort of protected environment immediately prior to despatch. I have experienced the disappointment of receiving such plants: the outside world is a shock for them and it takes them some little while to recover. There is no reason to suppose that they will not survive such an ordeal. It will produce no more than a slight and temporary setback from which they can be expected to make a full recovery.

If rains have consolidated the soil and only if conditions allow, fork over the surface, incorporating at the same time a general purpose fertiliser of some sort before planting. Plant in a slight depression in order that subsequent hand-watering will become more effective.

MAY

If the operations suggested for April have not for any reason been completed by May, have no fear. It is better to have postponed operations until May than to have pressed ahead in April if weather and soil conditions were not at that time suitable. The health and strength of rooted cuttings and seedlings can be maintained well into May by the occasional application of a liquid or foliar feed. This operation may well involve saturating flowers and buds, but it will be to the long-term benefit of the plant which should within a week or two be producing flowers in increased abundance. Warm weather may encourage slugs and snails to become more active. Steps should be taken to discourage them. Both cuttings and seedlings will already have begun to produce flowers by mid-May and these should be removed before they reach the stage of forming seed. It is best that all their strength be used to form a strong and stocky plant rather than seed. If healthy basal shoots are in evidence, a straggly plant can have its top growth pruned away. Plant out into final quarters at the earliest available opportunity, water well and begin the all-important task of keeping the viola bed free from weeds. At this stage, there is little else to be done for the month of May but to enjoy the early flush of blossom.

JUNE

June is the month in which the viola plant will, we hope, begin to make quite phenomenal growth and to produce the prodigious display of flowers that will delight us throughout the remainder of the summer. The tufted violas and violettas should require little further attention. Those varieties with more straggly or pansy-like habit will benefit from an occasional pruning of the growth – provided that the plants are growing freely and well and that there is evidence of healthy basal growth to take its place. This operation may involve sacrificing flowers and buds but it will be to the long-term benefit of the plant which should within a week or two be producing flowers in increased abundance. The soil should be maintained in moist, weed-free condition and if evidence suggests the necessity, they can be fed with a general liquid, powder or granular fertiliser. In a good, fertile, well-prepared soil, this will not necessarily be required. The occasional very light spray of insecticide or fungicide may be necessary, always remembering that prevention is infinitely preferable to cure.

JULY

July is perhaps the most spectacular month for violas and violettas. Provided the plants have received sufficient moisture and have been kept reasonably free from competing weed growth, the young plants will have formed robust cushions of growth a foot or more in diameter supporting a multitude of flowers and flower buds. The earliest flowers will be forming or in the process of forming seed capsules but there will be a constant succession of fresh flowers to replace those that fade away. The plants' appearance can be enhanced by carefully picking off faded flowers or seed heads unless of course it is the intention to save the seed for propagation. Unless seed is wanted, it can be assumed that food and energy will be concentrated into producing more flowers if the fading flowers are removed before seed formation can begin. It is by no means essential to remove spent flowers and this operation is perhaps only a practical proposition to those who grow relatively few plants that are accessible.

For those who can devote only a restricted number of hours to garden tasks, the plants can quite satisfactorily be left to their own devices. The soil should be maintained in a moist condition, using a light surface mulch for that purpose. If aphids are present, an application of insecticide will control the problem. Slugs are particularly fond of eating the flower petals of violas and if they are evident in any great numbers steps can be taken to discourage them. Fortunately the stems and foliage do not hold the same attraction for slugs and snails and although they will congregate by day in the shade of the violas' foliage, in my experience, they restrict any activity to the hours of darkness when they feast upon the petals of the flowers. At this time of year there is a great variety of other evidently more attractive food for slugs and snails.

Late July is probably the best time to identify those plants from which you would like to increase stock by way of autumn cuttings. In this case, the emphasis will be to produce strong, non-flowering basal shoots for autumn and this can perhaps best be achieved by trimming the plants to encourage such growth, though, unfortunately, at the inevitable expense of flowers. It is very much a case of sacrificing the present for the future, a situation for which there is unfortunately little or no alternative. A plant allowed to continue growing and flowering unabated may yield little or no suitable growth for autumn cuttings although different varieties will be found to react very differently one to another in this respect.

The basal shoots from which it is planned to produce new plants can be encouraged to form roots by gently sifting a light sandy soil or compost around their stems, or alternatively gently drawing surrounding soil towards the crown of the plant. If this is kept moist, it will be found that by autumn, many of the cuttings will have formed a little root growth and will therefore already be on the way to becoming self-supporting.

If seed pods have been allowed to ripen, now is the time to start collecting seed. When the pods start to open, they should be harvested complete with stalk and without delay. Place them straight into a paper bag which should then be placed in a warm, dry and well ventilated place. The seeds will be ejected from the pods with considerable force so that it is important that the bag is enclosed sufficiently to prevent their escape. After a few days, the bag can be given a thorough shaking and the shiny brown seed can then be separated from the chaff. You can either store it in a sealed container in a cool dry place or you can sow it immediately.

AUGUST

In August, we can expect no less than the profuse display of flowers that began in May and reached its zenith in July. If any particular variety is showing signs of easing up in its display of flowers it can benefit from being trimmed back with secateurs, scissors or shears. A gentle liquid feed will in all probability induce it to take on a new lease of life and once more start flowering with profusion. There is little to do in August other than to enjoy the flowers; water and spray them if necessary and keep the bed weed-free. You should at all costs avoid the possibility of weeds being allowed to seed. Unless the removal of spent flowers of violas and violettas has been thorough, seed will inevitably have ripened and fallen. Where conditions are to its liking it will germinate very readily and any resultant seedlings can, when large enough, be transferred to a nursery bed. It is unlikely that any seedlings produced in this manner will be superior or even comparable to the parent plant but one of the delights of gardening is that you can never be sure, and amongst such random seedlings there may be a gem that you can name and call your own. It is unlikely that a seedling will flower until the following spring and some sort of protection from excessive winter wet will enhance its chances of surviving the winter months.

Confusion can arise as a result of ripe seed falling into the crown of the parent plant, germinating, and producing sufficient vigour to overcome the parent plant in the following season. This, I suspect, could be one of the many reasons why differing plants in commerce are sometimes found to masquerade under the same name.

SEPTEMBER

September, in our ever unpredictable climate, can be little more than an extension of summer – or alternatively a foretaste of autumn and winter. Fine sunny weather will prolong the flowering display of violas seemingly endlessly until such time as a ground frost curbs their enthusiasm. You will notice that as the season progresses, the flowers – whilst still appearing in virtually endless succession – will become progressively smaller. For sheer size and quality, the flowers of early summer are supreme, later in the season, the size of subsequent flowers will become smaller, but they will appear in such profusion as to make this of little practical significance.

September is the month in which to prepare for, or even start, propagation from cuttings. No particularly sophisticated equipment is required. Some people strike viola cuttings without the assistance of any artificial protection. They simply choose an area of suitable soil, in an adequately shaded and protected corner of the garden and then, perhaps most important of all, they are blessed with suitable weather to render the operation a success. For those who prefer to maintain more control over the situation all that is needed is a reasonably weather-proof structure of glass or polythene, some form of adjustable shading, adequate natural daylight and reasonable access for watering. Artificial heating is entirely superfluous to the operation. In its simplest form, the propagation house need be no more than a bottomless box or a rectangle of building blocks covered by a sheet of glass, or alternatively, wires or piping supporting some clear polythene sheeting.

OCTOBER

If September weather has been fine and there have been no ground frosts, the violas may well still be blooming even if not with quite the same degree of vigour and profusion as before. The plants can be tidied up by carefully removing any spent flowers or developing seed pods, and any excessively lengthy growth can be trimmed back.

If the soil surface has become encrusted, it should be carefully broken, taking care that no viola roots are damaged and exposed. This should ensure that rain can penetrate freely and will not lie around the collar of the plant, thereby encouraging rot. Plants chosen for propagation purposes will have been trimmed hard in July or August and provided that they have not lacked moisture, they should by now be bristling with the non-flowering basal shoots which will form cuttings. October is an ideal month in which to take cuttings although in a reasonably mild autumn there is no reason why they should not be taken at any suitable time – until as late as mid-December.

Any seedlings can be potted up or transferred to nursery quarters where they can be afforded some protection from excessively cold or wet winter weather.

NOVEMBER

There is little if any essential work in relation to violas at this time of year. Preparation of fresh ground to take next year's crop can be undertaken. As with most crops it is unwise to plant violas in the same piece of ground in successive seasons, as this may encourage a build-up of any pest and diseases that have taken a liking to violas. Practice regular rotation of the viola crop in so far as space will allow. Even the most perennial of varieties will benefit from being lifted and replanted into fresh ground for the new season and there is no better time for this than during autumn when the soil is moist and growth has subsided. Tufted varieties, in particular the *cornutas*, can easily be divided at this time of year so that a small colony can with ease be created from one single, healthy one year old plant.

As already stated, cuttings can be taken successfully throughout November. Seedlings, if sufficiently advanced, can be planted out although it would perhaps be wise to pot them up or plant them in nursery quarters where it will be easier to protect them from excessive cold and moisture. They can then be bedded into their final quarters in spring.

DECEMBER

If you still wish to take cuttings, it is not too late to do so during the first half of the month. Lift any healthy self-sown seedlings, pot them up into a reasonably light compost, water gently and find a spot where they will have protection from excessive wet and cold. The resulting flowers may prove disappointing but alternatively there may well be a pleasant surprise in store. There is little doubt that many fine named varieties started life as nothing more than a random seedling and anticipation can be every bit as much fun as success. Such seedlings can also be lined out in nursery beds no more than 3in (7.5cm) apart, and given some very simple well-ventilated protection. By April, it will have become apparent whether there is anything amongst them showing sufficient promise to warrant further trial.

Cuttings should be inspected regularly to ensure that all is well. The rooting medium should be kept no more than moist – never saturated – and shading should be applied in sunny weather. A periodical light misting of insecticide and fungicide is a wise precaution. Rodents should be discouraged from taking up residence in the propagation frame. In severe weather hunger may drive rodents to turn to the violas in the absence of other available sustenance. Complete any winter digging, leaving the surface rough in the hope that winter frosts will penetrate – discouraging over-wintering pests and breaking down the soil into a crumbly structure. Prepare for spring in the knowledge that bad weather after Christmas may render planned progress impossible.

9

Floral Decoration

Apart from the various methods already discussed concerning presentation for competition there are many ways in which the pansy, viola and violetta can be used for decoration in the home.

It has to be appreciated that the flowers have a somewhat limited effective life of no more than a day or two when picked and placed in water. The plants bloom, however, with such profusion and for so long a season that this should be considered no serious obstacle. Since the plants bloom in such abundance, any that you pick for the house will not seriously diminish the garden display.

It is important when picking the flowers to choose perfect, unmarked blooms that have not gone past their peak of perfection. They should be cut with sharp scissors with the maximum length of stem, and placed immediately in water, taking care not to squeeze or damage the stem. A container of water should be taken to the plant to ensure that there is no delay between picking and immersing, otherwise an airlock will form at the base of the stem, reducing the eventual life of the flower. To lessen the risk of the petals becoming crushed or bruised, a piece of mesh or netting can be tied tautly across the top of the container and the flower stems inserted through to ensure that they are not only held securely but that they do not contact one another. An off-cut of woven shade netting is appropriate for this purpose.

Pansies and violas are at their most effective when used for small intimate vases or posies such as might be used for decorating the dining table. A container of neutral design and colouring should be chosen lest it detract from the flowers themselves. The flowers can be arranged as considered appropriate, being held in position either by a pin base, oasis foam, saturated silver sand or simply as an arrangement that is self-supporting. The flowers can be accompanied by their own foliage and can be harvested as growths whose foliage is intact. There is no reason why they should not be accompanied by other foliage, hawthorn for instance, to give a harmonious effect. The arrangement can be restricted to one variety, or a mixture may be preferred. Other flowers and foliage from the garden can be used in conjunction with the pansies and violas. It is all purely a matter of personal preference.

Flower decoration provides an ideal opportunity to appreciate all the charm and fragrance of the flowers at close quarters, in a totally relaxed and comfortable environment.

Pressed Flowers

There are few flowers that lend themselves so readily to pressing as those of the pansy and viola. The flowers, when mature, are already flat and when compressed and dried will retain much of their original character provided the operation is carried out with sufficient care. Flowers must be harvested when in the peak of perfection; unfaded and unmarked, and above all when completely dry. All preparations for pressing must be completed in advance of harvesting.

A flower press need only be of simple construction. Its main purpose is to hold the bloom flat and secure in order that all the moisture should dry from the flower without any shrinkage which would otherwise rapidly take place. The most simple press – if we are to disregard the book or telephone directory – will consist of two rigid boards linked by a nut and bolt at each corner, between which are placed sheets of clean, smooth, absorbent paper. Between each layer of flowers, it is advisable to incorporate at least one layer of lined fluted board, of the type commonly used for packaging boxes and cases. This material consists of a corrugated paper sandwiched between two flat, smooth, outer layers. Provided that undue pressure is not exerted in the press, it will allow a circulation of air which will hasten the drying process. It is advisable to use a superior quality, heavy duty card such as would be used for packaging wines and spirits as this will prevent any possibility of the corrugations appearing as parallel lines across the petals of the dried flower. It should also be borne in mind that any printed paper can disfigure the flowers by a transfer of ink brought about by chemical reaction during the drying process. Clean white paper is the wisest choice. A number of sheets of the absorbent paper should be placed above and below the flowers and each layer should be separated from the next by at least one sheet of the lined fluted board.

The preparation of the flowers requires care and patience. Using sharp scissors, the flower head should be severed from the stalk. This should be done at a height whereby any superfluous matter at the rear of the flower will be removed without causing the flower to disintegrate into its separate petals. In the case of the viola and pansy, this will involve removal of the spur. For white, cream, yellow and other pale colours, it is also advisable to remove the green sepals which – whilst invisible on the growing plant – will become all too apparent on the dried and pressed flower. You will need sharp, finely pointed scissors for this operation. Lay a sheet of lined fluted card on the bed of the press, then add a few sheets of clean absorbent paper and onto this surface the flower heads, face downwards, leaving sufficient space between each one to ensure that on expanding under pressure they will not touch one another. To ensure even pressure, it is advisable to fill each layer with flowers of one variety. Any slight flagging while this operation takes place will encourage the flowers to lay flat. They should not be permitted to flag to the point at which shrinkage commences. Add more sheets of clean absorbant paper followed by a sheet of lined fluted board. If more than one layer of flowers is to be pressed, apply weight to each completed layer to keep everything in place until all is finally ready. Tighten the press to ensure that the contents are under sufficient pressure to prevent any movement of the flowers. As the flowers gradually dry, tighten the press still further. Store the full press in a dry and well ventilated place. It will take some weeks, even months, before the flowers are sufficiently stable to be handled. When dry, they will be quite brittle and will need particularly gentle handling.

The pressed flowers can be used for a variety of purposes, the most common being to position them on some card with the tiniest drop of adhesive and then to seal them by overlaying a self-adhesive transparent sheet. Through the drying process, colours will have become subdued and a gloss adhesive film overlay will not only protect the flowers but will also enrich the colours. The colours of a pressed flower will eventually fade away if they are subjected to excessive sunshine, and so it is important that the finished product should be sited with this possibility very much in mind. Pressed flowers of this nature are commonly used for greetings cards, framed pictures and lampshades and there are doubtless many other ways in which they could be employed to good effect.

Pot-pourri

Pot-pourri is the traditional romantic attempt to preserve the scent of the summer garden to serve as a reminder of such pleasures during the dark days of winter.

The basic constituent of pot-pourri is flower petals and the petals of the pansy and viola (particularly those of strongest fragrance) are ideally suitable for blending with others.

In its most simple form, pot-pourri is no more than dried leaves and petals to which a chosen spice is added together with a little fixative. This ensures that when the ingredients are mixed together, all will be evenly distributed. Allow the mixture to stand for two or three weeks in a covered container. Stir or shake at frequent intervals, and it is then ready for transferring into jars, bottles and bowls or for sewing into sachets or tiny pillows.

There are other more complex methods of making pot-pourri. The success of these can only be gauged by experimenting – which is probably more than half the fun. If you wish to pursue this aspect, the tussie-mussie or nosegay and the pomander, historically employed to ward off unpleasant smells and hopefully offer protection from infection, may well lend themselves to an adaptation in which the pansy and viola could have a part to play.

In the belief that the pansy and viola are totally non-toxic, there is no end to the uses to which they might perhaps be put by those who wish to experiment with them in a culinary capacity. Attempts to distil and preserve their fragrance can surely be fun even if not wholly successful.

For the majority of us however, growing them successfully and appreciating them in the natural environment of the garden is as much as we ask.

10

Named Hybrids

There follows a list of the varieties of viola and violetta currently advertised as being available as young plants to the gardening public. The list is composed almost entirely of Bedding violas, Miniature violas and Violettas although a few of the larger-flowered varieties might be considered suitable for showing as Exhibition violas.

The size of flower will depend to some extent on the soil, the weather and the mode of cultivation. Most varieties have been classified into one of three flower sizes, all of which can only be considered approximate:

Small	1in (2.5cm) diameter or less
Medium	1–2in (2.5–5cm) diameter
Large	2in (5cm) diameter or larger

Strictly speaking, violetta flowers should measure no more than $1\frac{1}{2}$in (4cm) and no less than 1in (2.5cm) diameter, but there are now many varieties with smaller flowers classified by some as violettas. Whilst most violas and violettas possess at least some fragrance, the particularly pronounced fragrance considered essential to the violetta is sadly absent from some of these more recent introductions.

The term Miniature viola could be used to far greater advantage to differentiate many small-flowered violas from the true violetta, as was originally defined at the Viola Conference of 1894.

Precise classification of garden violas and violettas is sufficiently complex as to render the task almost impossible – and to beg the question as to whether there is any advantage in attempting to do so.

Names and addresses of the nurseries from which this list has been compiled will be found in Appendix I. Named varieties of Show pansy, Fancy pansy and Exhibition viola are listed in Chapter 11.

'Achilles': A white self with the faintest touch of mauve on all the petals. Medium.

'Adelina': Elongated white blooms with all the petals suffused with mauve. Very hardy. Medium.

'Admiration': A velvety, purple-blue self with a yellow eye. Compact habit. Medium.

'Agneta': A dark, violet-mauve self making a large vigorous plant. Large.

'Alanta': Very pale blue and white. Medium.

'Alcea': Pale yellow. Medium.

'Alethia': A deep violet-blue self with frilled petals and a yellow eye. Medium.

'Alma': A rich blue-purple self with good tufted habit. Large.

'Alwyn': Yellow, with all petals heavily suffused with violet-mauve. Medium.

'Alys': Dark purple splashed with a lighter shade. Medium.

'Amelia': Pale yellow with frilled petals margined with mauve. Good habit. Medium.

'Anita': Tiny blue and white flowers in profusion.

'Annabelle': A large mauve-blue self with good habit.

'Anne Mott': Violet with a yellow centre. Large. A seedling of 'Maggie Mott'.

'Anthea': A large silvery-mauve self.

'Aphrodite': A rich-yellow self. Medium.

'Apollo': Ivory with hint of blue, mauve. Medium.

'Arabella': White with all the petals marbled with a mixture of blue and mauve. Orange eye. Medium.

'Ardross Gem': Dusky gold and pale blue. Vigorous with very neat, compact foliage. Small to medium.

'Aspasia': Makes a large, vigorous plant. The top petals are creamy-white and the lower petals are deep-yellow. Small.

'Athena': Pale lemon-yellow with frilled petals. Large.

'Aurelia': A pale creamy-yellow self. Vigorous habit.

'Aurora': A medium-sized flower. White with blue mottling on all the petals. Slightly rayed.

'Avril': Yellow. Rayed. Small.

'Avril Lawson': Deep lavender-blue. Hardy and vigorous and will form a large clump.

'Barbara': A medium-sized flower. Combination of pinkish mauve-blue and yellow. Rayed.

'Benjie': A medium bloom. Blue-mauve with cream shading on the lower petals.

'Beshlie': Pale yellow flowers of medium size. Vigorous and floriferous.

'Bettina': Makes a large clump of white flowers with frilled petals. Medium.

'Betty': Purple with white centre. Medium.

'Black Diamond': So dark as to appear almost black.

'Black Panther': Jet black with yellow eye.

'Blue Carpet': Bright, almost royal-blue with a white eye. Neat habit. Medium.

'Blue Cloud': A very old variety. Pure white with all the petals margined violet-blue. Rayed. Medium.

'Blue Lace': A creamy-blue flower of medium size.

'Blue Tit': Mauve-blue with a yellow eye running into the bottom petal. Vigorous and floriferous. Medium.

'Bonna Cawthorne': A pure white self with a yellow eye. Medium size.

'Bonnie Heather': A large flower. White centre shading to mauve-purple. Top two petals royal purple.

'Bowles Black': Small, dark velvety-purple, almost black flowers with the character of the common Heartsease.

'Bronwen': Very pale mottled-mauve flowers held well above the foliage. Profuse blooms of a medium size.

'Bullion': A variety raised in 1867. A large, deep-yellow, heavily-rayed flower.

'Buxton Blue': Another old variety. A compact plant. Medium flowers, blue with a darker centre.

'Callia': A medium, pale creamy-yellow self of bushy habit.

'Calypso': A medium, violet-mauve self with an orange eye.

'Carola': Pale purple, white centre. Small.

'Caroline': Pink with a deeper pink-mauve centre. Medium.

'Charity': A mauve-violet flower with a pale yellow centre.

'Charlotte Mott': A compact plant with medium-sized flowers of pale blue-violet with a whitish centre. A seedling of 'Maggie Mott'.

'Chelsea Girl': Small flowers. Pale blue shading to cream.

'Cinderella': A robust, compact plant with medium-sized, soft mauve and cream flowers.

'Cindy': A small rayed flower with deep-purple upper petals and blue-mauve lower petals.

'Clementina': A vigorous plant with large flowers of rich purple-mauve held on long stems.

'Cleo': Medium-sized flowers of cream tinted with blue.

'Clodagh': Medium ivory-white blooms on long stems. Very hardy.

'Clover': Medium flowers in profusion. Yellowish-white ground, all petals suffused with pale violet.

'Columbine':   Lilac-white heavily veined with streaks of violet. The flowers are held high above low, compact foliage.

'Connie':   A small pale violet flower. Neat compact habit.

'Cordelia':   Medium-sized white flowers suffused with pale mauve. Prolific.

'Cream Sensation':   Medium-sized flowers. Cream with a yellow eye.

'Cressida':   A medium-sized yellow self. The top petals slightly paler.

'Cyril Bell':   Large flowers of rich purple-blue, rayed and with a yellow eye.

'Daisy Smith':   Small white flowers with a faint flush of blue on the upper petals in cool weather. Very neat compact habit.

'Dartington Hybrid':   A profuse bloomer. Medium-sized, mid-mauve, of compact habit.

'David Wheldon':   A canary-yellow self of medium size.

'Davina':   A small yellow-rayed self. Good habit.

'Deanna':   Yellow, margined and suffused with blue-mauve. Small.

'Decima':   A medium-sized flower, deeply veined violet-mauve on a yellow ground with a creamy yellow centre.

'Delia':   A mauve and cream combination. Small to medium. A compact plant.

'Delphine':   Neat habit. Medium flowers with elongated petals of pale maroon.

'Demeter':   Mid-yellow, long-stemmed blooms. Fragrant. Medium.

'Desdemona':   A large vigorous clump with small pale blue and white rayed flowers.

'Devon Cream':   A medium flower of soft cream, slightly rayed and strongly fragrant.

'Dobbies Bronze':   Rich bronze with mahogany centre. A distinctive colour but has comparatively short flowering season.

'Dobbies Red':   Mahogany-red with a dark centre. Medium.

'Dominique':   Mauve-blue. Small.

'Dulcie Rhoda':   A small mid-blue flower. Compact growth

'Dusk':   Dusky purple and yellow. Small.

'Eastgrove Blue':   Mid-blue. Particularly vigorous and fragrant.

'Elizabeth':   Compact and robust in growth. White ground with all petals heavily flushed with lavender and an orange eye. Medium size.

'Emily Mott':   A large, mid-violet self. A seedling of 'Maggie Mott'.

'Emma':   Medium flowers of cream with the top petals edged with mauve. Very hardy.

'Enterea':   Violet-blue. Small.

'Eris':   Rich ivory-white, the top petals slightly paler. Frilled petals. Long stems. Medium size.

'Eros':   Medium flowers, white with heavy blue marbling on all the petals.

'Etain':   Large flowers of pale lemon with all petals margined violet. Excellent habit.

'Ethena':   Soft-mauve, medium-sized blooms with an orange eye.

'Etienne':   Pale purple with a darker purple centre and a yellow eye. Medium.

'Evelyn Jackson':   Bright, pale mauve suffused and striped with purple. White centre. Medium size.

'Felicity':   Blue-mauve blooms, sometimes marbled. Yellow eye. Medium.

'Fiona':   Very hardy and highly scented with long stemmed flowers of white, all petals slightly suffused with the palest mauve. Medium.

'Florence':   Cream with all petals suffused with mauve. Vigorous. Medium.

'Francesca':   Creamy-white suffused with lavender-mauve. Medium.

'Gatina':   A yellow self and a compact plant. Medium.

'Gazania':   Silvery lilac-mauve flowers. Compact habit. Medium.

'Gemma':   A small to medium flower with mauve upper petals shading to blue.

'Genista Gambia':   Delicate lavender-pink flowers. Tall habit. Medium.

'Georgina':   Pale yellow with the top petals slightly suffused with pale mauve. A hardy plant. Medium.

'Giselle':   Red-purple self with a darker centre. Medium.

'Gladys Finlay':   White centre, all petals flushed with deep violet-blue. Tall habit. Medium.

'Grace':   Dusky yellow and blue. Waved edges to the petals.

'Grey Owl':   An unusual colour. All petals grey-mauve with a yellow centre. Medium.

'Helen':   A red-purple self of medium size.

'Hazelmere':   *see* Nellie Britten.

'Helena':   White with the top petals tinged with the palest mauve. A deep yellow blotch in the centre of the bloom. Medium.

'Hespera': Marbled blue on a white ground with a yellow eye. Medium.

'Hesperis': Apricot-orange. Good habit. Medium.

'Honey': A small, rayed, rich-cream flower.

'Huntercombe Purple': Purple-violet elongated flowers with a white eye. Compact, vigorous and hardy. Medium.

'Hyperion': White ground with bottom petals suffused with yellow. Medium.

'Iden Gem': Rich violet blooms on long stems. Vigorous and seldom without bloom throughout the year. Medium.

'Imp': A vigorous plant with flowers of warm red-purple. Medium.

'Inverurie Beauty': Exceptionally hardy and floriferous. A violet-mauve self, rayed, on 8in (20cm) stems.

'Inverurie Mauve': Violet, long-stemmed flowers. hardy and long-lived. Medium.

'Irish Molly': An old variety. An unusual combination of khaki-yellow and brown-violet. Medium.

'Ita': Creamy-white flowers with the top petals finely margined with mauve. Medium.

'Iver Grove': Top petals deep mahogany-chocolate. Lower petals yellow, each spotted with chocolate. Rayed. Medium.

'Ivory Queen': A pure-cream self. Vigorous, floriferous and most reliable. Medium.

'Ivory White': Ivory-white elongated flowers. Very floriferous. Medium.

'Jackanapes': Introduced by Gertrude Jekyll. Top two petals chocolate-brown. Bottom three petals yellow. Rayed. vigorous and eye-catching. Medium.

'James Pilling': An old variety. White suffused with warm violet-blue. Large.

'Jamie': A medium to large blue-purple self.

'Jane Askew': A violet-blue self with a yellow eye. Medium.

'Jane Mott': An extremely floriferous white self. A seedling of Maggie Mott. Medium.

'Janet': Rich medium-blue with a white centre. Large.

'Janna': A circular white flower sometimes faintly margined with mauve. Medium.

'Jeannie': A medium-sized flower with mauve upper petals shading to cream. Rayed.

'Jeannie Bellew': An elongated flower of the palest yellow with the habit of *V. gracilis*. Long stems. Medium.

'Jemma': A rounded bloom of lilac-mauve with a white centre. Large.

'Jersey Gem': Deep purple-blue self. Very floriferous. Medium.

'Joanna': White with the top petals suffused with pale-mauve.

'Jodie': Warm mauve, streaked with yellow. Medium.

'Joella': Top two petals pale purple with the bottom three petals a deeper purple. Medium.

'John Yelmark': Silver-mauve. Tall habit. Large.

'Johnnie Jump Up': Heartsease. A small flower in a combination of violet, mauve and yellow.

'Josie': Striped and marbled mauve on yellow. Medium.

'Joyce Grey': Yellow petals edged with blue.

'Julia': White suffused with pale mauve. Small.

'Julian': A clear mid-blue with a yellow eye. Compact and floriferous. Medium.

'Juno': Deep, rich violet blooms on 9in (23cm) stems above compact foliage. Hardy, Medium.

'Jupiter': Mid-mauve on long stems. Very hardy. Medium.

'Karen': Large, lightly rayed flowers of pale lilac.

'Kate': Deep lavender-blue with yellow eye over neat compact foliage. Small.

'Katerina': Blue-mauve. Small.

'Kilruna': Creamy-yellow with all petals heavily streaked with violet. Rayed. Medium.

'King of the Blues': An old variety. Rich-violet with a black face. Large.

'Kizzy': A small, slightly rayed flower of blue striped with white.

'Lady Tennyson': An old variety. A white self with slightly frilled flowers. Large.

'Larissa': A medium-sized flower of soft blue, making a large floriferous clump.

'Lavinia': An elongated speckled mauve and white flower carried well above the foliage. Neat habit. Medium.

'Leander': Violet-blue with deeper violet-blue veining. Good habit, blooms, held well above the foliage. Medium.

'Leda': A pure white with excellent hardy habit. Medium.

'Lee': A medium-sized, silvery-mauve self.

'Letitia': A small pink-purple self with deeper rays. A distinctive colour.

'Lewisa': A medium purple.

'Lilac Rose': A pale lilac-pink flushed yellow at the centre. It makes a compact vigorously spreading clump. Small.

'Liliana': Pale yellow heavily edged with violet-mauve and an orange eye. Large.

'Liriopa': Top petals creamy-white with a yellow bottom petal. A large plant with medium flowers.

'Little Johnny': Small, bright yellow rayed flowers to a height of 6in (15cm). Free-flowering.

'Little Liz': Small cream flowers, flushed yellow at the centre and rayed. It makes a large clump.

'Lola': Rich violet. Small.

'Lord Nelson': Violet-purple. Medium.

'Lord Plunket': Rich maroon-purple self with yellow eye. Excellent habit. Large flowers.

'Lorna' ('Lorna Doone'): A synonym of 'Mauve Radiance'.

'Lorna Moakes': A slightly frilled flower of pale yellow with all petals margined with mauve. Medium.

'Louisa': Carmine-purple-violet blooms with yellow centres. It makes a very large plant.

'Luca': A hardy variety with medium-sized purple-violet flowers held well above the foliage.

'Lulu': A small flower, the upper petals of which are a reddish-mauve and the lower petals mid-blue.

'Lydia': Good habit. A pale yellow flower with all petals margined lavender. Medium.

'Lysander': The top two petals are pale purple, the lower petals a deeper purple. Yellow eye. Medium.

'Madelaine': A small, elongated flower of pale blue. Very prolific.

'Magenta Maid': A magenta-purple flower with a small white centre and a yellow eye. Compact and floriferous. Medium.

'Maggie Mott': A popular old variety. Soft silvery-mauve with the palest cream centre. Tall habit and a particularly pronounced fragrance. Medium. Introduced 1902.

'Magic': A variety of *V. gracilis*. The early and late flowers are violet but in the height of summer they appear pure white.

'Margaret': A medium-sized creamy-white self.

'Mark Talbot': A large canary-yellow with good habit.

'Mars': Rich carmine self with a white eye carried on long stems above compact foliage. Medium.

'Martin': A medium, deep violet-blue elongated flower with a yellow eye. Compact habit.

'Mary Dawson': A large, pure white flower edged with violet-blue.

'Mattie': Pale lilac upper petals, rich yellow lower petals with a brown centre. A medium-sized flower.

'Mauve Beauty': A medium-sized, mid-mauve self. Hardy and of excellent habit.

'Mauve Haze': A subdued and delicate ivory-white flower flushed with mauve. Yellow eye. Small.

'Mauve Radiance': A lavender-violet self with a yellow eye. One of the most vigorous and reliable of varieties. Medium.

'Mayfly': Ivory-white with the upper petals delicately edged with amethyst-blue. Strongly fragrant.

'May Mott': Silvery-blue upper petals, lower petals cream-edged with blue. Superb fragrance. Undoubtedly a seedling of Maggie Mott. Large flowers.

'Megumi': A hardy variety with medium-sized, rich-violet flowers. Excellent habit.

'Melissa': Tiny dark-mauve blooms suffused with blue and cream in the centre and with an orange eye.

'Mercury': Medium-sized deep-crimson flowers with a darker centre. Long stems and a large plant.

'Midnight': A purple so dark as to be almost black. Medium, circular flowers. Compact, vigorous habit.

'Midnight Turk': small, elongated, almost black flowers.

'Milkmaid': Small creamy-white flowers flushed with the palest mauve.

'Minerva': A small pale-yellow flower with the upper petals margined mauve. Slightly rayed.

'Miss Brookes': An old variety and a striking colour. Fine, large, red-purple flowers with a yellow centre.

'Mistral': Large white blooms held well above the foliage.

'Monica': A large flower, white with all petals suffused with sky-blue.

'Moonlight': Medium, dainty elongated flowers of pale creamy-yellow on long stems. A variety of *V. gracilis*.

'Moonshine': A large pale creamy-primrose flower with an orange eye and a pronounced fragrance.

'Morwenna': Small. Pure white.

'Moseley Perfection': A very old variety. Large, deep-yellow flowers.

'Molly Sanderson': Virtually jet-black with a yellow eye. Low habit and compact. Medium sized flowers.

'Mrs Chichester': An old variety with large, white flowers heavily suffused with violet and rayed.

'Mrs Lancaster': A very compact plant with medium-sized white, slightly rayed flowers.

'Myfanwy': A medium-sized elongated flower of pale mauve marbled with white.

'Mysie': Compact foliage with flowers comparable to a small 'Mauve Radiance' held well above the foliage.

'Naomi': Small. Mid-blue.

'Nancy Jean': Pale blue and cream. Small.

'Natasha': Medium-sized white flowers heavily marbled with the palest violet.

'Nell': A compact vigorous plant with small violet flowers.

'Nellie Britten': A synonym of Hazelmere. A small rayed flower of soft lavender-pink. An unusual but welcome colour.

'Neptune': Medium-sized white flowers tinted with pale blue on all petals. Long stems held well above the foliage.

'Nicole': A rich violet-purple self. Compact foliage, long stems. Extremely vigorous and hardy.

'Nimrod': Red-orange striped blooms. Medium size.

'Nina': A medium-sized flower with yellow ground and all petals suffused with a pink-mauve.

'Norah Leigh': Medium-sized, lavender-blue rayed flowers over neat compact foliage.

'Olive Edmonds': A medium white self tinted with pale mauve and with a yellow eye.

'Oriana': Mauve-blue with white centre. Small.

'Palmer's White': An old variety. A medium, pure-white self with slightly frilled petals and a yellow centre. Dwarf and compact.

'Pamela': Mauve, blue and yellow. A rayed viola. Medium.

'Pam's Fancy': Pale yellow, streaked mauve and purple. A small exhibition viola.

'Pandora': A dark-mauve self with medium-sized blooms.

'Pat Creasey': Mid-blue circular flowers with a white centre. Fragrant.

'Pattie': Small. Pale blue and mauve.

'Peggy': Large Exhibition viola. Lilac-edged with deep purple.

'Phoebe': Small. Blue-mauve.

'Phyllida': A medium, violet-blue rayed self with a white centre and a yellow eye.

'Pickering Blue': An old variety with large, sky-blue, rayed flowers and an orange eye.

'Piper': A large red-purple self with a yellow eye.

'Pixie': Small flowers. The upper petals are cream with a tint of blue and the lower petals are yellow.

'Poppy': A prolific violet-blue self. Good habit and medium sized flowers.

'Priam': A pure-white, long-stemmed flower with a yellow eye. Medium.

'Primrose Cream': A sport of Primrose Dame with cream flowers.

'Primrose Dame':   An old variety. A medium-sized pale primrose yellow self.

'Purple Dove':   The upper petals are purple and the lower petals are creamy yellow.

'Purple Wings':   Upper petals violet-purple; lower petals dark blue, flushed with orange at the centre. Compact and vigorous.

'Ramona':   Medium-sized canary-yellow self. Compact and floriferous.

'Ravenna':   Medium sized lilac flowers on a yellow ground. A particularly attractive combination.

'Ray's Bedder':   Pale yellow streaked with mauve. A large-flowered exhibition variety.

'Rhoda':   Medium-sized pale yellow, slightly frilled, elongated flowers. A prolific bloomer.

'Richard's Yellow':   Medium-sized pure rich yellow flowers.

'Rio Rita':   Damson with pink rays. Large.

'Romilly':   Delicate violet stripes on a white ground.

'Rowan Hood':   A suffusion of yellow and mauve. A large flower.

'Ruth Blackall':   A lemon-yellow self with an orange eye and slightly frilled petals. Medium size.

'Ruth Elkins':   A particularly large flower of very pale yellow with a fine mauve edging. A variety suitable for exhibition.

'Sammy Jo':   Small, mauve.

'Sarah':   A large lilac and white striped flower.

'Saughton Blue':   A medium flower sky-blue with a small black face and an orange eye.

'Septima':   A pale lilac self of compact habit with medium sized flowers held well above the foliage.

'Serena':   A pale yellow self with a hint of mauve on the top petals. Medium.

'Sheila':   Medium sized circular flowers of mauve-purple with a yellow centre.

'Sissinghurst':   Dusky pink, slightly rayed, medium.

'Sky Blue':   A small sky-blue flower with a white centre.

'Sophie':   Small rayed flowers of pale yellow darkening to deep yellow on the lower petals.

'Steyning':   A medium mid-mauve.

'Sunshine':   Small, bright, golden-yellow with a white picotee edge. Floriferous.

'Susannah':   A very pale sky-blue fragrant flower with a faint marbling of white.

'Susie':   A large blue flower mottled with lilac and with a green tint in the throat.

'Talitha': A medium-sized, violet-blue, white-centred flower held well above the foliage. Particularly hardy.

'Tasmin': Mottled mauve. Medium.

'Thalia': Cream and mauve. Small.

'Thea': Small, rich violet flower on long stem.

'Thetis': Medium off-white blooms on long stems.

'Tiffany': Very pale lilac, medium-sized flowers over low compact foliage.

'Tina': A large marbled blue flower with a yellow eye and a good tufted habit.

'Titania': A medium-sized, deep, rich-violet-carmine self with an orange eye.

'Tom Tit': A compact and free-flowering plant with medium-sized elongated violet flowers with a white eye. Rayed.

'Una': A medium, pale yellow flower with all the petals margined with mauve.

'Venetia': A rich purple self with a yellow eye. A medium-sized, elongated flower.

'Virginia': An ivory-white self with small flowers. Forms a large clump.

'Virgo': Parchment-white, medium flowers. Good habit.

'Vita': A pale lavender-pink self with a small yellow eye. A medium-sized flower.

'Wanda': Medium-sized, purple-red with a white centre.

'Wendy': A pale lilac flower of medium size.

'White Gem': Similar to, if not the same as, *V. cornuta* 'Alba'.

'White Pearl': Small flower with orange eye.

'White Swan': An old variety. Medium-sized white flowers.

'William Wallace': Medium, mid-mauve with an orange eye.

'Winifred Jones': A large white flower flushed with blue.

'Winifred Wargent': A medium, flecked mauve-purple self with an orange eye.

'Woodland's Cream': A medium, cream self flower, compact and floriferous.

'Woodland's Lilac': A large flower marbled warm-grey and lilac on a yellow ground.

'Woodland's White': A medium, pure white self suitable for exhibition.

'Yoyo': A small flower with lilac-mauve upper petals, the lower petals being a shade lighter.

'Zara': A cream and mauve frilled flower. Medium.

'Ziglana': Small, deep-violet self. Good habit and a prolific bloomer.

'Zona': Large, rich, deep-velvety-violet with a yellow eye.

VIOLETTAS

This list contains varieties which would undoubtedly be considered unacceptable by those, who, in 1894, defined the violetta.

'Abigail':   Blue with white centre.
'Ann Kean':   White ground with all petals heavily suffused cornflower-blue.
'Atalanta':   White ground with a yellow centre. The top petals are margined with mauve.
'Beatrice':   Pure white.
'Bianca':   A perfect, pure-white self with an orange eye.
'Boy Blue':   A mid-blue self, very hardy and vigorous.
'Buttercup':   Rich, deep-yellow.
'Byrony':   A rich carmine self with a yellow eye.
'Calantha':   The top petals are pale yellow with the bottom petals a deeper yellow. Compact habit.
'Calliandra':   Deep violet-mauve flowers held well above the foliage. Prolific.
'Candida':   A small white self with a yellow eye.
'Carina':   White with mauve top petals and a yellow eye.
'Cassandra':   Small yellow flowers carried on long stems. Compact and highly fragrant.
'Chantal':   A combination of mauve, white and yellow.
'Chloe':   Pale yellow upper petals, deeper yellow lower petals. A small flower.
'Colleen':   Makes a large plant with pale mauve, white-centred flowers.
'Coralie':   Small violet-blue self with a yellow centre.
'Daena':   Violet-mauve with a white centre and an orange eye. Floriferous and of a good habit.
'Dawn':   A primrose-yellow self.
'Delicia':   Mauve on pale yellow ground. Hardy and compact.
'Dione':   Yellow.
'Dominy':   A mauve self with frilled petals.
'Fabiola':   A violet-mauve self producing a large plant.
'Gazelle':   Very pale yellow with an orange eye.
'Geraldine':   Pale yellow suffused with mauve.
'Gina':   A deep purple-violet self.
'Hebe':   Violet-mauve with a cream centre.
'Isla':   Primrose yellow.
'Iantha':   Deep violet-blue with an orange eye.
'Janine':   Pale yellow and white. A large floriferous plant.
'Jenelle':   Yellow.

'**Jenny**': Pure white flowers on 6in (15cm) stems. Compact and fragrant.
'**John Zanini**': Creamy-yellow, the top petals suffused with pale lavender.
'**Kathy**': Yellow and mauve. Prolific.
'**Lamorna**': Pale violet-mauve, white centre, orange eye.
'**Leora**': A rich yellow self.
'**Lerosa**': Tiny blue and white flowers.
'**Little David**': A creamy-white self with slightly frilled petals. Robust and hardy.
'**Livia**': Yellow with the upper petals tinted with lavender.
'**Luna**': A pale yellow self, fragrant, hardy and of good habit.
'**Maera**': A purple-violet self with a yellow eye.
'**Majella**': Palest blue and yellow.
'**Malvena**': A pure-white self with small flowers.
'**Meena**': A pure-white self with compact habit and flowers held clear of the foliage.
'**Melinda**': White ground, flushed mauve. Orange eye.
'**Mitzel**': Pale purple pink.
'**Myntha**': Yellow ground with all petals flushed violet.
'**Nerena**': White ground with all petals suffused pale mauve. Rich-yellow eye.
'**Nesta**': Soft lilac-mauve with a yellow centre.
'**Pandora**': Pale yellow. Frilled petals.
'**Petra**': Soft mauve with a pale centre; makes a large plant.
'**Pippa**': A mauve-blue self with a yellow eye.
'**Princess Mab**': An old variety. Soft flecked rosy-mauve. Low and compact.
'**Purity**': Pure-white self. Hardy and fragrant.
'**Queen Disa**': A clear-yellow self. Particularly floriferous.
'**Rebecca**': Deep flecks of violet on the outer edges of a cream-white ground. Slightly frilled petals. Fragant and of good habit.
'**Remora**': White with the upper petals margined with lavender. Orange eye.
'**Sally**': Yellow with all petals marbled violet. Compact and vigorous.
'**Samantha**': White, slightly flushed with pale lavender. Orange eye.
'**Soula**': White, the top petals slightly suffused with mauve.
'**Thalia**': Cream with the upper petals suffused violet-mauve.
'**Unity**': Mauve-violet.
'**Velleda**': A small white self with an orange eye.
'**Winona**': Pale mauve with a white centre and an orange eye.
'**Zoe**': Violet-mauve with a yellow eye.

V. CORNUTA

V. cornuta: Variable; commonly pale violet-blue, long stems.
'Alba':   A pure white variety.
'Belmont Blue':   A soft, pale sky-blue.
'Bessie Cawthorne':   Rich purple with white eye.
'Boughton Blue':   A vigorous pale blue.
'Daveron':   Soft yellow with tinge of mauve.
'Dr Smart':   Star-shaped flowers of mid-mauve.
'Elizabeth Cawthorne':   Blue.
'Emma Cawthorne':   Violet.
'Evelyn Cawthorne':   Cream.
'Foxbrook Cream':   A delicate pale cream.
'Geraldine Cawthorne':   Rich violet. Low and compact.
'Gustave Wermig':   Deep mauve-violet on long stems.
'Hextable':   Mauve-blue.
'Hyacintha':   A soft silvery-mauve.
'Kiki McDonough':   Pale purple-pink.
'Laura':   Golden variegated foliage with pale-blue flowers.
'Leora Hamilton':   White suffused with pale blue.
'Lilacina':   Soft silvery-lilac.
'Lisa Cawthorne':   White suffused with pale mauve. Yellow eye.
'Margaret Cawthorne':   Large, cream, star-shaped blooms.
'Mary Cawthorne':   Rich violet-purple. White eye. Long stems.
'Minor':   A neat compact miniature form. Pale violet flowers.
'Minor Alba':   A white-flowered version of the above.
'Netta Strachan':   Silvery-mauve.
'Pat Kavanagh':   Pale yellow, edged with mauve.
'Philippa Cawthorne':   Pale purple on a white ground. Star-shaped flowers.
'Rebecca Cawthorne':   White suffused with blue-mauve. Compact and floriferous.
'Rosea':   Glowing rose-purple.
'Tony Venison':   Golden variegated foliage. The pale blue flowers are delicately striped with white.
'Violacea':   A deep violet-mauve on long stems.
'Variegata':   Sky-blue. A variegated form of 'Belmont Blue'.
'Victoria Cawthorne':   Rose-pink. Vigorous and hardy.
'Winona Cawthorne':   Creamy-white with the upper petals suffused with pale mauve.
'White Gem':   A form of *V. cornuta* 'Alba'.

11

Recommended Varieties for the Beginner

Any list purporting to recommend varieties for a beginner will inevitably reflect the personal preferences of its compiler. It is appropriate that any such list should be restricted to varieties considered to be exceptionally robust, reliable and easy to cultivate and that it should represent a reasonable cross-section of the colours available. It will be assumed that a novice would only wish to start with a modest number of plants.

Bedding Violas

Bedding Violas constitute by far the largest section from which the following varieties can, with confidence, be recommended to a novice:

Admiration – rich purple-blue
Ardross Gem – gold and blue
Barbara – mauve-pink and yellow
David Wheldon – yellow
Hazelmere – lavender-pink
Huntercombe Purple – purple
Irish Molly – khaki and yellow
Ivory Queen – cream
Jackanapes – chocolate and gold
Letitia – purple-pink
Maggie Mott – silvery-mauve
Mauve Radiance – lavender-mauve
Palmers White – pure-white
Pickering Blue – sky-blue
Vita – soft dusty-pink

Violettas

Violettas form a smaller section with a more restricted range of colour from which the following can be recommended with confidence:

Buttercup – rich-yellow
Dawn – lemon-yellow
Little David – cream
Rebecca – cream, heavily flaked and edged with violet

Miniature Violas

Miniature violas are a less clearly defined group with small flowers from which the following varieties are to be particularly recommended:

Aspasia – cream and yellow
Connie – pale violet
Daisy Smith – creamy-white
Desdemona – pale blue and white
Fabiola – lavender-blue
Milkmaid – cream with a hint of blue

Viola Cornuta and all its many varieties are particularly suitable plants for the beginner. Not only are they very hardy and perennial in nature, but they will also self-seed most readily, rapidly forming colonies of plants where they are permitted to do so.

SHOW PANSIES, FANCY PANSIES AND EXHIBITION VIOLAS

Any attempt to recommend varieties under this heading must be modified by the warning that these varieties are by no means readily obtainable and if so certainly not in unlimited quantities.

Joseph Jackson of Kettleshulme list in their current catalogue a number of named varieties of Exhibition violas with the proviso that stocks are limited. They also offer a selection of Fancy pansies. Hazeldene Nurseries of East Farleigh list in their current catalogue a number of Bedding Violas, Fancy pansies. Show pansies and other violas all of which they consider worthy of consideration for exhibition. Wilfred Winstanley of Bolton offers violas, some of which he recommends as suitable for exhibition.

If your ambition is to acquire the best available named varieties of Show Pansies, Fancy Pansies and Exhibition Violas, the most appropriate course of action is to become a member of one of the specialist societies. You will thus secure an opportunity to meet other fellow enthusiasts and to acquire information, advice and hopefully, seed, cuttings and plants which can be utilised to form the basis of a collection.

The following is a list of just some of the varieties that have appeared on the competitive show bench in recent years. Most, if not all of these, have been and still are in the possession of individual growers but it is difficult to establish the extent to which they are still in more widespread circulation.

Show Pansies

Angela – cream with purple blotch and markings
Ann – pale yellow with dark blotch
Blackfaulds Gem – yellow with black blotch, all petals edged violet-blue
Jean Moir – pale yellow with black blotch
John Rodger – white ground, dark-purple blotch and belting
June – yellow with black blotch
Lynn – pale yellow with black blotch, upper petals violet-purple
Saughton Blue – sky-blue with black blotch
Susan – yellow with purple blotch
Sybil – yellow with dark blotch
Wendy – mid-yellow with violet-black blotch

Fancy Pansies

Bishop's Belle – purple blotch, primrose margin
Dean Ward – yellow margin, maroon upper petals, black blotch
Elizabeth Robb – purple blotch, cream margin
George Rowley – purple blotch, primrose margin
Jack Frost – dark blotch, reddish margin
James Christie – purple blotch, yellow margin
Joan Christie – dark blotch, cream margin
Joe Millett – plum blotch, rose margin
Peggy Brookes – purple blotch, pale yellow margin
Stewart William – dark blotch, reddish margin

Exhibition Violas

Agnes Cochrane – purple shaded with heliotrope
Alice Talbot – white-edged with blue
Alice Wood – pure-white
Andrew Jamieson – purple, striped amethyst and light purple
Betty Dale – heliotrope with white centre
Catherine Williams – deep cream, edged mauve
Cox's Moseley – pale yellow, suffused mauve
Glenroyd Fancy – dark plum self
H. H. Hodge – lemon with lavender picotee edge
Hugh Campbell – cream, heavily suffused light-blue
Jimmie's Dark – purple self
Kathleen Hoyle – rich-cream self
Kathleen Williams – deep cream, edged mauve
Mary Hatton – purple self
May Roberts – cream self
Mina Walker – rose-mauve with cream centre
Moseley Ideal – pale yellow, edged mauve
Mrs Alex Forrest – pale cream, suffused violet
Mrs Webb – cream, suffused mauve
R. N. Denby – pale lemon, edged with blue
Rowan Hood – pale yellow, suffused and edged mauve
Sarah Binnie – heavily striped amethyst and light-blue
Tom Bates – yellow
William Fife – silvery-white edged and suffused violet
William Jackson – yellow with white picotee edge
Woodsmoor – cream, edged and suffused sky-blue

12

Pansy and Viola
Seed Strains

There follows a comprehensive list of the pansy and viola seed strains currently available in this country, together with a very brief description and a key to those suppliers from whom the seed is obtainable.

Some of the information contained in this list may have altered before the publication date of this book, and it is therefore advisable to obtain an up-to-date catalogue from the suppliers in question. Those who find the choice bewildering will, I feel sure, not be alone. It is clear from the list that many of the names chosen by seed breeders for their pansies reflect an obsession, not necessarily shared by others, for the size of flower alone. The names and addresses of the suppliers will be found at the end of this list.

The culture of Pansies from seed

It is inadvisable to attempt to germinate pansy seed in temperatures above 73° F (23° C). Some colours within a mixture will take rather longer to germinate than others but all should show signs of germination within two to three weeks of sowing. Seed compost should not be rich in nutrient. Feeding should be postponed until the seedlings are established.

Growth Regulants

Be aware that pansy seedlings and young plants purchased from Garden Centres and other commercial outlets today may well have been treated with growth regulant to induce the plants to adopt a more compact habit of growth. The grower will have used these substances to produce a plant of greater initial visual appeal to the potential purchaser and it may well be that the effect of the growth regulant will become less apparent as the plant matures.

PANSY SEED STRAINS

'Aalsmeer Giant':   An early, large-flowered pansy, all with dark blotches. Mixed colours.
Supplier: 7
'Amsterdam Giant':   An early large-flowered pansy. Mixed colours.
Supplier: 14
'Armado':   Early flowering. Large.
Supplier: 19
'Artemis':   Violet with white centre.
Supplier: 11
'Aurora':   For spring or autumn flowering. A mixture of eight colours.
Supplier: 3
'Azure Blue':   Flowers in early spring.
Supplier: 6
'Baby Lucia':   A miniature pansy. Lavender-blue.
Supplier: 1
'Banner F_1':   An all season variety which comes in a wide range of colours.
Supplier: 8
'Black Pansy':   A selected form of 'King of the Blacks'. Rich velvety-black.
Suppliers: 7, 11, 18
'Bluebird':   Small-flowered blue and white combination.
Supplier: 10
'Blue Laser':   An early flowering variety of recent introduction. Lower petals deep blue, upper petals azure-blue with a white margin.
Supplier: 17
'Blue Wings F_1':   Blue and yellow.
Supplier: 15
'Bravissimo Super Giant':   Large flowers. A range of mixed colours.
Suppliers: 4, 7
'Brown's Prizewinner':   Mixed colours.
Supplier: 4
'Brunig':   Mahogany edged with gold. *See* Roggli Elite.
Supplier: 10
'Carter's Choice':   Early, large-blotched flowers on compact plants. Mixed colours.
Supplier: 5
'Chalon Giant':   Waved and frilled petals, dark blotches.

Mixture including deep shades of blue, mahogany-red and yellow.
Suppliers: 2, 8, 9, 16
'Clarion': Bright, rich, medium-sized, blotched flowers. Mixed colours.
Supplier: 18
'Clear Crystals (Holland Giant)': Self colours, no blotches. Compact plants with long flowering season. Space-blue, azure-blue, carmine-rose, golden-yellow, red, orange, paper-white, cream-white, black, mahogany-red, purple, wine-red, sulphur-yellow, violet-blue.
Suppliers: 1, 2, 3, 4, 6, 11, 13, 14, 15
'Colossal F_1': Very large flowers. Mixed colours.
Supplier: 10
'Colour Festival F_2': Early-flowering, large blotched blossoms. Mixed colours.
Suppliers: 1, 8, 14, 16, 17
'Coronation Gold': Rich yellow.
Suppliers: 1, 10, 13
'Crown F_1': Azure, blue, cream, gold, orange, rose, scarlet, white, yellow and mixed.
Suppliers: 14, 16
'Crown Exhibition'; Large-flowered. Mixed colours.
Supplier: 14
'Crown Special': Early, large-flowered. Mixed colours.
Supplier: 14
'Crystal Bowl F_1': Medium-sized flowers. Selfs with yellow eye. No blotches. Primrose, deep-blue, true-blue, orange, rose, scarlet, white, yellow, purple and mixed.
Suppliers: 4, 18
'Delft F_1': A recent large-flowered introduction. Creamy-white lower petals, deep-blue upper petals. Rayed.
Suppliers: 3. 11
'Delta F_1': Large flowers.
Supplier: 3
'Disco F_1': Self colours. Medium flowers. Yellow, blue, wine-red, white and mixed.
Supplier: 18
'Dobies Emperor': Large blotched flowers with velvety petals. Mixture of reds, bronzes, yellows, violets and blues.
Supplier: 9
'Dream': Clear self colours early to flower. Apricot, blue, primrose, red, yellow, dark blue, white and mixed.
Suppliers: 12, 16

'Dream Giants':   Plain faces, no blotches. Mixed colours.
Suppliers: 4, 17, 18
'Early Alaska':   Large-flowered. Mixed colours.
Suppliers: 11. 14
'Early Giant':   Early-flowering and bright. Mixed colours.
Supplier: 16
'Eclipse':   A recent introduction. Early flowering, long season. Purple blue with white margin.
Suppliers: 1, 11, 18
'Englemann's Giant':   Mixed colours.
Supplier: 2
'Felix':   Whiskered faces. Mixed colours.
Supplier: 2
'Flame Princess F₁':   A perpetual-flowering variety. Cream or yellow, medium flowers, with scarlet or mahogany blotch.
Supplier: 10
'Floral Dance':   Hardy, winter-flowering, mostly blotched. Ruby, violet, white, yellow and mixed.
Suppliers: 1, 10, 16, 17
'Forerunner':   Winter-flowering, some blotched, some fancy, some selfs. Blue, blue and white, dark-eyed orange, golden-yellow, golden-orange, red and gold, ruby, tangerine, white and mixed.
Suppliers: 9, 14, 16
'Gay Jesters':   Spring and summer-flowering. Self colours in a mixture of reds, oranges, yellows, apricots, violets, blues and white.
Supplier: 9
'Giant Fancy':   Large, blotched flowers.
Supplier: 1
'Giant Forerunner':   Hardy and floriferous with upright growth. Red and gold, blue and white, tangerine, blue, celestial blue, golden-yellow, dark-eyed golden-yellow, dark-eyed orange, white, dark-eyed white, and mixed.
Suppliers: 4, 19
'Giant Mixed':   Large flowers. Mixed colours.
Supplier: 6
'Giant Pastels Mixed':   Large flowers. Pastel shades.
Supplier: 11
'Glacier Ice':   Large flowers. Blue with dark blotch, and yellow and white centre.
Suppliers: 10, 14
'Golden Champion':   Without blotch. Rich yellow.
Supplier: 1

'Golden Crown (Majestic Giant)': Dwarf habit, large early flowering. Rich yellow.
Supplier: 16

'Gypsy Dance': Orange with dark centre.
Supplier: 17

'Hamlet F_2': Large, blotched flowers. Mixed colours.
Suppliers: 11, 19

'Happy Flower F_2': Medium-sized, blotched flowers. Mixed colours.
Supplier: 18

'Herald': Winter-flowering. A mixture of six colours.
Supplier: 3

'Holland Giant': Self colours. Golden-yellow, sky-blue, space-blue, orange, scarlet, violet, white, black and mixed.
Suppliers: 14, 19

'Ice Queen': A recent introduction. Winter hardy. Medium, large flowers, most with small blotching. Red, yellow, blue, dark blue, wine-red, brilliant red, pure white (no blotch), white, blue and white and mixed.
Supplier: 3

'Imperial Antique Shades F_1': Mixed colours.
Suppliers: 8, 11

'Imperial Blackberry Rose F_1': Very large flowers. Velvet-red with blotch.
Supplier: 10

'Imperial F_1': Mixed colours.
Suppliers: 1, 3, 14, 16, 18

'Imperial Frosty Rose F_1': Rose and white.
Suppliers: 8, 10, 11, 19

'Imperial Gold Princess F_1': Golden yellow with deep red blotch.
Suppliers: 4, 8, 19

'Imperial Light Blue': Pale lavender-blue; violet centre.
Suppliers: 4, 17

'Imperial Orange (Prince)': Apricot orange; black blotch.
Suppliers: 4, 10, 11, 16

'Imperial Pink Shades F_1': Large flowers. Bicoloured light pink and rose.
Suppliers: 1, 8, 11, 16, 18, 19

'Imperial Rose F_1': Deep rose with purple blotch.
Supplier: 11

'Imperial Silver Princess F_1': Creamy-white with deep rose blotch.
Suppliers: 10, 15, 18

'Imperial Sky Blue F₁': Large flowers. Azure-blue with a blotch.
Supplier: 10

'Jamboree F₂': With and without blotches. Mixed colours.
Supplier: 7

'Joker F₂': Winter-flowering. Light blue, mahogany-red, violet and gold and mixed.
Suppliers: 1, 4, 5, 8, 9, 11, 16, 17, 18

'Jolly Joker': A recent award-winning introduction. Orange with purple belting.
Suppliers: 4, 7, 8, 11, 14, 15, 16, 18, 19

'Jumbo F₁': Giant flowers of good substance. Mixed colours.
Supplier: 18

'King of the Blacks': Virtually black.
Suppliers: 2, 16

'Lac de Zurich': Very large flowers. Azure-blue.
Supplier: 10

'Large-Flowered Early Giant': Mixed colours.
Supplier: 4

'Love Duet': Large flowers. Creamy-lemon with raspberry blotch.
Suppliers: 5, 6, 9, 10, 11, 13, 16, 17

'Lyric Turbo F₁': Available to special order as 'Activa' seed for faster germination. Blue, cream, purple, red, white, white with blotch, yellow or mixed.
Supplier: 8

'Magnum F₁': Large flowers, both blotched and self coloured.
Supplier: 5

'Majestic Giant F₁': Very large, blotched flowers. Vigorous. A favourite variety. Mixed colours.
Suppliers: 1, 2, 4, 7, 8, 9, 10, 11, 13, 14, 15, 16, 17, 18, 19

'Mammoth': Early, large-flowering. Mixed colours.
Supplier: 14

'Mammoth Giant F₁': Mixed colours.
Supplier: 8

'Maxim': Blue, orange, red, red and yellow, rose, sherbet, white, yellow and mixed.
Suppliers: 14, 16, 18

'Mello 21 F₁': Wide range of colours.
Supplier: 10

'Monarch (Swiss) Giant': Large, heavily blotched flowers on compact plants. Mixed colours.
Supplier: 16

'Nene Giant': Large flowers, most with blotches. Golden-yellow, deep blue, orange sun (no blotch) or mixed.
Supplier: 15

'Padparadja': Intense orange.
Suppliers: 1, 7, 8, 10, 11, 14, 16, 18, 19

'Paper White': Large flowers. Pure-white with yellow eye.
Supplier: 10

'Paramount F_1': Medium-sized flowers, early to flower. Vigorous and hardy. Azure-blue, apricot, deep blue with blotch, red king (red and yellow), river gold (yellow with blotch), super Beaconsfield (light and dark blue), fire-flame, true-blue, pure white, yellow, white with blotch and mixed.
Suppliers: 4, 14, 16, 19

'Premiere F_2': Winter hardy. Medium-sized flowers both plain and faced. Azure-blue, dark blue, red and bronze shades, yellow with eye, white with eye, white and mixed.
Suppliers: 7, 8, 9, 18, 19

'Premiere Giant': Large flowers. Early-flowering. Mixed colours.
Supplier: 4

'Prima Bella': Medium flowers, compact. Mixed colours.
Supplier: 14

'Queen of the Planets': Very large flowers. Fancy pansies in warm, rich combinations of colour.
Supplier: 10

'Radar F_1': Medium large flowers. Sturdy, compact habit. Clear blue, pure yellow, rich yellow with blotch, red with blotch, white with blotch, dark blue with blotch, white, carmine-rose and mixed.
Supplier: 18

'Redwing': Large flowers. Upper petals chocolate-red, lower petals yellow with blotch.
Supplier: 10

'Raspberry Rose': Large flowers. Carmine-pink.
Supplier: 10

'Regal F_1': Large, blotched flowers.
Supplier: 16

'Reveille F_1': For winter and spring-flowering. Beaconsfield (light blue and dark blue), dark blue with blotch, mid-blue, clear blue, orange, yellow with blotch, yellow, red with blotch, purple, red wing, white and mixed.
Suppliers: 11, 18

'Rhine Gold': Large flowers. Yellow with black blotch.
Supplier: 10

179

'Rippling Waters':   Large flowers. Rich purple; petals edged with white.
Suppliers: 10, 11
'Rock':   Early, large-flowered. Light blue, blue, gold, orange, raspberry, red, white, yellow, yellow/red and mixed (also pastel mixture).
Supplier: 3
'Rococo':   Large flowers in rich colours with waved, ruffled petals. Mixed colours.
Suppliers: 8, 13
'Roggli Elite':   Large-flowered Fancy pansies of great merit. The genuine original Swiss Giants. Alpengluhn, bern, blumlisalp, brunig, eiger, gemmi, grimsel, hohenfeuer, jungfrau, kander, monch, thunersee, super blend.
Supplier: 8
'Roggli Giant':   *See* Roggli Elite.
Suppliers: 8, 9, 10
'Royal Mixed F_1':   Blotched and self.
Supplier: 11
'Scala F_1':   A choice of seven colours, some blotched. Medium to large blooms.
Supplier: 18
'Senator':   Small to medium flowers. Blue with blotch, celestial-blue, golden-yellow, orange with blotch, red, ruby, white, white with blotch, yellow with blotch and mixed.
Supplier: 8
'Shades of Blue':   A mixture of blues, purples, violets, lilacs and a few cream.
Supplier: 10
'Silver Princess':   Large flowers. White with raspberry-rose blotch.
Supplier: 15
'Soham Surprise':   A selection of the larger-flowered pansies. Mixed colours.
Supplier: 2
'Spanish Sun':   Circular, rayless flowers. A tangerine-orange self.
Supplier: 10
'Spring Magic Moonlight':   Without rays or blotches. Creamy-yellow self.
Supplier: 10
'Spring Ovation':   A hardy mixture.
Supplier: 1
'Springtime F_1':   A hardy pansy for spring and summer

display. Azure-blue, deep blue with blotch, lemon with purple blotch, orange, primrose-yellow, purple, red, red and yellow-rose with blotch, white, yellow with blotch, yellow, yellow marble, white with blotch, and mixed.
Suppliers: 8, 19
'St Tropez F$_2$': Large flowers in a wide range of colours.
Supplier: 3
'Super Beaconsfield': Large flowers. Lower petals rich-purple, upper petals very much paler.
Supplier: 10
'Super Chalon Giant': Large, ruffled, blotched and early-flowering. Mixed colours.
Suppliers: 1, 10, 11
'Super Majestic Giant Colossal': The flowers are described as gigantic! Mixed colours.
Supplier: 16
'Super Swiss Giant': Mixed colours.
Supplier: 3
'Superb Giant': Mixed colours.
Supplier: 17
'Supreme Early': All Blotched. Mixed colours.
Supplier: 1
'Sutton Giant Fancy': Large blotched flowers. Mixed colours.
Supplier: 1
'Swiss Giant': Alpen glow (cardinal) – rich cardinal shades; berna – deep velvet-blue; claret – wine-red; coronation gold – pure rich yellow; flame – orange-scarlet; island mist – white or cream with purple-pink centres; king of the blacks – black; Laurea – rosy-lilac; Lake Constance – bright blue with blotch; Lord Beaconsfield – purple and white; Mont-Blanc – creamy-white; orange sun – apricot-orange; purity – white with yellow eye; raspberry rose – raspberry-pink; red wings – yellow and crimson; rheingold – yellow with blotch; silver bride – white with violet blotch; Ullswater – rich blue with dark blotch; white lady – ivory-white; yellow master – golden-yellow.
Suppliers: 2, 4, 7, 11, 12, 13, 14, 15, 16, 17
'Swiss Giant Elite': A mixture of the previous variety.
Suppliers: 7, 16
'Swiss Giant Southbank': Mixed colours.
Supplier: 8
'Swiss Master': Giant flowers. Mixed colours.
Supplier: 8

'Swiss Velvet':   Very large velvety flowers. Mixed colours.
Supplier: 5
'Tiara F$_2$':   Large blotched flowers. Mixed colours.
Supplier: 6
'Tivoli':   Early-flowering. Mixed colours.
Supplier: 16
'Toto F$_1$':   Bright colours, winter-flowering.
Supplier: 4
'True Blue':   Medium-sized flowers. Pure sky-blue.
Supplier: 10
'Turbo F$_1$':   Large flowers. Spring-flowering.
Supplier: 8
'Tuttifruitti F$_1$':   Creams and yellows. Blotched.
Supplier: 11
'Ullswater Blue':   Large flowers. Deep blue with black blotch.
Supplier: 10
'Ultima F$_1$':   Mixed colours.
Suppliers: 4, 5, 7, 8, 15, 16, 19
'Ultima Pastel F$_1$';   Pastel shades.
Supplier: 5
'Ultima Pink Shades F$_1$':   Various shades of pink.
Supplier: 18
'Universal':   Winter-flowering. Some clear, some faced. Purple, Beaconsfield, blue blotch, true-blue, light blue, red, red wings, orange, deep yellow, yellow with blotch, white with blotch, white, violet and mixed.
Suppliers: 1, 4, 5, 8, 9, 10, 11, 12, 13, 17
'Vernale F$_1$':   Winter-flowering to end of May. Bright red with blotch, clear blue, dark blue with blotch, golden-yellow with blotch, medium-blue, true white, vivid orange, yellow and mixed.
Supplier: 16
'Watercolours F$_1$':   Pastel shades.
Suppliers: 11, 16
'Winter Flowering (Hiemalis)':   Medium-sized blooms with and without blotches., Mixed colours.
Suppliers: 1, 4, 5, 11, 15

VIOLA SEED STRAINS

'Admiration':   Deep violet-blue.
Suppliers: 3, 14

'Alpine Summer':   Small, bicoloured blue and yellow.
Supplier: 3
'Arkwright Ruby':   Ruby-crimson.
Suppliers: 7, 8, 10, 12, 14, 16, 19
'Avalanche':   Large, pure-white flowers.
Suppliers: 12, 14, 16
'Azurella':   Small, azure-blue flowers. Rayed.
Suppliers: 10, 12, 16
'Baby Franjo':   Small yellow flowers, dwarf habit.
Suppliers: 10, 16
'Baby Lucia':   Small, lavender-blue, on 4in (10cm) stems.
Suppliers: 10, 12, 13, 16, 18, 19
'Bambini':   Pastel shades with golden-yellow centres and rays.
Suppliers: 2, 4, 7, 10, 11, 12, 13, 14, 15, 16, 17, 19
'Blue Gem (Jersey Gem)':   Rich purple-blue.
Suppliers: 4, 10
'Blue Heaven':   Large, sky-blue with yellow eye. Neat and compact.
Suppliers: 1, 4, 8, 12
'Blue Perfection':   Pale blue.
Suppliers: 3, 8, 14, 16
'Blue Princess':   Small violet-blue.
Supplier: 8
'Bowle's Black':   Small, almost black flowers.
Supplier: 7
'Campanula Blue':   Soft clear blue.
Suppliers: 9, 12
'Chantreyland':   Apricot-yellow, suffused with orange.
Suppliers: 2, 3, 4, 8, 9, 10, 12, 14, 16, 19
'Choice Mixture':   Large selfs; faced and whiskered flowers.
Supplier: 5
'Choice Mixture':   Large self colours.
Supplier: 17
'Cornuta':   Small, lavender or violet flowers on compact perennial plants.
Supplier: 7
'Cornuta Alba':   As above but white.
Supplier: 7
'Crown Blended Mixed':   An unspecified mixture.
Supplier: 14
'Cuty':   Small flowers of purple and creamy-yellow similar to the wild pansy or heartsease.
Suppliers: 8, 10, 16, 17

'Dobie's Bedding Mixed':   Rounded flowers and compact foliage.
Supplier: 9
'Elatior':   Pale blue flowers in May and June.
Supplier: 7
'Fancy Shades Mixed':   Medium; bicoloured and tricoloured.
Supplier: 1
'Funny Face':   A range of colours with intriguing faces and markings (similar to Bambini).
Suppliers: 5, 9
'Golden Yellow'
Supplier: 4
'Goldie':   Large, rich-yellow, velvety flowers.
Supplier: 16
'Helen Mount':   A synonym of Johnny Jump Up, the wild pansy or heartsease.
Supplier: 4
'Johnny Jump Up':   *See* above.
Suppliers: 4, 8, 11, 12, 14, 16, 18, 19
'King Henry':   Small purple flowers on compact plants.
Supplier: 3
'Large-Flowered Mixed':   A mixture of more than one large-flowered variety. Mostly self coloured.
Suppliers: 1, 8, 11, 16
'Large-Flowered Bedding Mixed':   Large bright flowers. Mixed colours.
Supplier: 18
'Lucea':   *See* Baby Lucia.
Supplier: 19
'Lutea Splendens':   Rich yellow.
Supplier: 8
'Macedonica':   Small violet flowers.
Supplier: 7
'Maroon Picotee':   Mahogany with yellow margin.
Suppliers: 8, 10, 16
'Nigra':   *See* Bowle's Black.
Supplier: 7
'Pretty':   Top petals purple, edged with yellow. Lower petals yellow.
Suppliers: 10, 11, 16
'Pretty':   Mahogany and golden-yellow.
Supplier: 8
'Prince Albert':   Violet and white. Small.
Supplier: 18

'Prince Henry':   Small rich violet-purple flowers with a yellow centre.
Suppliers: 1, 2, 3, 4, 7, 8, 9, 12, 14, 16, 17, 18, 19
'Prince John':   A companion to Prince Henry with small yellow flowers.
Suppliers: 2, 3, 4, 8, 9, 11, 12, 14, 16, 17, 18, 19
'Princess Blue':   A large-flowering viola. Blooms appear early in violet-blue.
Suppliers: 8, 9, 15, 16, 18
'Princess Cream':   Cream flowers.
Supplier: 18
'Princess Deep Purple':   Deep purple flowers.
Supplier: 8
'Princess Yellow':   Yellow flowers.
Supplier: 8
'Purple Bedder':   Large, rich, wine-purple flowers.
Suppliers: 2, 14, 16
'Purple Picotee (Picotee Princess)':   Large, rich, warm, purple flowers with a fine white outer margin.
Suppliers: 12, 16
'Rose Picotee':   Rose-coloured flowers.
Supplier: 16
'Royal Blue':   Deep blue with paler margin.
Supplier: 12
'Royal Formula':   Rounded; mixed; compact habit.
Supplier: 3
'Royal Picotee':   Dark brown with gold margin.
Supplier: 12
'Rubin':   Dark red, almost claret.
Supplier: 10
'Ruby Queen':   Large velvet-red.
Supplier: 10
'Sawyer's Black':   Small velvety purple-black.
Supplier: 14
'Scotch Hybrids':   A mixture of established old varieties.
Supplier: 2
'Sutton's Apricot':   Medium-sized flowers.
Supplier: 1
'Toyland Mixed F$_2$':   Large flowers.
Suppliers: 2, 4, 7, 8, 12, 14, 16
'Valentine Mixed':   Mixed colours.
Supplier: 5
'White Perfection':   Rounded; creamy-white or white.
Suppliers: 3, 8, 10, 16, 17, 19

'Yellow Perfection': Rich yellow.
Suppliers: 2, 3
'Yellow Prince': Similar, if not the same, as Prince John.
Suppliers: 1, 10
'Yellow Queen': Deep yellow.
Supplier: 14

Remember that with all seed, there will be a certain amount of variation amongst the seedlings. The more expensive first generation (F_1) seed will produce vigorous and reasonably consistent seedlings. F_2 or open-pollinated varieties will exhibit greater variety. Only by propagating vegetatively from cuttings or by employing micropropagation techniques can all the progeny be expected to be identical to the parent plant.

Key to the Names and Addresses of Suppliers of Pansy and Viola Seed

1 Suttons Seeds Ltd, Hele Road, Torquay TQ2 7QJ.
2 J. W. Boyce, Seedsmen, Bush Pasture, Lower Carter Street, Fordham, Ely, Cambridge CB7 5JU.
3 Breeders' Seeds Ltd, 17 Summerwood Lane, Halsall, Ormskirk, Lancashire L39 8RQ.
4 D. T. Brown & Co Ltd, Station Road, Poulton-le-Fylde, Blackpool BY6 7HX.
5 Carters Tested Seeds Ltd, Hele Road, Torquay, Devon TQ2 7QJ.
6 Chelsea Choice, Regal Road, Wisbech, Cambridgeshire PE13 2RF.
7 Chiltern Seeds, Bortree Stile, Ulverston, Cumbria LA12 7PB.
8 Colegrave Seeds, West Adderbury, Banbury, Oxon OX17 3EY.
9 Dobies, PO Box 474, Bristol BS99 1HA.
10 Thompson & Morgan, London Road, Ipswich, Suffolk IP2 0BA.
11 Mr Fothergill's Seeds Ltd, Kentford, Newmarket, Suffolk CB8 7QB.
12 Hazeldene Nursery, Dean Street, East Farleigh, Maidstone, Kent ME15 0PS.
13 W. W. Johnson and Son Ltd, London Road, Boston, Lincolnshire PE21 8AD.
14 E. W. King & Co Ltd, Monks Farm, Pantlings Lane, Coggeshall Road, Kelvedon, Essex CO5 9PG.

15 S. E. Marshall & Co Ltd, Wisbech, Cambridge PE13 2RF.
16 J. W. Moles & Son, London Road, Stanway, Colchester, Essex CO3 5PD.
17 Unwins Seeds Ltd, Histon, Cambridge CB4 4LE.
18 Samuel Yates Ltd, Withyfold Drive, Macclesfield, Cheshire SK10 2BE.
19 Royal Sluis, PO Box 34, Unit 24, Marathon Place, Moss Side Estate, Leyland, Preston PR5 3QT.

13

Species

The genus *Viola* consists of well over 400 species, subspecies and varieties. The section Melanium, in which we find pansies, violas and violettas forms no more than a small part of the genus.

The majority of viola species are plants more akin to what a gardener would consider to be violets, as opposed to pansies, violas and violettas. Most violets have a rather more demure and elusive charm than the bolder pansies, violas and violettas (with their significantly larger, more prominent flowers), and their culture calls for a somewhat different technique.

It will be apparent from the following list of species – which can by no means be considered to be complete – that there are many significantly similar violets with subspecies and varieties in which the differences are not altogether pronounced. It is not unusual to find more than one name ascribed to a particular plant.

The plant descriptions are deliberately brief in the belief that many of the species listed will only be of marginal interest to the reader of this book.

V. accrescens: A violet similar to *V. pumila* but with larger leaves and usually white flowers.
V. adriatica: A violet with the characteristics of *V. suavis* and *V. alba*. Native to north-western Yugoslavia.
V. adunca: A native violet of North America which grows to a height of 3 or 4in (8 or 10mm) and produces deep violet flowers in the spring. It is considered to be closely related to *V. riviniana*.
V. aethnensis: Related to *V. calcarata*.
V. aetolica: Sometimes referred to as *V. saxatilis aetolica* or *V. aetolica saxatilis*. A perennial sub-species of *V. saxatilis* closely related to *V. tricolor*, a native of eastern Europe with small yellow or lavender-lilac flowers and grey-green foliage.
V. affinis: Sometimes referred to as *V. venustula*. A North American violet with purple, white-eyed flowers.
V. alba: Also referred to as *V. scotophylla*. A variable species native to central and eastern Europe. Closely related to *V. odorata*. Fragrant white or violet flowers in late spring.
V. albanica: A synonym for *V. magellensis*.

V. albiflora: A white-flowered variety of *V. cucullata.*

V. allchariensis: A perennial about 4in (10mm) in height. Native to Yugoslavia. Grey-green felted leaves and large blue-violet flowers.

V. allegheniensis: A violet native to the USA. It is believed to be related to three other species: *V. conspersa, V. walteri* and *V. appalachiensis.*

V. allionii: A form of *V. rupestris.*

V. alpestris: A synonym for *V. saxatilis.* An annual with yellow flowers. It has been described as a form of *V. tricolor.*

V. alpina: A perennial alpine pansy native to the Austrian Alps, the Carpathians and Transylvania, producing rich violet or purple flowers with a white or gold throat in May or June.

V. altaica: A perennial pansy native to the Crimea, Turkistan and the Atlas Mountains. The flowers are yellow, sometimes violet and appear between March and June.

V. ambigua: The Austrian violet with dark violet, fragrant flowers. It appears between March and June.

V. amoena: A blue-purple variety of *V. lutea.* Native to Scotland. Also considered a synonym of *V. blanda,* the sweet white violet of the USA and Canada.

V. appalachiensis: A variable American violet which has been likened to *V. allegheniensis, V. conspersa* and *V. walteri.*

V. arborea arida: Sub-species of *V. praemorsa.*

V. arborescens: A dwarf shrubby plant about a foot in height with whitish or pale violet flowers on long stalks. Native to the Eastern Mediterranean region.

V. arenaria: A synonym for *V. rupestris,* the Teesdale violet. A dwarf violet with pale blue-violet flowers, native to Europe, Asia and North America.

V. arenicola: A violet akin to the wood violet. *V. silvestris.* A synonym of *V. rupestris.*

V. argentea: An Antarctic violet.

V. arizonica: A variety of *V. nephrophylla* with hairy leaves and blue and white flowers lined with violet. Native to the western USA.

V. arsenica: A perennial species from Yugoslavia with relatively large, yellow, rayed flowers.

V. arvensis: The field pansy. A variety of *V. tricolor* with tiny creamy-white flowers with an orange or yellow eye. Native to Europe and Asia.

V. athois: A small pansy with lilac flowers originating from Greece.

V. atlantica: A synonym for *V. Brittoniana.*

V. atriplicifolia: A North American violet with small yellow flowers similar to, if not the same as, *V. venosa.*

V. aurea: A variety of *V. purpurea.*

V. austimae: Similar to, if not the same as, *V. nephrophylla.*

V. beckiana: A pansy native to southern Yugoslavia and Albania with flowers of yellow or deep violet.

V. bakeri: A small violet with pale yellow flowers considered to be a variety of *V. nuttallii* and native to western America.

V. bannatica: A form of *V. tricolor.*

V. beckwithii: A violet native to western America with long-stemmed flowers, the upper petals of which are a dark red-violet and the lower petals lilac with a small yellow blotch. A violet similar to *V. trinervata* but with more divided leaves.

V. bellidifolia: A tiny violet with purple-veined petals found growing in the lower regions of the Canadian Rocky Mountains. Akin to *V. adunca* and *V. flettii.*

V. bertolonii: A synonym for *V. heterophylla.* A pansy from Italy and the Maritime Alps with long-spurred lilac, yellow or white flowers; blooms on 9in (23mm) stems during July and August.

V. betonicifolia: An Australian species of tufted habit with rich purple flowers on short stems.

V. bicolor: A form of *V. pedata.*

V. bielziana: A Rumanian species very similar to *V. tricolor.* Considered a synonym of *V. tricolor* sub-species *subalpa.*

V. biflora: The yellow wood-violet. A low creeping perennial with bright yellow flowers, widespread throughout northern Asia, Europe, Scandinavia and North America.

V. blanda: A dwarf violet native to the USA with glossy-green leaves and fragrant white flowers veined with lavender, appearing in April and May.

V. bosniaca: A synonym of *V. elegantula* and *V. latisepala.* A species from Yugoslavia with flowers, in May and June, which vary in colour but are commonly rosy-mauve.

V. brachyphylla: A sub-alpine pansy from southern Yugoslavia and maritime Greece with yellow flowers.

V. brevifolia: A form of the dog violet, *V. canina.*

V. brainerdii: A violet akin to *V. renifolia.* Eastern USA.

V. brittoniana: A violet native to the eastern United States of America with flowers of bright warm violet in May, June and beyond.

V. brevipes: A variety of *V. palustris.*

V. bubanii: Species akin to *V. lutea.* Native to the Pyrenees and

Cantabrian Mountains of northern Spain with prostrate creeping habit and long-spurred, rayed flowers of a rich purple.

V. cadevallii: A variety of *V. alba* sub-species *V. dehnhardtii*; native of south-eastern Greece.

V. caespitosa: Has been described as an alpine pansy from the east, not unlike a dwarf form of *V. tricolor*, a synonym of *V. langeana*.

V. calaminaria: A sub-species of *V. lutea* or *V. tricolor subalpina* found in the vicinity of La Gueule in Belgium where the soil is rich in zinc. Rare.

V. calcarata: The long-spurred pansy which is native to central Europe, the Alps and the Apennines. Flowers between April and October, yellow or violet.

V. calcarea: A synonym of *V. hirta*.

V. calycina: A pansy with small yellow flowers native to Pisidia.

V. canadensis: A North American violet with long-stalked white flowers sometimes tinted violet and with distinct purple veining on the lower petals. It flowers from spring through to autumn.

V. candida: A form of the dog violet, *V. canina*.

V. canina: The heath dog violet. It is common throughout the temperate regions of Europe and Asia and produces its pale blue flowers between April and June. A synonym of *V. flavicornis*.

V. cascadensis: A variety of *V. adunca* native to the Pacific north-west of the United States of America.

V. cassinensis: A sub-species of *V. pseudogracilis* native to central western Italy.

V. catalonica: A violet akin to *V. suavis* from north-eastern Spain.

V. cavanillesia: A synonym of *V. catalonica*.

V. cavillieri: A variety of *V. bertolonii* native to western Italy.

V. cazorlensis: A shrubby species from southern Spain with long-stalked, long-spurred, rosy-lilac or reddish-violet flowers in June.

V. cenisia: The Mount Cenis pansy is a small tufted plant from the European Alps which has bright violet flowers between June and September.

V. cephalonica: A species related to *V. athois* and *V. gracilis* and native to western Greece.

V. chaerophylloides: A south-east Asian species with violet or white fragrant flowers. Considered by some to be a variety of *V. pinnata*.

V. chalcosperma: A violet from the eastern United States of America with long-stemmed pale violet flowers.

V. chamissoniana: A woody violet from Hawaii.

V. chelmea: A Greek violet not unlike *V. palustris*.

V. chrysantha: A synonym for *V. douglasii*.

V. clabrata: A variety of *V. hirta*.

V. clementiana: A synonym for *V. grandiflora*. A variable Alpine species not unlike *V. altaica* with smaller, yellow flowers. Native to Greece.

V. cognata: A form of *V. nephrophylla*. From the western USA, produces pale violet flowers in June.

V. collina: A European species not unlike *V. hirta*. The flowers are pale blue and fragrant.

V. comollia: A species from the Alps of northern Italy similar to *V. cenisia* with pale purple or whitish, yellow-centred flowers.

V. compacta: A perennial pansy with violet-blue flowers.

V. congena: A synonym of *V. triloba*.

V. coniophila: A variety of *V. curtisii*.

V. conspersa: The American dog violet. A species common throughout the central and north-eastern USA with pale blue or pale violet flowers. Synonymous with *V. muehlenbergii*.

V. contempta: A variety intermediate to *V. tricolor* and *V. arvensis*.

V. cornuta: A vigorous tufted species native to the Pyrenees with violet or lilac, narrow-petalled flowers. Widely cultivated in gardens.

V. corsica: A vigorous variety of *V. bertolonii* native to Corsica and Sardinia with blue or violet-mauve flowers.

V. cotyledon: A rosulate viola native to South America which forms a compact rosette of leaves; in habit, not unlike a Sempervivum.

V. crassa: A Japanese species of very neat tufted habit with rich yellow rayed flowers.

V. crassifolia: A tiny tufted pansy with glossy leaves and purple flowers found in the Lycian Alps. The name has also been used for a variety of *V. canina*.

V. crassiuscula: A Spanish species with violet or occasionally pink or whitish flowers on 9in (23cm) stems. A synonym of *V. nevadensis*.

V. cretacea: A pansy from the Ukraine similar to *V. hymettia*.

V. cretica: A species not unlike *V. alba* with small pale lilac flowers. Native to Crete.

V. cryana: A diminutive version of *V. hispida* from northern central France – believed to be extinct.

V. cucullata: A violet which is widespread in the USA from New England to Arkansas and Georgia. The flowers are usually lavender, occasionally white (or white with a violet centre), or blue and perhaps even rose-pink.

V. cuneata: Very similar to *V. ocellata.*

V. cunninghamii: A small neat creeping plant native to New Zealand whose small white or lilac flowers with yellow veining appear in May.

V. curtisii: A sub-species of *V. tricolor* and synonymous with *V. sabulosa.* A native to the sand dunes of the west and south coast of Great Britain, western Europe and the Baltic region. Flowers are purple and yellow and occasionally white.

V. cyanea: A violet sometimes referred to as a sub-species of *V. sepincola.* It is native to eastern Europe and produces blue or violet flowers in the spring.

V. dacica: A species with violet or yellowish flowers found growing in grassland and forest margins in the mountain districts of Albania, Bulgaria and north-eastern Poland.

V. declinata: A short-lived little pansy with violet, yellow-throated flowers which has been compared to *V. cenisia, V. tricolor* and *V. valderia.* A native to eastern Europe and the Alps of Lombardy in particular.

V. dehnhardtii: A Mediterranean sub-species of *V. alba* with lilac flowers.

V. delphinantha: A shrubby species native to Greece and Bulgaria with rose-lilac or reddish-violet flowers in June and July. It makes its home in rocky crevices.

V. delmonden: A hybrid violet with deep lavender flowers on 4in (10cm) stems akin to *V. pedata* and *V. septentrionalis.*

V. delphinifolia: A synonym of *V. pedatifida.*

V. demetria: Akin to *V. tricolor.*

V. dilitata: This American violet is a variety of *V. triloba* with lilac-blue flowers and ragged leaves.

V. dichroa: An Alpine pansy from Turkey and Armenia with tiny circular yellow and pale blue flowers.

V. disjuncta: A species native to central Asia.

V. dissecta: A Siberian violet not unlike *V. pedata.*

V. diversa: A variety of *V. riviniana.*

V. diversifolia: A tufted perennial from the central and eastern Pyrenees with fragrant violet flowers in mid-summer. A synonym of *V. lapeyrousei.*

V. doerflerii: A viola from the eastern Alps and southern Yugoslavia with deep violet, long-spurred flowers and tufted, felted leaves.

V. domestica: A synonym of *V. papilionacea.*

V. drepanophora: Similar if not the same as *V. adunca.*

Viola declinata, Viola chrysantha, Viola cornuta, 1838

V. douglasii: A synonym of *V. chrysantha.* A yellow-flowered violet from the western USA where it enjoys hot, dry conditions.

V. dubyana: A native of the Italian Alps. Violet flowers.

V. dukadjinica: A pansy akin to *V. brachyphylla* located in northern and central Albania and possibly north-western Greece.

V. dumetorum: A variety of *V. odorata.*

V. ebracteolata: A form of *V. tricolor.* A synonym of *V. modesta.*

V. eburnea: A form of *V. splendida* with creamy-white flowers.

V. egglestonii: A violet from central Tennessee with lavender-blue flowers.

V. eizanensis: A variety of *V. dissecta* which is very similar to *V. chaerophylloides.* It originates from Japan and produces fragrant, pale rose flowers in March and April.

V. elatior: A violet with soft blue flowers widespread throughout western Asia, France, Germany and Scandinavia. It is akin to *V. canina* and *V. pumila* but larger in all parts.

V. elegans: A blue and yellow pansy from Switzerland comparable to *V. lutea.*

V. elisabethae: A synonym of *V. tricolor* sub-species *subalpina.*

V. elegantula: A neat, tufted plant from eastern Europe with flowers that vary in colour from violet, yellow (or a combination of both) to rose-red. A synonym of *V. bosniaca* and *V. latisepala.*

V. elongata: Has been described as a larger form of *V. calcarata* and a synonym of *V. eugeniae.*

V. emarginata: A violet from the eastern USA with triangular leaves and deep violet flowers in March and April.

V. epipsila: Considered to be a form of *V. palustris.* It grows wild in Alaska.

V. erecta: A synonym of *V. elatior.*

V. erectifolia: A native of the Alps of Colorado with large narrow leaves and relatively large yellow, veined flowers. A synonym of *V. gomphopetala.*

V. ericetorum: A variety of *V. canina.*

V. eriocarpa: A synonym of *V. pensylvanica* and considered to be a variety of *V. pubescens.*

V. esculenta: A violet native to the south-eastern corner of the USA with pale violet or white flowers and a preference for wet but not saturated soil.

V. euboea: A sub-species of *V. heterophylla* from eastern Greece.

V. eugeniae: A pansy from the Apennines, similar to *V. tricolor* but with larger, broader-petalled flowers of violet or yellow. A synonym of *V. elongata.*

V. eximia: A species from Greece with dark leaves, yellow flowers and prostrate habit.

V. falconari: A Himalayan violet which has been compared to *V. canina,* but with larger, finer flowers.

V. filifolia: A native of New Zealand.

V. fimbriatula: A small violet with soft, downy leaves and rich violet-purple flowers from the United States of America.

V. flavicornis: A synonym of *V. canina.*

V. flavovirens: A synonym of *V. linguaefolia.* A tall form of *V. nuttallii.* Western USA.

V. flettii: Warm violet flowers with yellow centres and creeping habit. It thrives in shady crevices in the mountains of Washington and the north-western corner of the USA.

V. florariensis: A Swiss hybrid whose parents were *V. cornuta* and *V. tricolor,* or *V. hispida.* The flowers are purple with a yellow centre.

V. floribunda: A variety of *V. odorata.*

V. floridana: A violet from the south-eastern USA with white-centred flowers in shades of lavender. It shows a preference for rich, moist soil.

V. fragrans: Narrow leaves and short-stemmed yellow or pale violet fragrant flowers. A native of Greece and Crete.

V. fraterna: A form of *V. hirta.*

V. frondosa: A pansy with yellow or violet flowers native to Alpine pastures of Yugoslavia.

V. foudrasi: A variety of *V. hirta.*

V. geminiflora: A violet akin to *V. canadensis* variety *rugulosa.*

V. glabella: A woodland violet widespread throughout the northern and eastern USA with rich lemon-yellow, purple-veined flowers in April and May.

V. glaberrima: A variety of *V. tripartita,* from which it differs by its uncut leaves. It has relatively small yellow flowers and is native to the south-eastern USA. Also the name used for a variety of *V. rupestris.*

V. glabra: A variety of *V. adunca* with smooth leaves.

V. glabrata: A variety of *V. hirta.*

V. glabrescens: A variety of *V. rupestris.*

V. gmeliniana: A species native to Siberia.

V. gomphopetala: A synonym of *V. erectifolia* and a variety of *V. chrysantha.*

V. gostivarensis: A sub-species of *V. allchariensis* with small yellow flowers. Native to Albania and Yugoslavia.

V. gracilis: A synonym of *V. olympica.* A dainty species with rich violet flowers native to the region around Bursa in Turkey.

V. gracillima: A form of *V. lutea* but with larger, purple, long-stemmed flowers.

V. graeca: A variety of *V. Bertolonii* native to south-eastern Italy, Albania and Greece.

V. grandiflora: A synonym of *V. clementiana.*

V grayi: A synonym of *V. sylvestris.*

V. grisebachiana (V. grisebachii): A small pansy from the Balkan Peninsula which has been compared to *V. cenisia.* Its rounded flowers are of violet or soft blue.

V. grypoceras: A synonym of *V. sylvestris.*

V. guitteaude: A form of *V. canina* variety *lanceolata.*

V. hallii: A species closely related to *V. beckwithii* and *V. douglasii* with purple upper petals and cream or yellow lower petals. Native to the borders of Oregon and California.

V. hastata: A species from the eastern USA, similar in many ways to *V. glaberrima.* Its bright yellow flowers are tinted on the lower petals with purple and it blooms during April and May.

V. hederacea: A small, rather tender Australian violet with violet-blue flowers fading to white at the tips of the petals.

V. heldreichiana: A pansy native to the mountain rocks and screes of Greece and Crete with lilac-blue flowers.

V. helenae: A woody violet from Hawaii.

V. hertzogii: A variety of *V. allchariensis* with narrower leaves and smaller, yellow flowers.

V. heterophylla: A synonym of *V. bertolonii.*

V. hirsuta: A variety of *V. hirta.*

V. hirsutula: A small violet native to the eastern USA with hairy, silvery leaves, purple beneath, somewhat like those of a cyclamen. Warm, rich purple flowers appear in April and May.

V. hirta: A species found throughout central and northern Europe including the British Isles. It is not unlike *V. odorata* except that the young leaves and stems are hairy, the flowers have no fragrance and the plant is compact and does not spread by way of stolons.

V. hispida: The Rouen pansy. A synonym of *V. rothomagensis* and with many of the characteristics of *V. lutea* and *V. tricolor.* It produces pale violet, rayed flowers between May and August. In its wild state it is restricted to north-eastern France.

V. hondoensis: A violet native to Japan and China. Related to *V. odorata.*

V. hornemannii: A synonym of *V. canina rupii.* A variety of *V. canina* which flourishes in damp meadows and has clear blue-violet flowers with particularly broad petals.

V. hortensis: A synonym not only of the group of plants called *V. x wittrockiana,* but also confusingly applied by some to a form of *V. odorata.*

V. howellii: A woodland or meadow violet from Oregon and California which has been compared to both *V. adunca* and *V. conspersa*. Versions of this plant have been found with rose-madder, violet or soft blue and white flowers.

V. humilis: A form of *V. stagnina*.

V. hymettia: A species similar to *V. tricolor*.

V. imberbis: A form of *V. hirta* and of *V. odorata*. A synonym of *V. selkirkii*.

V. ignobilis: A form of *V. odorata* from Romania.

V. ilvensis: A sub-species of *V. corsica* from Corsica and Sardinia.

V. incognita: An American violet very similar to *V. blanda* and *V. pallens* but more prostrate in habit and with greener stalks. It has been found from New York State westwards to as far as the region of the Great Lakes.

V. inconcinna: A variety of *V. hirta*.

V. inexpecta: Generally accepted to be a variety of *V. pubescens*, although some suggest that it is a separate species. Its likeness to *V. glabella* only serves to add further confusion. *V. inexpecta* is a white-flowered form found in Pennsylvania.

V. inodorata: A form of *V. odorata*.

V. integrifolia: A variety of *V. lobata* with toothed but undivided leaves, native to the deep ravines of Mallorca.

V. intemedia: A natural hybrid between *V. riviniana* and *V. reichenbachiana*.

V. ircutiana: A violet with red or pale purple flowers and tufts of leaves which are similar to those of the common daisy, *bellis perennis*.

V. jagellonica: A violet akin to *V. suavis* from Poland.

V. jaubertiana: A violet with bright violet flowers. Similar to *V. prionantha*. Related to *V. alba*. Majorca.

V. jooi: A violet from Romania with reddish or violet-purple fragrant flowers. A synonym of *V. transsilvanica*.

V. jordanii: A variety of *V. canina* with longer leaves.

V. juressii: A variety of *V. palustris* from which it differs by having more pointed leaves. Native to western Europe and Ireland.

V. kamtschatica: Similar if not the same as *V. selkirkii*.

V. kauaiensis: A violet native to Hawaii. Deciduous with glossy green leaves and creamy-white flowers.

V. keiskei: A species native to Japan.

V. kitaibeliana (v. kitaibeli):   A tiny pansy sometimes called *V. nana*; somewhat like a miniature version of the already small *V. arvensis*, with pale creamy-white flowers. It has been found in the Channel Islands, the Isles of Scilly, France, Germany and Southern Europe.

V. kosaninii: A dwarf, shrubby violet about 5in (13cm) high from south-eastern Europe with long-stalked, lilac-pink flowers.

V. kutzingiana: A variety of *V. montana.*

V. labradorica: A violet of creeping habit similar to *V. adunca* with violet flowers. It is native to the northern USA, Canada and Greenland.

V. lactea: Commonly called the pale dog violet. It is similar to *V. canina* and *V. stagnina* but it has pale bluish-white flowers in May and June. It is native to Great Britain and north-western Europe.

V. lacteoides: A variety of *V. persicifolia.*

V. lactiflora: A variety of *V. hirta.*

V. lanceolata: A violet from the eastern USA. The flowers are white with purple veining.

V. lancifolia: A synonym of *V. lusitanica,* a variety of *V. lactea.*

V. langeana: A pansy with yellow flowers, native to the sandy acid soils of the mountains of central Spain and central Portugal.

V. langloisii: Similar to *V. affinis,* a violet from the southern USA whose flowers vary from purple to white.

V. langsdorfii: A violet with lavender-blue, violet or white flowers native to Alaska, the west coast of Canada and the USA.

V. lapeyrousei: A form of *V. cenisia* native to the Pyrenees and with stouter, more tufted habit. Possibly a synonym of *V. vestita.* See *V. diversifolia.*

V. latifolia: A variety of *V. stojanowii* which is very similar to *V. saxatilis.*

V. latisepala: A sub-species of *V. elegantula* native to Albania.

V. latiuscula: A large-flowered, North American woodland violet.

V. lavrenkona: A plant very similar to *V. hymettia.* Native to the Ukraine.

V. lepida: A perennial form of *V. tricolor.*

V. leucantha: A form of *V. silvestris.*

V. levieri: A sub-species of *V. eugeniae* native to the lower regions of the Apennines.

V. libanotica: This species has been described as a smaller version of *V. hirta.*

V. lineariloba: A form of *V. pedata.*

V. linguaefolia: So named due to its tongue-shaped foliage. A violet with bright yellow flowers making a plant about 12in (30cm) high. A synonym of *V. erectifolia, V. gomphopetala* and others.

V. lobata: A violet native to the Pacific Coast of the USA with purple stemmed, lobed leaves and yellow flowers with brown veining. Flowers from March to July.

V. longifolia: A variety of *V. canina*.

V. longipes: Similar if not the same as *V. adunca*.

V. lovelliana: A species similar to but smaller than *V. sagittata* from the south-eastern USA. White buds give way to warm lavender-violet flowers in March.

V. lucitanica: A synonym of *V. canina lancifolia*.

V. lucorum: A variety of *V. canina*.

V. lutea: A species native to upland areas of northern England, Scotland and western and central Europe. The flowers are pale yellow, purple or a combination of the two. It has a creeping, perennial habit.

V. luteola: A synonym of *V. tricolor* sub-species *tricolor*.

V. luxurians: A form of *V. riviniana*.

V. lyallii: A New Zealand violet with white flowers.

V. macabeiana: Similar if not the same as *V. nephrophylla*.

V. macedonica: A synonym of *V. saxatilis madeconica* and similar to *V. tricolor* except that the petals are more separated from one another and the plant is more perennial. Native to the meadows and hills of the Balkan Peninsula.

V. macloskeyi: A small, neat violet with white flowers, native to bogs and wet areas of the western coast of the USA.

V. macroceras: A species virtually the same as *V. jooi*.

V. maculata: A form of *V. silvestris*, variety *punctata*.

V. macrantha: A pansy akin to *V. calcarata*.

V. maderensis: A synonym of *V. odorata*.

V. magellensis: This pansy has been described as a miniature ***V. cenisia***. It is native to sandy soil in the Apennines and the Balkans. A synonym of *V. albanica*.

V. magellanica: Considered to be a synonym or sub-species of *V. tricolor*.

V. mamillata: Similar if not the same plant as *V. adunca*.

V. mandshurica: An Asiatic violet akin to *V. sagittata*.

V. masonii: A white-flowered variety of *V. conspersa*.

V. matutina: A sub-species of *V. tricolor*, usually with yellow flowers, native to southern and eastern Ukraine, northern Moldavia and parts of southern Russia.

V. mauritii: A violet with pale violet flowers found in the coniferous woodlands of eastern Russia.

V. maviensis: A woody violet native to Mavi, Hawaii.

V. maxima: An attractive variety of *tricolor* synonymous with *V. wittrockiana*.

V. maymanica: A species native to Afghanistan.

V. mercurii: A yellow-flowered pansy native to southern Greece.

V. messanensis: A sub-species of *V. bertolonii* found in southern Italy.

V. methodiana: A synonym of *V. scorpiuroides*.

V. militaris: A violet found in the south and west of England. It combines the characteristics of its two parents *V. canina* and *V. lactea*.

V. minor: A synonym of *V. adunca* minor and *V. labradorica*.

V. minuta: A tufted alpine species intermediate to *V. cenisia* and *V. alpina*. It has grey leaves and purple flowers and is native to the Caucasus mountains.

V. mirabilis: A European and north Asian woodland species with fragrant pale violet flowers.

V. missouriensis: A violet from the southern USA where it grows in moist woodland and on the banks of rivers. The flowers are lavender with a white eye, these two colours sometimes being divided by a band of rich purple.

V. modesta: A type of *V. tricolor*.

V. montana: A tall form of *V. canina* from the temperate areas of Siberia and Europe with pale blue flowers between May and July.

V. montanensis: An American violet similar to *V. adunca* but of more compact habit and with paler flowers and longer, narrower leaves.

V. montcannica: A viola from northern and central Spain with flowers similar to *V. cornuta* but of half the size.

V. monticola: Some claim this to be a synonym of *V. tricolor* sub-species *subalpina*. Other authorities say it is similar if not the same as *V. adunca*.

V. Muehlenbergii: Var. minor – a synonym of *V. labradorica*.

V. multicaulis: A synonym of *V. walteri*. Also the name for a hybrid of *V. hirta* and *V. odorata*, and *V. alba* and *V. odorata*.

V. multifida: A violet very similar in all respects to *V. pinnata*.

V. munbyana: A pansy with relatively large flowers of violet or yellow, recorded as native to North Africa, Spain and Greece.

V. nebrodensis: A form of *V. calcarata*.

V. nemausensis: Synonym of *V. tricolor* sub-species *tricolor*.

V. nemoralis: A form of *V. montana*.

V. nemorosa: A form of *V. riviniana*.

V. nephrophylla: A variable species widespread throughout the USA with violet or purple flowers. It flourishes in wet, boggy ground.

V. nevadensis: A pansy from the high screes of the Sierra Nevada of southern Spain with reddish, violet-blue, green-eyed flowers. A synonym of *V. crassiuscula.*

V. nicolai: A sub-species of *V. orphanidis* with violet flowers from the mountains of Yugoslavia.

V. novae angliae: An American violet somewhat similar to *V. septentrionalis* but with more triangular pointed leaves. The flowers are lavender with a white, green-tinted centre.

V. nummularifolia: A violet restricted in the wild to the Corsican Mountains and the Maritime Alps. It is a compact, creeping plant with short-stemmed flowers of clear, bright blue.

V. nuttallii: A violet which thrives in the dry environment of the American prairies. It has bright yellow flowers. Akin to *V. purpurea.*

V. oahuensis: A woody stemmed violet from Hawaii.

V. obliqua: A violet naturalised from gardens in Switzerland and Italy. Derived from the American *V. cucullata.*

V. obtusifolia: A variety of *V. arvensis* with smooth oval leaves.

V. ocellata: An American violet native to California and Oregon which has been likened to *V. canadensis* and *V. cuneata.* The flowers are white with lavender tinting and some purple striping.

V. occidentalis: This is considered to be a sub-species of *V. lanceolata.* It is native to the west coast of America. The flowers are pure white with rich purple lines.

V. occulta: An annual akin to *V. tricolor.*

V. odontocalycina: An Alpine pansy from Armenia, similar to *V. cenisia.* It has fleshy grey-green foliage and large bright purple-blue flowers.

V. odontophora: Similar if not the same plant as *V. adunca.*

V. odorata: The well-known sweet violet of which there are many varieties. The flowers are usually dark violet, occasionally white, sometimes blue, rose or apricot. Widely cultivated in gardens.

V. oenochroa: A variety of *V. hirta.*

V. olympica: A name used erroneously for *V. gracilis.*

V. orbelica: A pansy from southern Bulgaria related to *V. tricolor.*

V. orbiculata: A mountain violet from the north-western USA. The name is a reference to its orbicular leaves. Its flowers are yellow and it compares with *V. sempervirens* except that it is not evergreen and does not spread by way of stolons.

V. orbiculoides: A variety of *V. sempervirens.*

Viola nummularifolia, Viola alpina, Viola calcarata, Viola zoyssii,
1838

Viola rothomagensis, Viola bannatica, 1838

V. oreades: A pansy with yellow or violet flowers from Alpine meadows and rocky areas of the Caucasian region of Russia.

V. oregana: A variety of *V. praemorsa*.

V. oreocallis: An American violet of tufted habit.

V. orphanidis: A viola of loose, lank habit from the Balkan Peninsula with flowers, that have been likened to those of a small *V. cornuta*, over a long season.

V. orthoceras: A plant of prostrate, spreading habit from the area that includes Greece, Armenia and the Caucasus. The flowers are of yellow and purple with wide, spreading petals.

V. ovalifolia: An Antarctic violet.

V. ovata: An American violet. The flowers have slender petals and are of a pinkish mauve and the leaves are small and oval.

V. oxyceras: Similar if not the same as *V. adunca*.

V. paliens: An American sub-species of *V. macloskeyi* with white flowers.

V. palentina: A pansy from north-western Spain, similar to *V. bubanii*.

V. pallida: A form of *V. silvestris*.

V. palmata: A violet widespread in the eastern USA. It has deeply segmented hairy leaves and large, usually violet flowers in April and May. In nature it chooses to live in dry woodland.

V. palustris: The marsh violet is widespread throughout temperate regions where it flourishes in mainly boggy land. It produces lilac or occasionally white flowers in March and April.

V. papilionacea: A synonym of *V. sororia*, the most common of all the species of the USA.

V. parva: An annual akin to *V. tricolor*.

V. parvula: A pansy with small creamy-white flowers found amongst rocks and screes in the mountains of southern Europe, southern Yugoslavia, Corsica and central Spain.

V. pascua: A pansy from Macedonia with the characteristics of *V. beckiana*.

V. patrinii: A small violet of tufted habit with white, lavender or purple flowers. It is distributed in the wild from Russia through China to Japan.

V. pectinata: A form of *V. brittoniana* native to the eastern USA. The flowers are large, bright violet with a white beard and light centre.

V. pedata: The 'bird's foot violet' from the USA. The variety *lineariloba* has lilac flowers; the variety *bicolor* has flowers of which the top petals are rich purple and the lower petals lavender or white. There is also a white form of *lineariloba*.

V. pedatifida: A synonym of *V. delphinifolia*. A violet from the

United States of America with deeply cut leaves and violet flowers between April and June.

V. pedatiloba: A vaiety of *V. langloisii.*

V. pedunculata: A perennial violet with rich yellow flowers from the west coast of the USA.

V. pensylvanica: A synonym of *V. eriocarpa.*

V. pentadactylis: A variety of *V. tricolor.*

V. pentelica: A variety of *V. alba* sub-species *dehnhardtii* from south-eastern Greece.

V. perinensis: An eastern European violet with yellow or sometimes white flowers on 5in (13cm) stems.

V. permixta: A variable plant resulting from the hybridisation of *V. hirta* and *V. odorata.*

V. persicifolia: A European violet of fens and marshes with white flowers tinted with blue and violet with violet veins. Considered by some to be a synonym of *V. stagnina.*

V. petraea: Rosulate violet from the Andes of South America.

V. philippica: Not unlike *V. sagittata.*

V. physaloides: A synonym of *V. vallicola.*

V. picta: A variety of *V. alba* and/or *V. hirta*, with white flowers suffused with lilac or violet.

V. pinetorum: A variety of *V. purpurea*. Also a variety of *V. hirta.*

V. pinnata: A violet from the European Alps with distinctive fan-shaped, divided leaves. The pale violet, fragrant flowers appear between June and August.

V. pinnata chaerophylloides: A more robust form of *V. pinnata* from Japan which has been compared to *V. pedata*. The flowers are larger than those of *V. pinnata* and have been described as translucent, amethyst-lilac.

V. poetica: A small dainty mountain pansy from Greece with fleshy leaves and rich blue-purple flowers.

V. polychroma: An Austrian version of *V. tricolor.*

V. polydonta: A variety of *V. dacica* from Yugoslavia.

V. pontica: There are those who consider this violet to be a sub-species of *V. sepincola* or even a synonym of *V. sepincola*. Others have compounded the confusion by suggesting that it is the same as *V. suavis* – a species which others claim to be a synonym of *V. odorata*. They have however agreed that it has pale blue fragrant flowers and can be found in southern Europe, Russia, the Caucasus, Asia Minor, Turkestan and Kashmir.

V. praecox: A variety of *V. odorata.*

V. praemorsa: A variety of *V. nuttallii* and similar in many ways to *V. vallicola*. It originates from the western USA and has hairy leaves and bright yellow flowers.

V. pratensis:　A synonym of *V. pumila* and similar to *V. persicifolia*.

V. pratincola:　A violet from the mid-western USA not unlike *V. sororia* and commonly with purple flowers.

V. prenja:　A variety of *V. pyrenaica* but with smaller flowers. Native to western Yugoslavia.

V. priceana:　The Confederate violet. A variety of *V. sororia* with white flowers with a purple centre common from the eastern to the central and upper mid-western USA.

V. primulifolia:　A variable species from the eastern USA and Asia with leaves a little like those of a primrose. It inhabits boggy ground and produces small, fragrant white purple-veined flowers.

V. pringlei:　A Mexican violet closely related to *V. blanda*.

V. prionantha:　A dainty little violet with purple flowers and heart-shaped, toothed leaves from northern China and Japan.

V. prionosepala:　A form of *V. cucullata* from the eastern United States of America.

V. prolixa:　A synonym of *V. dacica*.

V. propera:　A variety of *V. hirta*.

V. pseudo-gracilis:　A variety of *V. gracilis* from southern Italy with bright, blue-purple flowers.

V. pseudo-mirabilis:　A variety of *V. riviniana* or hybrid of *V. mirabilis* and *V. riviniana*. A synonym of *V. subvestita*.

V. pseudo-munbyana:　A variety similar to *V. munbyana* but the leaves have waved or incised edges and the flowers have a shorter, thicker spur. It is believed to be of North African origin.

V. puberela:　A variety of *V. canina*. A synonym of *V. subvestita*.

V. pubescens:　A very hairy tall violet from dry woodlands in the eastern USA. It has bright yellow flowers with brown veins between May and July.

V. pubescens eriocarpa:　A variety of *V. pubescens* which is less tall and hairy and grows in open meadow land.

V. pubescens inexpecta:　A white form of *V. pubescens*.

V. pubescens peckii:　A variety of *V. pubescens*.

V. pumila:　A synonym of *V. pratensis*. A violet likened to a dwarf *V. elatior*. A small perennial violet from Europe and western Asia with blue or violet flowers in May and June.

V. pumiliformis:　A variety of *V. lactea*.

V. purpurea:　A confusing name for a violet with yellow flowers although there are purple veins and a rusty purple to the reverse of the upper petals. Native to the north-western USA.

V. pusilla: A variety of *V. canina*.

V. pyrenaica: A species from the Pyrenees, Alps, Jura and central Apennines with shiny heart-shaped leaves and fragrant pale violet flowers with a white throat from March to July.

V. pyrolaefolia: A Patagonian violet with hairy toothed leaves and yellow flowers veined with dark red on slender 4in (10cm) stems.

V. raffinesquii: An annual pansy similar to *V. tricolor* with blue and cream flowers in April and May. It has been described as the only native American wild pansy.

V. raunsiensis: A violet akin to *V. allchariensis* and a native of northern Albania.

V. reichenbachiana: The early pale wood violet or dog violet of Great Britain, Europe, North Africa and Asia with pale warm purple flowers between March and May. It can be compared to *V. riviniana* but is of more dwarf habit and prefers soil with a high lime content. This violet is sometimes referred to as *V. sylvestris*.

V. relicta: A sub-species of *V. rupestris*.

V. renifolia: A violet from Alaska, the Rocky Mountains, Colorado and northern Washington State with small white slightly fragrant flowers and kidney-shaped leaves.

V. reniformis: A violet native to Australia and New Zealand with dainty foliage and rich violet flowers edged with white on wiry 3in (8cm) stems.

V repens: A variety of *V. epipsila* from the eastern USA.

V. retroscabra: Similar, if not the same as *V. adunca*.

V. retusa: A violet with stout well-branched habit and violet flowers in May and June – Kansas and Colorado.

V. revoluta: A variety of *V. hirta*.

V. rhodopeia: A pansy with yellow flowers from the damp mountain pastures of southern Bulgaria.

V. riviniana: The common dog violet of woodland and hedgerow with blue-purple flowers between April and June. It is comparable to *V. reichenbachiana* but for its bluer flowers and preference for less alkaline soil. It can be found growing throughout the British Isles, Europe and North Africa.

V. rivularis: A woody violet from Hawaii.

V. rostrata: A violet from the eastern USA and Canada with long-stemmed blooms varying from white or pale lavender or purple to almost pink. The spur on the reverse of the flower is notoriously long and the leaves can be tinged with violet.

V. rosacea: A rosy-red form of *V. affinis* from the United States of America.

V. rothomogensis: A synonym of *V. hispida* the Rouen pansy.

V. rotundifolia: A stemless yellow, brown-veined violet with rounded, downy leaves. It is closely related to *V. orbiculata*, and is native to the eastern USA. It flourishes in acid, woodland soil and flowers in May.

V rubra: A variety of *V. alba* with reddish flowers.

V. rugulosa: Similar and undoubtedly closely related to *V. canadensis*. It will grow as high as 2ft (61cm) and spreads by way of long underground stolons which *V. canadensis* does not. The flowers are of white tinted by the purple of the reverse side of the petals. It is native to the Rocky Mountains and the northern USA.

V. rupestris: The Teesdale violet. A synonym of *V. arenaria*. Not unlike a dwarf form of *V. riviniana* with downy leaves and pale, violet-blue flowers in May and June.

V. ruppii: A synonym of *V. hornemannii*, a variety of *V. canina* with broad-petalled flowers of clear violet-blue.

V. ruprechtiana: A cross between *V. epipsila* and *V. palustris*.

V. rydbergii: Described as a particularly fine form of *V. canadensis* from the USA.

V. sabulosa: A synonym of *V. curtisii*. Also, confusingly, a variety of *V. canina*.

V. sagittata: A varied and adaptable violet from all but the far west of the USA. The flowers are of pale violet with darker veins and appear in April and May. The long-stalked, arrow-shaped leaves can be either smooth or downy.

V. sarmentosa: A synonym of *V. sempervirens*, *V. alba* and *V. odorata*.

V. saxatilis: A synonym of *V. alpestris* and *V. tricolor alpestris*. It is a perennial pansy. The flowers are usually yellow and appear throughout the summer. It is a native of eastern Europe and Asia Minor, considered by some to be a synonym of *V. tricolor* sub-species *subalpina*.

V. schultzii: A sub-species of *V. canina* found in central Europe, northern Italy and southern Romania.

V. sciaphila: A form of *V. hirta* with larger flowers and noticeably less hairy foliage.

V. scopulorum: A smaller, more compact and richly coloured form of *V. canadensis*.

V. scorpiuroides: A semi-shrubby violet from Crete, Greece and North Africa with yellow flowers.

V. scotophylla: A sub-species of *V. alba* from south-eastern Europe.

V. scrabriuscula: A synonym of *V. pensylvanica* and sometimes considered a variety of *V. pubescens.*

V. segetum: A variety of *V. tricolor.*

V. selkirkii: A small species found in Scandinavia, North America and Alaska. It has heart-shaped leaves and pale violet, veined flowers in April and May. It spreads by way of runners.

V. semialba: A variety of *V. trinervata.*

V. sempervirens: An American species with small lemon-yellow, brown-veined flowers from March to June. The almost evergreen leaves have reddish stalks.

V. sepincola: Originally considered to be a hybrid arising from *V. hirta* and *V. odorata* but now re-classified as a separate species. A synonym of *V. suavis.*

V. septemloba: A violet from the eastern USA. It has large, red-violet flowers on long stalks. The deeply incised leaves do not necessarily always show the seven lobes that this violet's name would imply.

V. septentrionalis: A violet from the northern USA with rich violet, white-bearded flowers. There is also a rare, white-flowered form. The leaf stalks and the under-surface of the leaves are downy.

V. sericea: An Antarctic violet.

V. sheltonii: A violet native to the western USA. The distinctive leaves are deeply incised and have purple veining on the under-surface. The flowers are yellow with purple veining and appear between March and June.

V. sieberiana: A synonym of *V. hederacea.*

V. sieheana: A south-east European violet. It thrives in woodland and shaded areas amongst rocks and has pale blue or whitish flowers.

V. silvatica: A synonym of *V. silvestris.*

V. simulata: A violet with violet flowers, ovate leaves and thick creeping stems, from the western USA. Akin to *V. langsdorfii.*

V. sororia: The most common violet native to the USA where it is called 'the sister violet'. The colour of the flowers is normally purple but can vary. There is a speckled variety 'freckles', rosy-red shades, blue shades, white with a purple centre (the Confederate violet, *V. priceana*) or pure white (*V. sororia albiflora*).

V. spathulata: A Caucasian violet.

V. speciosa: This violet has been likened to *V. macedonica* but with larger flowers. A synonym of *V. elegantula.*

V. splendida: A species from southern Italy described as being like a 'looser and more prostrate *V. cornuta* with some of the character of *V. gracilis*'.

V. spuria: A synonym of *V. riviniana* variety pseudo-mirabilis. A hybrid of *V. mirabilis* and *V. sylvestris.*

V. stagnina: Considered by some to be a synonym of *V. persicifolia* and a form of *V. canina.* A European violet of fens and marshes with very pale blue almost white flowers with violet veins. Closely related to *V. elatior.*

V. stenochila: A variety of *V. curtisii.*

V. stewardiana: A species native to China with bright green pointed leaves and small white flowers.

V. stojanowii: A pansy originating from the Balkan peninsula with small yellow flowers and hairy grey-green leaves making a plant about 4in (10cm) high.

V. stoneana: Similar to *V. palmata* but the leaves are less hairy. A violet from the USA which is considered to be a natural hybrid rather than a specific species.

V. striata: A violet from the eastern USA with white or creamy-white flowers with purple veins in April and May. As the season progresses it can reach a height of 2ft (61cm).

V. stricta: A more upright form of *V. canina.* It has been suggested that it is a synonym of *V. stagnina.*

V. suavis: Said by some to be a synonym of *V. odorata*, by others of *V. sepincola* and yet others of *V. pontica.* Some consider it a separate species. It has pale blue, fragrant flowers in the spring and has been recorded growing in southern Europe, Russia, Caucasus, Asia Minor, Turkestan and Kashmir.

V. stuartii: A synonym of *V. williamsii.*

V. subalpina: A sub-species of *V. tricolor* with yellow flowers, the upper petals sometimes violet. Native to the Alps, the Pyrenees and the Apennines.

V subcarnea: A variety of *V. odorata.*

V. subjuncta: Similar to, if not the same as, *V. nephrophylla.*

V. subsagittifolia: Similar if not the same as *V. vallicola.*

V. subvestita: A violet native to the Rocky Mountains of Canada and the United States of America. Similar to *V. rupestris.*

V sudetica: A tall white-flowered violet; native to the Vosges Mountains of eastern France and the mountains of central Europe. A sub-species of *V. lutea.*

V. sulfurea: A synonym of *V. vilmoriniana*, a variety of *V. odorata* with small apricot-yellow flowers.

V. superodorata: A cross between *V. hirta* and *V. odorata.*

V. sylvestris: A synonym of *V. reichenbachiana.*

V. tanaitica: A violet from deciduous woodland and scrubland areas of central Russia.

V. tenella: An American species believed to be a variety of what has been called their 'field pansy'. The flowers are about $\frac{1}{3}$in (0.8cm) wide, the top petals are pale lilac and the lower petals are white with purple veining. It enjoys hot, dry conditions.

V. tenerrima: A synonym of *V. odorata*.

V. thasia: A pansy possibly related to *V. tricolor macedonica*.

V. thessala: A sub-species or synonym of *V. alba* from Greece.

V. thibaudieri: A Japanese violet.

V. thomasiana: One authority describes it as a violet from the central and southern Alps with heart-shaped leaves and very pale lilac fragrant flowers on 6in (15cm) stems; whilst another source describes it as a minutely small and neat form of *V. hirta* with almost triangular hairy leaves and fragrant flowers of lilac or rose or mauve-rose. Related to *V. ambigua* and considered to be a separate species.

V. thorii: A variety of *V. purpurea*, similar if not the same as *V. venosa*.

V. thurstonii: A mottled blue and white-flowered variety of *V. cucullata*.

V. trachellifolia: A woody stemmed Hawaiian violet that will grow as much as 6ft (183cm) high.

V. transsilvanica: A synonym of *V. jooi*.

V. tricolor: The wild pansy or heartsease of the British Isles, Europe and Asia. An annual or short-lived perennial pansy with flowers of which the top two petals are usually mauve or violet, the two lateral petals pale with dark rays the bottom petal blotched with rich yellow and rayed. An ancestor of the garden pansy (*V. wittrockiana*) native to most of Europe..

V. triloba: A woodland violet native to the Appalachian mountains of the USA. It is similar to *V. palmata* with deeply lobed leaves and flowers in shades of blue and violet in April and May.

V. trinervata: An American species with fragrant flowers very similar to those of *V. beckwithii*. The leaves are thicker and more broadly segmented. The plant dies back to below ground level in summer to reappear in the spring when in March it produces its flowers: the upper petals are rich, warm violet and the lower petals lilac with a yellow centre.

V. trinitatis: A large-flowered, long-spurred pansy, similar to *V. bubanii* from the Zamorra province of Spain.

V. tripartita: A long-stemmed violet from the western USA with small yellow flowers which grow from the leaf axis at the top of the stem. The leaves are divided into three segments. It spreads by way of runners or stolons.

V. uechtritziana: A synonym of *V. riviniana* variety *pseudomirabilis*. A hybrid of *V. mirabilis* and *V. riviniana*.

V. uliginosa: A rare species of marsh violet similar to *V. palustris* with heart-shaped leaves and large violet flowers. It is native to parts of northern Europe, Scandinavia and Russia.

V. umbrosa: A form of *V. stagnina*. Also claimed to be a synonym of *V. hirta, V. pyrenaica* and *V. selkirkii.*

V. uncinulata: A violet with characteristics of *V. adunca* and *V. flettii.*

V. uniflora: A Siberian violet with small yellow flowers on 4in (10cm) stems in spring.

V. vagula: A synonym of *V. nephrophylla.*

V. valderia: An Alpine pansy closely related to *V. cenisia*, native to the granite region of the Maritime Alps of Italy and France. Usually the flowers are a combination of purple and soft lavender-violet, although white forms have been recorded. It flowers between June and September.

V. vallicola: A variety of *V. nuttallii*, a synonym of *V. physaloides*. It is a species from the mid-western USA. It produces relatively large rich yellow flowers in abundance in spring.

V. variata: A variable natural hybrid of *V. arvensis* and *V. tricolor.*

V. variegata: A Siberian violet that has been compared to *V. dissecta* but with undissected leaves. Also a variety of *V. hirta.*

V. velutina: A synonym of *V. gracilis.*

V. venosa: A variety of *V. purpurea* with similarities to *V. trinervata*. It is a mountain species from the western USA. The flowers are yellow with bright rusty-red on the reverse of the petals.

V. venustula: A synonym of *V. affinis.*

V. verbascula: Similar if not the same as *V. adunca.*

V. verecunda: A very small species from Yaku-shima, southern Japan, with smooth rounded leaves and tiny white purple-veined flowers on $\frac{1}{2}$in (1cm) stems.

V. vestita: A pansy from the Pyrenees, similar if not the same as *V. lapeyrousei* and closely akin to *V. cenisia*. It is of robust, tufted habit and the leaves are a silky grey-green. The flowers are purple with a golden eye.

V. viarum: A violet of the mid-western USA which is possibly no more than a variety of *V. missouriensis*. It has indented long-stalked leaves and flowers of lavender or lilac.

V. vicinta: A variety of *V. riviniana nemorosa.*

V. vilaensis: A variety of *V. chelmea* native to Albania. The flowers are pale lilac or white with dark veins.

V. villarsiana: A sub-species of *V. calcarata* from the south-western Alps with yellow, blue or white flowers.

Viola cenisia, Viola valderia, 1838

V. villosa: A violet from the southern USA with woolly pubescent foliage and small, long-spurred lavender-purple flowers with pale centres. A form of *V. riviniana*.

V. vilmoriniana: A synonym of *V. sulfurea*.

V. violacea: A variety of *V. alba* with violet flowers.

V. vittata: A sub-species of *V. lanceolata* native to the eastern and southern USA. Its white flowers have lines of purple.

V. visseriana: A synonym of *cornuta hybrida* and *gracilis hybrida*. A collective name for all the hybrids of which *V. cornuta* and *V. gracilis* are the parent plants.

V. vivariensis: A perennial pansy from southern France with clear blue, long-stemmed flowers, the lower petals rayed with gold.

V. volcanica: A rosulate viola from the Andes of South America.

V. vratnikensis: A sub-species of *V. chelmea*, native to western Yugoslavia.

V. wailenalenae: A woody violet from Kauai, Hawaii.

V. walteri: A synonym of *V. multicaulis*. This violet makes its home in selected areas of the southern USA. The leaves are coated with tiny white hairs which give an overall silvery appearance. The flowers, which appear in March and April, are a delicate lavender with a white centre.

V. wiedemannii: A more spectacular form of *V. palustris*, native to the mountains of Turkey.

V. williamsii: A synonym of *V. stuartii*. A collective name for all the violas (tufted pansies) and violettas descended directly from the crossing of *V. wittrockiana* and *V. cornuta*.

V. willkommii: A violet that has been likened to *V. mirabilis*. It is a native of Spain and produces blue flowers.

V. wittrockiana: A synonym of *V. tricolor hortensis* and *V tricolor maxima*. The generally accepted name for the garden pansies derived mainly from *V. tricolor*, *V. lutea* and possibly *V. altaica*.

V. xylorrhiza: A synonym of *V. erectifolia*, *V. linguaefolia* and others.

V. yakusimana: A synonym of *V. verecunda*.

V. yedoensis: A rare Japanese species of tufted habit with arrow-shaped leaves and blue flowers.

V. zoysii: A sub-species of *V. calcarata*. It originates from limestone regions of the eastern Alps and the Balkan Peninsula and has long-spurred yellow, occasionally lilac flowers.

14

Diseases and Pests

No book of this nature is deemed to be complete without a section somewhat ominously entitled 'diseases and pests', the very title suggesting that both pests and disease are inevitable evils against which the gardener will have to wage war. In the case of the pansy, the viola and the violetta any such fears are to a very great extent unfounded in that they are plants which show quite remarkable resistance to such problems.

Provided the plants start their life free from infection and are well cultivated in a healthy, fertile soil from which unwelcome intruders are discouraged, there is no particular reason to suppose that they will fall victim to either pest or disease. Prevention is, of course, immensely more effective than cure and there is no shortage of readily available concoctions which can be employed as protection against the possibility, however remote, of attack.

The best approach may be to list the most common pests and diseases that might conceivably pose a threat to the pansy, viola and violetta. Together with the list are some suggestions as to how to prevent or – if the worst should happen – attempt to overcome the problem.

DISEASES

Stem rot or Pansy sickness

Stem rot is the common name for an affliction of the pansy or viola. In the midst of the active growing season, the plant may partially or totally collapse quite suddenly without any prior warning. The first indication that the plant is not well will manifest itself in the foliage which will flag and lose colour. Flowers will fade and shrivel prematurely and the plant will leave you in no doubt whatsoever that it is sick. If gentle upward pressure is applied to such a plant it will fracture and break at the point at which the stem contacts the surface of the soil and on close inspection the stem at this point will look lifeless. The plant will have reacted as though it had been severed from its roots at ground level. Plants of tufted habit with more than one stem arising from ground level may not be totally affected. The diseased portion of such a plant can quite easily be removed and the remaining unaffected parts may well continue to grow on in a healthy manner. A pansy affected by stem rot will therefore probably constitute a total loss whereas a tufted viola or violetta has a reasonable chance of surviving such a set-back.

It is generally agreed that stem rot is a soil-borne disease, as opposed to an infection that is passed directly between plants and it is believed to be transmitted more freely in wet soil. It is a fungus organism within the soil which invades the stem tissue of the plant, destroying its ability to transmit moisture from the roots upwards. This disease may become active when the soil has reached the level of temperature that might be expected by early June – a time when the plant growth is at its most active. Research into this particular problem was undertaken initially over fifty years ago with results which indicated that the culprit was a complex of more than one organism or fungus. One of these fungi was isolated as *Myrothecium roridum* which was found to be active just a little above and below soil level. It was established that this particular fungus has the ability to attack uninjured growth and did not require damage to gain access. A second group of fungi held responsible for attacking both the stem and the root are *Pythium, species corticium (rhizoctonia) solani* and *Pythium species phytophthera*. Further research has suggested that root and stem rot was most prevalent on heavy, wet clay soils or wet soils carrying excessive organic matter. More recent research has produced another name – *fusarium* wilt – as the identity of the culprit. It is quite possible that the spores of this and other fungi are introduced to the soil by way of animal manures and other unsterile organic matter and it is therefore a wise precaution to drench such soils with fungicide prior to planting.

Steps can be taken to reduce the risk of root and stem rot. The soil should be fertile and cultivated sufficiently to ensure good ventilation and drainage. The soil surface should be mulched to prevent overheating from the sun, and both the soil and the plants can be dosed quite liberally with either the traditional 'Cheshunt' compound or modern day systemic fungicides such as Benomyl. Young plants may be totally immersed in the solution before planting out as a precautionary measure. Benomyl is purchased as a powder to be dissolved, as instructed, in water.

For traditionalists wishing to produce their own Cheshunt compound the recipe is as follows:

2 parts finely ground copper sulphate
11 parts fresh ammonium carbonate

Mix thoroughly and stand the mixture for 2 hours in a sealed container. Dissolve 1oz (28g) of this mixture in a little hot water and add this to 2 gallons (9 litres) of cold water. The solution should then be used immediately.

It goes without saying that any infected plant, together with its roots, should not only be removed but destroyed, preferably by burning, at the very earliest opportunity in an effort to prevent the spread of the disease.

Where soil-borne disease is suspected it is important to rotate the crop – not allowing the pansies and violas to occupy the same area of soil for more than two consecutive seasons.

Rust

Rust is another fungus disease, the culprit this time bearing the name *Puccinia aegra*. It manifests itself in the form of yellowish-brown spots on the leaves and stems of the plant. A proprietory systemic fungicide such as Benomyl may discourage it and an alternative more traditional answer is to spray the plants with a solution of sulphide of potassium which must be first dissolved in hot water and then diluted at the rate of 1 oz (28g) to $2\frac{1}{2}$ gallons (11 litres) of cold water.

Leaf Spot

Leaf spot is caused by the fungus *Ramularia deflectens*. Dark spots first appear on the leaf margins, then gradually spread inwards and a white web eventually covers the leaf. It is a disease associated with cool, damp weather in spring. A similar disease is identified by the name *Phyllosticta violae*. Both of these fungi should be discouraged by application of fungicides similar to those previously mentioned.

Mildew

Mildew is caused by another fungus, *Oidium*, which forms a violet-grey powder on the under-surface of the leaves. It is a disease fostered by stagnant air and can be discouraged but not necessarily cured by spraying thoroughly with fungicide taking particular care to coat the under-surfaces of the leaves.

Cucumber Mosaic Virus

Cucumber Mosaic is a disease transmitted by aphids and therefore is best prevented by precautionary applications of insecticide. The disease can be recognised in pansies and violas by fine yellow veining on young leaves, stunted growth and uncharacteristic flowers. It is a disease by no means restricted to pansies and violas and infection can spread readily throughout a garden of mixed plants.

Viral and bacterial diseases, unlike fungal diseases, can be transmitted from one generation of the plant to another and their effect is registered throughout the whole plant as opposed to being confined to a particular portion of it. An unfortunate characteristic of a virus is that it can lie dormant in a host plant or within the soil without any manifestation of its presence only to be transmitted at some later stage to another plant which will then fall victim to the disease. The elimination of any latent virus within a plant can have a quite remarkable effect upon its vigour and growth potential. Undoubtedly, much research into the complex world of such plant diseases is being, and will continue to be, undertaken.

It is fortunate that, provided pansies and violas are cultivated in an appropriate manner, there should be no undue risk of their contracting disease. In order to reduce any risk to a minimum, it is wise to bear in mind the following fundamental points:

– Always purchase healthy, disease-free stock and reject and totally destroy any plant that exhibits signs of sickness.
– Plant into well-cultivated, fertile, disease-free soil which will hold moisure whilst draining sufficiently to avoid water-logging.
– The soil should be neither excessively alkaline nor acid.
– The nutrients in the soil should be well balanced in nitrogen, phosphate and potash but without excessive trace elements which can cause toxicity.
– Regular inspection should reveal evidence of any serious disease and an occasional precautionary spray of insecticide and fungicide is all that should be required.

PESTS

There are few pests for the pansy and viola grower to fear and never assume that a visitor to the pansy and viola bed is necessarily there with evil intent. The average garden will undoubtedly be

home to a countless variety of interesting insects and other creatures all of whom have every bit as much right to be there as we
ourselves. It is inevitable that their various activities will, on
occasions, come into conflict in some way with those of the
gardener. It is only reasonable that we should attempt to reach
an acceptable compromise and live in harmony. There is little
need for the sometimes almost hysterical response to the arrival
of some of our more common garden visitors. The ready avail-
ability of so many pesticides and insecticides has made wholesale
annihilation all too easy for those who lack conscience in such
matters. The recent realisation that we may now be consuming
the residues of such concoctions not only on and in our food but
also in our drinking water may well bring about a substantial
change of attitude amongst us all. The introduction to a crop of
a predatory creature which will feed upon and destroy an insect
that is causing damage – whilst being a more natural solution –
is, none the less, an unpleasant concept to have been engineered
in a supposedly civilised world.

Alternative solutions to the problem are by no means simple
but steps can be taken to discourage pests rather than necessarily
resorting immediately to a campaign of extermination.

Slugs and Snails

Slugs, and sometimes snails, are probably the most common
visitors to the pansy and viola bed. The lush foliage of a mature
viola or pansy plant provides the damp, shady conditions that
appeal particularly to the slugs who must necessarily find day-
time shelter from the drying heat of the sun. It is not an uncom-
mon sight when lifting the foliage of such a plant to find a large
colony of resting slugs of the smaller varieties. There is little in
my experience to suggest that the taste of any part of the viola
or pansy appeals to them other than that of the flower petals. On
summer evenings when the sun goes down they will come out
from their dark retreat, climb up the flower stems and feast on
the petals. Their activity will be most pronounced in mild or
warm, damp weather but in hot, dry weather their activity and
the consequent damage to the flowers will be negligible.

A traditional method of discouraging the slugs and snails is to
lay a surface dressing of sharp gritty sand or clinker around the
plant in the belief that the creatures will find progress across it
uncomfortable and go elsewhere. If the soil surrounding the plants
is top-dressed with chipped bark, the natural volatile oils within
the bark are claimed to deter the slugs and snails. Slugs and snails

can be further discouraged by ensuring that the surrounding area is not unduly hospitable to them. The soil should be kept clean of weeds and of any superfluous matter which will form alternative day-time shelter for slugs and snails. If left unmolested they will form partnerships and lay eggs which will of course exacerbate the problem in succeeding seasons. A clean and tidy garden will be less attractive to slugs and snails than one in which there is undisturbed debris in which they can take up permament residence.

There are various insecticides designed to rid the garden of slugs and snails but there is a measure of doubt as to whether they may be harmful to other more welcome creatures. Frogs, toads, thrushes and other creatures which consider slugs and snails a delicacy can be encouraged.

Aphids

The common greenfly and blackfly are just two of more than 500 species of aphids that can be found in Britain and Northern Europe. They are weak fliers but they can be carried for many miles on thermals and air currents, descending to feed and breed where instinct tells them that conditions are right. They feed on the sap of young growth and have the ability to give birth to live young which reach maturity within a week. This explains why a colony can appear as if from nowhere. When aphids attack the violas and pansies, they are not as apparent to the naked eye as on many other plants and a quite detailed and close inspection will be necessary to spot them. A stunted and ailing plant may well be found to be infested with aphids. A traditional treatment against this pest is a soft soap solution made by dissolving 2oz (56g) of soft soap in a gallon (4.5 litres) of water. There are many other chemical insecticides both systemic and contact which may be used. Unfortunately, there are few alternatives to discourage the aphids other than predators which can be introduced to tackle the problem in a slightly more natural manner.

Another theoretical suggestion is that by reducing the nitrogen available to a plant, the latter will produce less attractive young growth for the aphids, but this can hardly be considered a practical solution to the problem.

There is no reason to suppose that aphids will attack a healthy, vigorous viola or pansy, certainly not with the predictability with which they will attack roses, broad beans and many other common garden plants.

Apart from aphids, slugs and snails there are, in my experience, no other insects which pose a particular threat to the viola and pansy. Wireworms, cut worms, leather jackets, red spiders, amongst countless others, may or may not test the viola and pansy for flavour but woodlice and ants are among those which I believe to be quite harmless.

Mice and Voles

Under conditions of harsh weather, when the ground is frozen and covered by snow for any length of time, mice and voles may consume the contents of the cold frame and over-wintering cuttings can quite simply disappear in this way. If pansies and violas were particularly attractive to mice and voles they would undoubedly consume them other than on these occasions when there is perhaps no other available food to sustain them. A mouse or vole-proof structure would be the only alternative to more drastic and unpleasant methods of control.

Rabbits

I have had no direct experience of wild rabbits feeding on violas and pansies but have every reason to suppose they will. If rabbits pose a threat the most positive solution is to enclose the area in question with rabbit-proof netting to exclude them.

Biological Control

There are now available a number of predatory and parasitic insects that can be introduced to a crop which is suffering from the attention of pests. The parasite or predator will attack and kill the insect that is causing the trouble and poisonous sprays will therefore not be necessary.

It is unlikely that forms of biological pest control for pansies, violas and violettas need be considered.

Appendix I

SPECIALIST NURSERIES

List of nurseries specialising in the propagation and sale of pansies, violas and violettas.

Bouts Cottage Nurseries, Bouts Lane, Inkbarrow, Worcestershire WR7 4HP.
Richard G. M. Cawthorne, Lower Daltons Nursery, Swanley Village, Swanley, Kent BR8 7NU.
Hazeldene Nursery, Dean Street, East Farleigh, Maidstone, Kent ME15 0PS.
Joseph S. Jackson & Son, Post Office Nurseries, Kettleshulme, Whaley Bridge, Nr Stockport, Cheshire SJ12 7RD.
Elizabeth MacGregor, Ellenbank, Tongland Road, Kirkcudbright, Scotland DG6 4UU.
Tom Thumb Nursery, Woolram Wygate, Spalding, Lincolnshire PE11 3PA.

Appendix II

SPECIALIST SOCIETIES AND ASSOCIATIONS

The National Viola and Pansy Society, Hon. Secretary, Mr T.H. Pitt, 28 Carisbrooke Road, Edgbaston, Birmingham B17 8NW.
The Scottish Viola and Pansy Association, Secretary, Ms S. Ferguson, 1 The Loaning, Marybole, Ayrshire, Scotland.
(My requests for current information regarding this Association have so far met with no response).

Appendix III

BIBLIOGRAPHY

The following list includes just some of the literature that would be of interest to a student of pansies, violas and violettas.

Barillet, J., *Les Pensées* (Paris, 1869)
Becker, W., *Violae Europeae Systematische Bearbeitung der Violen Europas* (1910)
Brett, W., *Pansies, Violas and Violets* (Newnes, n.d.)
Brunfel, O., *Herbarium Vivae Eicones* (1536)
Cook, E. T., Sweet Violets and Pansies (*Country Life*, 1903)
Crane, D. B., *Violas, Pansies and Violets* (1908)
Crane, D. B., *Violas, Pansies and Violets* (1921)
Crane, H. H., *The Book of the Pansy, Viola and Violet* (The Bodley Head, 1908)
Crane, H. H., *Violas and Pansies* (*Country Life*, 1921)
Crane, H. H., *Pansies and Violas* (Collingridge, 1951)
Curtis, *'Flora' Londinensis* (1835)
Cuthbertson, W., *Pansies, Violas, Violets* (T. C. & E. C. Jack, 1910)
Farrer, R., *The English Rock Garden* (T. C. & E. C. Jack Ltd, 1919)
Fitter, R., Fitter, A., Blamey, M., *The Wild Flowers of Britain and Northern Europe* (Collins, 1974)
Fuchs, Leohart, *De Historia Stirpium* (1542)
Genders, R., *Pansies, Violas and Violets* (The Garden Book Club, 1958)
Gerard, *General Historie of Plants* (1597)
Glenny, G., *The Culture of Flowers and Plants* (1861)
Glenny, G., *The Properties of Flowers and Plants* (1863)
Grey-Wilson, C. and Blamey, M., *The Alpine Flowers of Britain and Europe* (Collins, 1974)
Icones Florae Germanicae (1938–1940)
Icones Plantarum, vol. II
Kay, C., *Notes on the propagation and cultivation of the Pansy* (Stirling, 1890)

Keble Martin, W., *The New Concise British Flora* (Michael Joseph, 1986)

Klaber, Doretta, *Violets* (Thomas Yoseloff Ltd, 1976)

Lister A., *The Pansy, how and when to cultivate it* (Glasgow, 1896)

McIntosh, *The Flower Garden* (1839)

Parkinson, *Paradisus Terrestris* (1629)

Ponsort, Baron De, *Traité de la culture de la pensée* (Paris, 1844)

Ragonot-Godefroy, *La Pensée* (Paris 1844)

Royal Horticultural Society, *Dictionary of Gardening* (RHS)

Sanders, T. W., *Violas and Pansies* (W. H. & L. Collingridge, n.d.)

Simkins, J., *The Pansy and how to grow and show it* (Simpkin, Marshall & Co, 1889)

Sinclair, J. and Freeman, J., *A History and description of the different varieties of the Pansey or Heartsease now in cultivation in the British Gardens* (Effingham Wilson, 1835).

Sowerby, J., *English Botany*, Vol. XI (1800)

Stuart, Dr Charles, *Pansies and Violas* (Dobbie & Co 1892–1898)

The Pansy, its propagation, cultivation and general treatment in all seasons (Houlston & Stoneman, 1844)

Tutin, ed., *Flora Europea* (Cambridge University Press, 1968)

Wittrock, V. B., *Viola Studier* (Stockholm, 1895–1896)

Various issues of the following publications contain interesting details relating to pansies, violas and violettas:

The Floricultural Cabinet and Florists Magazine
The Garden
The Gardeners Chronicle
The Florist
Ladies Flower Garden of Ornamental Annuals
Glennys Garden Almanack
The Floral Magazine
Viola Conference Reports
Journals of the Royal Horticultural Society

Appendix IV

PUBLICATIONS AND ORGANISATIONS OF REFERENCE

The Plant Finder

For those who are anxious to acquire a particular variety of viola or violetta and are experiencing difficulty in locating a source of supply *The Plant Finder*, a book of reference revised and updated annually, lists most if not all currently available plants with the full details of those who stock them. *The Plant Finder* is published by Headmain Ltd for: The Hardy Plant Society, c/o Lakeside, Gaines Road, Whitbourne, Worcestershire WR6 5RD.

The National Council for the Conservation of Plants and Gardens

The National Council for the Conservation of Plants and Gardens, commonly abbreviated to the initials NCCPG, is an organisation dedicated to conserving and maintaining plants which might otherwise be lost to cultivation. The NCCPG's collections of violas and violettas are currently held by: R. G. M. Cawthorne, Lower Daltons Nursery, Swanley Village, Swanley, Kent BR8 7NU. and: T. Exley, Leeds City Council, Department of Leisure Services, City Hall, Leeds, West Yorkshire LS1 4DG.

Enquiries relating to NCCPG collections should be addressed to: R. A. W. Lowe, NCCPG Secretary, c/o Wisley Gardens, Woking Surrey GU23 6QB.

Appendix V

GLOSSARY

Annual   A plant which completes its life cycle in one year.

Anther   The tip of the stamen which contains the pollen grains.

Axil   The angle formed by a leaf, leaf-stalk or lateral shoot to the main stem.

Bearded   Furnished with hair-like structures.

Bicolor   A flower in a combination of two distinct colours.

Biennial   A plant with a complete life cycle of two years.

Calyx   The outer part of a flower; the sepals.

Capsule   A ripe seed pod.

Clone   A group of identical plants maintained by vegetative propagation.

Corolla   The petals or inner part of a flower.

Crenate   Scalloped; with rounded marginal teeth.

Cultivar   A garden plant maintained as a clone.

Cutting   A portion of living plant detached for propagation purposes.

Deciduous   A plant that sheds foliage in winter.

Dehiscent   A capsule in the process of shedding ripe seed.

Family   A group of related genera.

Fertile   A plant which produces viable pollen or seed.

Floriferous   Free-flowering.

Florist   One who cultivates flowers to perfection for competitive exhibition.

Foliar Feed   A liquid fertiliser designed for application to, and absorption by, the leaves.

Fungicide   A compound designed to deter, prevent or cure fungal attack.

Glabrous   Without hairs.

Glaucus   Bluish-grey.

Herbaceous   A plant of soft, leafy growth.

Hormone Rooting Powder   A chemical substance which encourages the formation of root growth of cuttings.

Hybrid   A plant that is the result of the cross-breeding of two different species.

Hybridisation   The natural or deliberate cross-pollination of two species or varieties.

Inorganic   A substance of non–organic origin.

Mulch   Material applied to the soil surface in order to retain moisture, stifle weed growth or maintain soil temperature.

Nectary   The part of a flower which produces nectar, attracting pollinating insects.

Node   The point on the stem from which a leaf emanates.

Open Pollination   Natural pollination without interference from man.

Organic   Derived from naturally-occurring animal and vegetable matter.

Ovary   The part of the flower in which the seeds develop.

Perennial   A plant which lives for more than two years but usually conforms to an annual cycle.

Petal   An individual portion of the corolla, usually of distinctive colouring.

Petiole   The stalk of a leaf.

Pistil   The female portion of a flower comprising ovary, style and stigma.

Pollen   Spores or grains produced in the anthers of the male portion of a flower.

Pollination   The process during which the pollen makes contact with the stigma.

Pot on   To transfer a growing plant to a larger pot to allow for extending root growth.

Prick out   To transfer young seedlings into another container to allow greater room for development.

Procumbent   Lying or creeping.

Propagation   The multiplication of plants by a variety of means.

Prostrate   Lying flat on the ground.

Pubescent   Covered with down or short soft hairs.

Self-Pollination   The process of a plant producing seed without the intervention of another plant.

Species   A basic wild plant that has not hybridised with other species.

Spur   The protuberance at the back of a pansy or viola flower which encloses the nectary.

Stamen   The male portion of the flower comprising the filament and anther.

Stigma   The extremity of the pistil on which pollen alights at the pollination stage.

Stipule   A leaf-like structure at the junction of the petiole and stem.

Stolon   A creeping stem which will root when in contact with the soil.

Style   That part of the pistil which separates the stigma from the ovary.

Systemic   A compound which is absorbed into the plant structure.

Top Dressing   The application of fertiliser or mulch as a surface layer over the soil.

Viscid   Sticky.

Index

Other Gardening books published by The Crowood Press

1 85223 182 3	Begonias	Catterall
1 85223 366 4	Camellias	Edgar
1 85223 744 9	Carnations and Pinks (pb)	Hughes
1 85223 745 7	Fuchsias (pb)	Bartlett
1 85223 034 7	Geraniums & Pelargoniums	Taylor
1 85223 313 3	Primulas	Robinson
1 85223 411 3	Water Garden Plants	Case

Crowood Gardening Guides

1 85223 669 8	Alpines (pb)	Robinson
1 85223 353 2	Bedding Plants (pb)	Murray
1 85223 128 9	Bonsai (pb)	Pike
1 85223 264 1	Cacti & Succulents (pb)	Keen
1 85223 284 6	Clematis (pb)	Fair
1 85223 165 3	Climbing Plants & Wall Shrubs (pb)	Taffler
1 85223 304 4	Conservatory Gardening (pb)	Rees/Palliser
1 85223 303 6	Container Gardening (pb)	Rees/Palliser
1 85223 505 5	Flowering Shrubs (pb)	Carr
1 85223 259 5	Fuchsias (pb)	Bartlett
1 85223 149 1	Garden Design (pb)	Leverett
1 85223 576 4	Garden Trees (pb)	Carr
1 85223 575 6	Greenhouse Gardening (pb)	Edwards
1 85223 207 2	Ground Cover Plants (pb)	Taffler
1 85223 506 3	Heathers & Conifers (pb)	Carr
1 85223 410 5	Herb Gardening (pb)	Houdret
1 85223 504 7	Houseplants & Bottle Gardens (pb)	Murray
1 85223 254 4	Indoor Bonsai (pb)	Pike
1 85223 465 3	Organic Gardening (pb)	Pike
1 85223 507 1	Patio Gardening (pb)	Rees/Palliser
1 85223 278 1	Pelargoniums (pb)	Taylor
1 85223 295 1	Water Gardens (pb)	Leverett
1 85223 524 1	Wildflower Gardening (pb)	Rees

Practical Gardening Series

1 85223 661 2	Practical Bonsai (pb)	Lewis
1 85223 730 9	Practical Cacti Growing (pb)	Johns
1 85223 656 6	Practical Clematis (pb)	Murray
1 85223 621 3	Practical Container Gardening (pb)	Carr
1 85223 736 8	Practical Conservatory Gardening (pb)	Rees
1 85223 774 0	Practical Flowering Shrubs (pb)	Johns
1 85223 619 1	Practical Fruit Growing (pb)	Leverett
1 85223 632 9	Practical Fuchsia Growing (pb)	Toogood
1 85223 624 8	Practical Garden Design (pb)	Rees
1 85223 739 2	Practical Greenhouse Gardening (pb)	Murray
1 85223 619 1	Practical Fruit Growing (pb)	Leverett
1 85223 632 9	Practical Fuchsia Growing (pb)	Toogood
1 85223 626 4	Practical Herb Gardening (pb)	Houdret
1 85223 622 1	Practical Organic Gardening (pb)	Palliser
1 85223 631 0	Practical Propagation (pb)	Toogood
1 85223 657 4	Practical Pruning (pb)	Murray
1 85223 660 4	Practical Rock Gardening (pb)	Johns